The English Reformation

Religion and Cultural Adaptation

Norman Jones

First published 2002

2 4 6 8 10 9 7 5 3 1

Blackwell Publishers Ltd
108 Cowley Road
Oxford OX4 1JF
UK

Blackwell Publishers Inc.
350 Main Street
Malden, Massachusetts 02148
USA

Library of Congress Cataloging-in-Publication Data
Jones, Norman L. (Norman Leslie), 1951–
    The English Reformation : religion and cultural adaptation / by Norman Jones.
        p.   cm.
    Includes bibliographical refeences and index.
    ISBN 0–631–21042–3 (alk. paper)—ISBN 0–631–21043–1 (pbk. : alk. paper)
        1. Reformation—England.   2. England—chruch history.   I. Title.
    BR375 J66   2001
    274.2'06—dc21

                                                                                        2001025599

British Library Cataloguing in Publication Data
A CIP catalogue record for this book is available from the British Library.

Typeset in 10.5 on 12.5pt Octavian
by SetSystems Ltd, Saffron Walden, Essex
Printed in Great Britain by TJ International Ltd, Padstow, Cornwall

This book is printed on acid-free paper.

Contents

List of Illustrations

Acknowledgments

The seeds for this book were planted in me by long talks with my friends Professor Kurt and Gwynneth Lipstein. Their long experience of the twentieth century reminded me that history is made by people whose lives reach far before and behind events, and that people can and do adapt to rapid and even catastrophic changes in their lives.

Its intellectual conception took place at an NEH Summer Seminar "Religion in Early Modern England," run by David Cressy and Lori Anne Ferrel, at Claremont in 1993. I deeply appreciate the stimulation they and the other members of the seminar provided.

I have benefitted from the kindness and generosity extended to me by Roy Ritchie, Mary Robertson, and the rest of the staff and donors of the Huntington Library. As a Mayer Fellow in the summer of 1999, they provided me with money, time, and the wonderful Perkins House on Poppy Peak, as well as access to their collections.

I owe the Huntington redoubled thanks for naming me the Huntington Library Exchange Fellow to Lincoln College, Oxford. Mark Goldie, the Acting Rector, Joy Makin, the Steward, and the Fellows and staff of Lincoln made my wife and me comfortable and welcomed me into their pleasant society.

By electing me a Fowler Hamilton Visiting Fellow, Christ Church, Oxford allowed me to pursue my research in comfort. I am especially appreciative of the kindnesses shown by the students and staff of Christ Church when I arrived with a broken shoulder. And I owe a special debt to Christopher Haigh and Alison Wall for their many kindnesses.

My special thanks go to Steve Gunn, who suggested that I look at Merton College's superb records, and to the Warden and fellows of Merton for allowing access to them. Likewise, I appreciate the willingness of the Benchers of the Inner Temple to allow me access to the Petyt Manuscripts. The staffs of the Public Record Office, the British Library, the London Guild Hall, the Bodleian, and the Huntington Library have provided their usual, unsung, help and insights.

All authors incur deep debts to their colleagues for conversations, inspirations, helpful hints, and critical readings. A book of this breadth makes me grateful to a host of people. At the head of the list I must place Sir Geoffrey Elton, who taught me so much, and who encouraged me in the exploration of this topic. After him, I owe thanks to many, many others. In no particular order I thank Dale Hoak, Susan Wabuda, James Day, Chris Kyle, Felcity Heal, Clive Holmes, Ian Archer, John Cooper, Henry Summerson, David Dean, Marjorie McIntosh, Bob Tittler, Stan Lehmberg, Roger Schofield, Phebe Jensen, Peter MacCullough, Ethan Shagan, Peter Marshall, Victoria de la Torre, Peter Kaufman, Ralph Houlbrooke, Wallace Mac-Caffrey, Caroline Litzenberger, SusanWabuda, Eric Carlson, Peter Cunich, David Skinner, John Guy, Fred Schnable, Keith Wrightson, Patrick Collinson, Paul White, Diarmaid MacCulloch and the late Bob Scribner. They all, wittingly and unwittingly, helped me. Of course the faults of the book are entirely mine, but it would have been much worse without their generosity.

Susan Brigden read the manuscript, saving me from some silly errors and forcing me to clarify my arguments.

As all teachers know, you often learn more from your students than they learn from you. For me, this is especially true of Julie Mackin, Brandon Hartley, Susan Cogan, Debbie Luke Hirschi, Eric Olsen, DeAnn Lester and Emily Allen, all of whom helped me work out ideas in this book, and from whose theses I learned a great deal.

I could not have done this book, or retained my sanity, without the superb organizational skills, technical sophistication, and good humor of Carolyn Doyle and Monica Ingold. They make it possible for me to remain active as a scholar while chairing a department. I am deeply indebted to Carol O'Connor, Fran Titchener, and Ann Leffler who have voluntarily taken my administrative burdens upon themselves, freeing me for research and writing. Dean Stan Albrecht has supported my pursuit of scholarly opportunities while department head, and has contributed his own scholarly insights to this work.

The final touches were added to this book at the Baja Outpost in Loreto, Mexico. There, Leon and Noelia Fichman supplied superb food, intelligent conversation, a stream of fascinating human and piscatorial encounters, and all the quiet an author could want. Humphrey Bogart and Lauren Bacall, their dogs, supplied soft ears.

Books, like biographies, mirror the things that shape an author. My vision of people, politics, and community are deeply influenced by my parents, Leslie and Charlotte Jones. Whatever empathy I have for the problems of people trying to make a living was given me by them. In the substrata of this book a biographer would find the Bean Growers Co-op, the Knull Grange, the Salmon River Canal Company, the First Methodist Church, LRJ Inc., and two of the finest examples a child could have.

The bedrock upon which this book and I rest is provided by my wife, Lynn

Meeks. Intelligent, interested, caring, and willing to live anywhere my research has taken me, her questions, insights, and patience have kept me growing and writing. She is the audience in my head. Her fine sense of language, her high standards for rhetoric, and her impatience with dry historical persiflage have made this book much better than it might have been.

I dedicate this work to my mother, my father, and my wife.

Abbreviations

BL = British Library, London

Bodl. = Bodleian Library, Oxford

CSP Dom. Ed. = C. S. Knighton, ed. *Calendar of State Papers Domestic Series of the Reign of Edward VI 1547–1553.* London: HMSO, 1992.

CSP Dom. Mary = C. S. Knighton, ed. *Calendar of State Papers Domestic Series of the Reign of Mary I 1553–1558.* London: Public Record Office, 1998.

Cal.Pat.Rolls = *Calendar of the Patent Rolls Preserved in the Public Record Office. Edward VI,* 5 vols. London: HMSO, 1924–9.

CSP Spain = Martin A. S. Hume, and Royall Tyler, eds. *Calendar of Letters, Despatches, and State Papers Relating to England and Spain, Preserved in the Archives at Vienna, Simancas, and Elsewhere. Vol. IX Edward VI 1547–1549.* London: HMSO, 1912.

CSP Ven. = Rawdon Brown, ed. *Calendar of State Papers and Manuscripts, Relating to English Affairs, Existing in the Archives and Collections of Venice.* London: HMSO, 1892.

CUL = Cambridge University Library

DAMC = John M. Fletcher, and Christopher A. Upton, eds. *The Domestic Accounts of Merton College Oxford 1 August 1482–1 August 1494.* Oxford Historical Society, NS XXXIV (1996).

ER = *English Reports, The* Edinburgh: W. Green and Sons, 1900–.

Foley = Henry, Foley, ed. *Records of the English Province of the Society of Jesus.* London, 1877.

Hartley, Proceedings = T. E., Hartley, ed. *Proceedings in the Parliaments of Elizabeth I.* 3 vols. Leicester: Leicester University Press, 1981–95.

Hooker = Richard Hooker. *The Works of Richard Hooker,* 3 vols. John Keble, ed. Oxford: 1845.

HEH = Henry E. Huntington Library, San Marino, CA.

HMC = Historical Manuscripts Commission

HPTD = *The History of Parliament on CD-ROM.* Cambridge: Cambridge University Press for The History of Parliament Trust, 1998. This incorporates, and in some cases corrects *The History of Parliament: The House of Commons, 1509–1558,* S. T. Bindoff (ed.) (London: Secker and Warburg, 1982) and *The History of Parliament: The House of Commons, 1558–1603,* P. W. Hasler (ed.) (London: Her Majesty's Stationery Office, 1981).

H&L = P. L. Hughes, and J. F. Larkin, eds. *Tudor Royal Proclamations,* 3 vols. New Haven: Yale University Press, 1969.

ITL = Inner Temple Library, London

ITR = F. A., Inderwick, ed., *The Inner Temple: Its early History, as Illustrated by its Records, 1505–1603.* London: Stevens and Sons, 1896.

L&P = John Sherren Brewer et al., eds. *Letters and Papers, Foreign and Domestic of the Reign of Henry VIII, Preserved in the Public Record Office, the British Museum, and elsewhere in England,* 21 vols. London: HMSO, 1862–1932.

LIBB = *The Records of the Honorable Society of Lincoln's Inn. The Black Books. Vol. 1 from* A.D. *1422 to* A.D. *1586.* London: Lincoln's Inn, 1897.

LGL = London Guildhall Library

OHS = Oxford Historical Society

Parker Corres. = John Bruce, and T. T. Perowne, eds. *Correspondence of Matthew Parker, D. D. Archbishop of Canterbury. Comprising Letters Written by and to Him, from* A.D. *1535, to his Death,* A.D. *1575.* Cambridge: Parker Society, 1853.

Perkins = *The Workes of that Famous and Worthie Minister of Christ, in the University of Cambridge, Mr. W. Perkins,* 3 vols. Cambridge: 1608–9.

PRO = Public Record Office, London

RACM 1483–1521 = H. E. Salter, ed. *Registrum Annalium Collegi Mertonensis 1483–1521* Oxford Historical Society LXXVI (1923).

RACM 1521–1567 = John M. Fletcher, ed. *Registrum Annalium Collegii Mertonensis 1521–1567.* Oxford Historical Society, NS XXIII (1974).

RACM 1567–1603 = John M. Fletcher, ed. *Registrum Annalium Collegii Mertonensis 1567–1603.* Oxford Historical Society XXIV (1976).

1

Post-Reformation Culture

Once upon a time the people of England were happy Medieval Catholics, visiting their holy wells, attending frequent masses, and deeply respectful of Purgatory and afraid of Hell. Then lustful King Henry forced them to abandon their religion. England was never merry again. Alternatively, once upon a time the people of England were oppressed by corrupt churchmen. They yearned for the liberty of the Gospel. Then, Good King Harry gave them the Protestant nation for which they longed. Neither of these myths is about real people, though our historiographies are still caught up in disputes about which is right. They are the myths created by conflicting parties and creeds in the aftermath of the Reformation.

The sixteenth-century generations caught in the vast social upheaval that changed English religion could not experience it as pious myths and simple histories have portrayed it. For them the story was more individual, more complex, more difficult to tell. When I think of those people, I invite myself to a wedding feast in the late 1570s. There they sit, three generations of family and friends met to celebrate the union that would produce a fourth generation. The eldest participants had been genuinely Medieval Christians, the Reformation coming in their middle age. Their children, born in the 1520s or 1530s, had religious habits formed in the confusing 1540s, only to see them further confused by the wild variations of the 1550s. The marrying couple, remembering only the late 1550s and 1560s, were different again. Ideologically these people should not have been able to speak with one another. Some were inclined to puritanism, despising their neighbors' moderation and their grandparents' Catholicism. Some thought of others as schismatics and heretics. They might not be able to agree on even the form of the wedding, except that it was established by law. But they were all there. They were living as a family and community despite mutually exclusive religious opinions.

This book is about the creation of post-Reformation English culture. It is a history of what the Reformation did, not a history of what it failed to do. As a religious reform it was never fully successful. England never became a godly commonwealth with a single faith. But the events we call the Reformation, beginning with Henry VIII's rejection of the papacy and ending with the establishment of the Elizabethan Settlement, changed English culture forever. Over the course of three generations the way the English worshiped, did business, governed themselves, and related to their places in the universe underwent a sea change. This book is an effort to explain how that change occurred.

It is an attempt to inject new questions into the discussion of sixteenth-century England, and answer some already on the table. As the historiography now stands, there is broad agreement that, although there were some English people excited about Protestantism in Henry VIII's reign, there was not much popular support for a change. The society portrayed by Eamon Duffy and John Scarisbrick was contentedly, habitually Catholic.[1] The attempts of the reformers to change this seemed, in Christopher Haigh's analysis, to make very slow in roads into that world of habitual Catholicism. And the change came at various points and to various degrees.

This historiography, however, meets another historiographical tradition coming from the other way. Duffy sees mid-Tudor England as more akin to the fifteenth century than the seventeenth. But Patrick Collinson and his students have documented a Protestant culture in operation in the Elizabethan age.

I am asking how a nation of habitual Catholics turned into Protestants. But as this work has progressed, I have become convinced there is another question more important than what theology best describes the beliefs and practices of sixteenth-century English people. For the men and women living through the Reformation the question was more often "What do I do now?" than "What do I believe now?" They were not consulted about their theological opinions by the people who imposed Reformation upon them, but they had to adapt to the changes in order to continue the business of living. English people did not have the option of ignoring the Reformation. It touched them in too many different ways.

Many of those impacts came suddenly and hard. The death of monasticism, the erasure of the culture of purgatory, the war on "superstitious" custom, amounted to the intentional introduction of religious and social amnesia. But as the Crown took the property more was destroyed than purgatory. Power relationships were radically altered, schools and hospitals disappeared, and conceptions of virtue were turned upside down. Communities had to respond to these changes, their responses initiating new political and social realities that altered the culture. Queen Mary's attempts to undo those effects often heightened them, since what had been undone by royal order was now restored by royal order. Until, that is, Parliament permitted Elizabeth to order them undone once more.

Sharp blows followed by prolonged confusion hit English culture like a series of earthquakes. Things slowly fell apart as public commitment and certainty waned. And it was not just the physical apparatus of late Medieval religion that was being dismantled. Intellectual certainty, habits of obedience, the very definitions of virtue and truth were under attack. Consensus was disappearing in a welter of competing voices that would have made it impossible to return to the Catholic world of the 1520s, even if Mary Tudor had not died when she did. People were learning to doubt, they were forgetting, and many had nothing to remember. The people under 30 in 1559 had spent their childhoods barraged by contradictory religious and political messages, exposed to successive waves of destruction, denunciation, and persecution.

And they had seen a different world. Although some churchwardens rushed to restore their rood lofts and altars and the mass was "up again" in some places by popular demand, those Catholics had seen a world in which priests married, in which worship was in English, in which they had read the Bible in their own tongue. Their shrines were no more, and they showed little interest in monasticism. The genie was out of the bottle of late Medieval religion. Had Mary lived, her Catholic subjects would never have recreated the "merry England" of their grandparents.

The power of corrosive ideas prompted Henry and Mary to burn heretics, but too many had heard and seen the alternatives to simply pretend they did not exist. By the 1550s the English were living in a world which was irretrievably multi-theological.

By 1580 they were living in a world where very few people had clear memories of a time without religious confusion. Traditional, pre-Reformation Catholicism was dying of natural causes by then. To the Elizabethan grandchildren of people who had lived in that world, it was as far away as Camelot and as exotic as Xanadu. It had become history, and, as a time of superstition and ignorance, it was tidied away by Protestant folklore and history.

By the late sixteenth-century England was living in a post-Reformation culture that was distinctly different from that of 1530. Every sort of institution and every person within those institutions had adjusted, one way or another, to the impact of the Reformation, and, as they lived with those adjustments, they found themselves thinking and behaving in new ways.

They had quickly become used to the idea that people had conflicting religious values, and that those values had to be appreciated and avoided if business was to be done. As a dying Catholic usurer said to his neighbors in 1561, "Masters, I cannot tell of what religion you be that be here, nor I care not, for I speak to tell you the truth. . . ."[2] The truth was greater than individual religion, and the key to life in this world was to cooperate with your neighbors.

In families we can see this in the ways in which family authority was undermined by claims of religious conscience, while family lore was reinvented to stabilize family solidarity. Most of all, families, like other organizations, found that, although they could not pray for one another's souls, they could see to it that family property, power, and honor were maintained, that family memory was perpetuated. The family unit was being reconstructed and redefined as having a secular history and purpose.

Institutions, if they survived, were going through the same process. Stripped of their "superstitious" functions, some simply died, but most concentrated on those elements of their role in society that all members could accept. Livery companies became increasingly secular organizations, concentrating on policing their trades, reinventing their company histories as they went. They no longer invoked their saint, and they avoided religious actions that were either costly or divisive, concentrating on charity.

Educational institutions passed through the Reformation more quickly than most. Of course the dissolutions killed many grammar schools, which led to the creation of new schools. The Edward VI schools were built directly on the ruins of the monasteries and chantries, as were Repton and many more created by charitable donors. In the universities Reformation could be brutal, and the short tenure of most fellows meant that colleges rapidly changed their ideological spots. The Inns of Court preferred to ignore religion when they could, acting against Catholic members half-heartedly. But in all cases, the nature and self-definition of the community was affected by the Reformation in ways that narrowed interests.

Oddly, this was true of the church, too. The property laws governing benefices and prebends guaranteed that many livings were occupied by men who were not zealous adherents of any theology. Acting as stabilizers, these priest-ministers often served through successive regimes, trimming their habits to fit the times, setting an example of conformity for their parishioners. Even in Cathedrals the prebendaries settled for talking about property management more than theology in order to reduce religious friction.

Property was the great sweetener of the Reformation, and it guaranteed the royal supremacy. One of the least noted but most important impacts of the Reformation was the power over the church and local institutions that passed into lay hands during the dissolutions. The laity emerged victorious and powerful, uninterested in any church that tried to take back their power. For many "How should I live now?" became "How shall I get mine?" And once they had it, they were scarcely enthusiastic about any ecclesiastical establishment that claimed authority over them. Perhaps they were not anti clerical, but they were opposed to clerics who were unwilling to practice apostolic poverty.

The rapid adaptations made by institutions and individuals in the middle years of the century left a virtue deficit. So much energy had been expended on undermining religious authorities, destroying the ecclesiastical institutions, and grasping their property that there was little consensus about positive behavior. The readiest answer was that the good person did not disturb "order." In the absence of priests and penances, pilgrimages and penitentials, monasteries and sacrificial masses, Elizabethans had to discover new ways of recognizing the Christian life. But there was no consensus among them. They followed alternatives paths, crisscrossing one another, but disagreeing on which authority was supreme. Emphasis fell on the individual conscience, but when and how conscience was to be applied became a vexing question. Should conscience test and possibly reject custom and law? Or were custom and law appropriate guides to the conscience? The English Civil War would test this.

But there was no Elizabethan civil war. Why? Because in all this confusion the Crown only demanded minimal outward conformity, allowing local groups to work out their own *via media*, substituting political loyalty for religious orthodoxy. These local adaptations permitted the conservatives of the north and west to remain yoked to the Puritans of East Anglia in a single state church. Run by local authorities responding to local conditions, these little commonwealths conformed but mitigated or ignored the deviation of their neighbors. Of course, on one level, conformity was not a choice, but the working out of the meaning of conformity was the job of governing groups in institutions. They had the latitude to fit the Reformation to the realities of their institutions. Most chose a conformity that fit local conditions, working with the expectations and aspirations of the people in their communities, while avoiding, as much as possible, external intervention. This meant that institutions responded in ways that best suited the generation in control at a given point.

By the time Elizabeth died a generation was in power that had only the vaguest recollections of Mary's reign, if any, and a lifetime worth of anti-Catholicism. Its members had created their national identity in relation to their great enemy, the Pope, and they lived in a Protestant state whose most important religious demand was *politique* conformity, masking confessional confusion.

The most important element in this world was the possibility of choice. The possibility of conversion, the awareness of alternatives, the idea of vocations grounded in conscience, meant nothing was static anymore. Although the governing classes were deeply concerned with order, the ground of order was the conscience rightly informed. This undermined their willingness to enforce certain sorts of rules, and strengthened their fear of those who refused to obey their consciences. This changed the regulation of behavior, and government's relation to God's law. Magistrates sought to ensure that the community did nothing to insult God's honor, while leaving many sins, previously regulated, to God for punishment. This changed the purpose of government. Now that the two swords were united in the Crown, heresy was no more, and secular order was the primary reason for governance.

In this study there is always a tension between institutional responses and individual choices, as there was in the sixteenth century. No single institution represents or rules an individual. Personal choices are always possible. However, institutions have to be prepared to respond to those choices, and personal choices are brought to the table in consensual processes. Which means that the churchwardens, justices of the peace, clergy, aldermen, wardens, and masters, who interpreted and carried out policy produced local regimes that reflected their choices and shaped those of their communities.

Grasping at process rather than hunting for belief, this book pays less attention than usual to the noisy minorities. Certainly Puritans and seminary priests are important, but I am attempting to understand how the rest of English society avoided the division inherent in their radical impulses. In some parishes godly ministers excluded most of their parishioners from communion for failure to meet their high standards, complaining of their hardness of heart and ignorance. But the excluded were the majority, and they are the people whose culture I am attempting to understand. They may well have been religious in their way, but their religion was only a part of their way of life. And no matter what individuals chose to believe, they lived in communities and participated in institutions, so that their personal choices overlapped and were circumscribed by their places and roles.

It took three generations for the effects of the Reformation to be assimilated in English institutions. Although it is currently fashionable to talk about the "long Reformation," this was a moderately short one, whose impact is visible in the reconstruction of English institutions. By the early seventeenth century English people were living in a reconstructed culture that was, to them, clearly Protestant. Perhaps they were not good Protestants, but they knew they were not Catholics, and they related together in ways that used Protestant language. The reconstructed culture was, in most cases, an adaptation of older forms, but it was vastly different because of those adaptations.

Unfortunately, this new culture contained within it seeds of violence. Because the Elizabethan style of religious settlement allowed for vast local differences, the nation was unprepared for the Stuart style of government. The contradictions in values carefully glossed over by Elizabethans came to deeply trouble their children.

This book is the story of how the English, learning to live with religious diversity, reconstructed their culture. It takes the known historical facts and asks how the English culture evolved as the English people found ways to carry on their daily lives in the face of the changes that engulfed them. Not knowing how the story would end, they each learned to be aware of difference, to live with it, to oppose it, to embrace it, but most of all, to get through their lives in a reasonable way.

2

Choosing Reformations

In the fall of 1531 Robert Joseph, the novice master of the Benedictine monastery of Evesham, was corresponding with Thomas Marelborow, a brother Benedictine, about the attacks on the church made by evangelicals. Joseph, an Oxford educated humanist who made his novices read Terrence's *The Eunuch* as fitting for men who made themselves eunuchs of God, took a wry, world weary view of the Protestant agitation. "*O saeculum corruptissimum*," he wrote, counseling patience. God will bring this to an end in His own time. In the meantime, we must remain calm, taking refuge in Blessed Jesus.

Joseph's sanguine expectation that all would be well rested on his certainty that God was in His Heaven and the world was as He wanted it to be. As he told another friend about the attacks on the veneration of the Virgin and the ancient order of the Church, "God who so loved His Church, would never have permitted it to fall into error for so many years."[1]

But God failed Robert Joseph. He did not chastise those who slandered His clergy and church. On January 27, 1540 Joseph, by then a Bachelor of Theology and the Prior of Evesham, left his monastery, pensioned off when the house was dissolved. A year later he got a job as chaplain of All Saints, Evesham, rising to be vicar there in 1546. Conforming to the Edwardian changes, perhaps he welcomed the Marian restoration, but after Mary died he got a better job, as vicar of Cropthorne, Worcestershire. There he read the liturgy of the Book of Common Prayer until he died, aged 69, in 1569.

Joseph's letters portray a man who joined in the humanist critique of the late Medieval church, but who saw no reason to tear it down. As others destroyed it, he had to adapt. Forced from the monastery, he chose to become a priest serving a cure. When he took his vows as a monk in 1517 he never expected that he would live in the world again, but he learned to do it. Nor did he expect to see the Pope banished from England, but he was. Nor did he expect to say mass in English, but he learned to do it in 1549. He once expected to pray for the souls of the departed, and to be prayed for in his turn, but he was forbidden to pray and could expect no prayers. Perhaps in 1553 he felt justified at last when God killed Edward VI and brought back the Catholic liturgy and the Pope, but, if he was, he must have been horrified when Queen Mary met the angel of death on November 17, 1558, after a reign even shorter than that imp of Satan, King Edward. Certainly, by the time the Elizabethan Settlement was imposed in June 1559, Robert Joseph met it with resignation.

At any point along the line he could have reacted differently. He could have taken a public stand in the early 1530s, but he did not, counseling his students to passivity. In 1540 he might have gone into exile in a Benedictine house in some other country, but he did not. In 1549 he could have resigned his cure, but he chose to temporize. In 1559 he might have refused to conform, but he chose not to. Robert Joseph's course through the Reformation changes was pragmatic, prudent, and unheroic.

Every one of his contemporaries confronted choices of conformity, resistance, or assistance. For the first time in centuries, English people had to choose how they were to live their religion. But religion was not a private matter. As practiced in the late Medieval church, religion was very public, requiring participation in communal activities. Even those who chose, for religious reasons, to separate themselves from the rest of society by becoming hermits or anchorites did so within a highly developed structure that placed the Church between heaven and earth. Its clergy, its altars, and its shrines, mediated between the two realities, modeling behavior and providing alternative routes to heaven while invoking the aid and protection of the divine court.

The Reformation confused the paths to salvation, rejecting the mediation of the Church, debunking the saints, ridiculing works of piety, and exalting the individual's right to go directly to God. But even within the Protestant community there was much confusion about authority and behavior. "How should we live?" becomes, on the individual level, "How do I behave?" and "How do I know what is right?" Those questions, in turn, become social and political questions, since they must be answered in public contexts.

In the sixteenth century people believed in God. And they agreed that God had revealed himself in the Bible and history. The problem was authority. Which authority was the right one to explain the meaning of scripture and tradition? The established Catholic model demanded acceptance of a hierarchy containing Christ's Vicar on Earth the Pope, apostolically descended bishops, and ordained priests who held the monopoly on the sacraments necessary for salvation. The courts of the church, separate from those of the secular world, were charged with keeping the faithful on the straight and narrow, elaborating and enforcing the codes of behavior expected of the righteous. No one could come to the Father except through Christ; no one could come to Christ except through Christ's church; no one could be saved without obedience to the Church.

This Catholic paradigm managed, and adapted, the popular religious expressions, while providing moral definition. Managerially this meant an emphasis on observable behaviors that conformed to the Church's mandates. The church courts could not judge intentions; they could judge what could be observed. Consequently, though theologians might believe otherwise, people were given the impression that they could, and should exercise their free will and choose to be good, behave meritoriously, and be saved. Saints' tales provided the models, and preachers confirmed them. Choose to be good, choose the right, work toward salvation, repent your sins, and Heaven will be yours, even though most of us, imperfect souls, must first spend time in Purgatory expiating our sins. As Everyman learns, only good works go with you to Heaven.

This ideology placed the church in the heart of the authority system. Protestant theology rejected the church's authority, seeking truth unmediated by corruptible humans. For Luther and his heirs salvation comes through faith alone. It can not be earned, it is a gift from God. If it is a gift from God, God does not expect you, sinner that you are, to earn salvation. He saves you because he loves you, not because you can perfect yourself. God's grace gives you faith, and faith is enough to justify you before the divine tribunal. But the gift of faith, provoking you to love God, makes you anxious to please God by obeying him like you would your loving father, doing good works out of love rather than fear.

This personal bond with your loving Father in Heaven allows you to go directly to Him with your problems, so you do not need a priest any more. The office of the priest, and his authority, is abolished in Protestant theology. His authority to mediate with God was inherited by every individual, male and female, and each individual had to guide his or her life according to their love of God and their understanding of His will as expressed in the Bible. In this model the role of the church, and the role of its clergy, became that of the school master, aiding the faithful to understand the faith awakened in them. The church no longer mediated between the faithful and God, and it had lost the right to trump conscience.

These two models of authority are not always mutually exclusive, but in the era of the Reformation they were assumed to be, in large part because the great wealth and power of the Church was appropriated by secular authorities who used Protestant theology to justify its expropriation. Henry VIII was hardly a Protestant in his heart, but he nationalized the church in order to get what he wanted. In the process, he encouraged people to question religious authority – even, unwittingly, his. No matter what your theology was, you had frequent opportunities to confront the issue of authority in your life. The righteous life required that you defend your self-defined moral universe.

But that was precisely the problem. One had to make choices, and there were few certain guides beyond your own conscience. Consequently, the worlds of righteousness and secular self-interest became confused as never before.

Most people chose, reasonably, to go along with changes imposed from above because it was convenient, and because Tudor culture stressed obedience and order so much that it was the preeminent godly virtue, inculcated by priests who demanded respect. But as the century matured the nature of the choices became clearer. By Elizabeth's reign the younger generation made personal conviction the ultimate authority defining proper behavior.

Philip Howard, earl of Arundel, expressed this attitude neatly in a letter to the Queen in 1585. Suspected of being a treasonous Catholic, and highly aware of that his father and grandfather had been executed for treason, Howard decided to go into religious exile. He explained that his belief that he must live by the Catholic faith or face eternal damnation forced him to abandon his duty to Queen Elizabeth.[2]

Philip Howard became a Catholic saint, with counterparts in people like the Protestant separatist John Penry, executed for plotting against the Queen in 1593. Penry died, he proclaimed, "for the name and truth of the Lord Jesus which now I maintain and whilst I acknowledge with a loud and triumphant voice that the affections of this present life are not worthy of the glory which shall be revealed unto us."[3] He died because of his conviction that the state church, in its structures and liturgy, was "derived not from Jesus Christ but from the kingdom of Antichrist . . ."[4] Unable to obey the Queen and God, he chose God.

Most people, however, were not martyrs. They found it possible to keep their desire for salvation from overwhelming their sense of self-preservation. How they squared their timorous behavior with God and their consciences is important because the habits they were forming became new cultural norms. For the most part, they compromised, collaborating enough with the changes to allow them to become natural to their children.

Of course the choices were modulated by the age, gender, social position, educational level, and personal situation of each person, making broad generalizations only partially valid. However, broad patterns do appear that clarify the nature of the choices presented by events and personal ideologies.

Men born in the late fifteenth and early sixteenth centuries caused, tolerated, benefitted the most, and lost the most from the attack on the church in the 1530s and 1540s. Henry VIII was born in 1491, and he and his contemporaries made the choices that shaped the Reformation. They dominated Tudor England until the end of the 1550s, slowly disappearing so that, by about 1570 power was in the hands of people who had no active memories of a time before the royal supremacy. Lacking memory of an alternative, they had a very different view of themselves, the state, and the church, though continuing to follow the patterns of response sketched by their parents.

Of course, every generation is a product of the complicated dance of acceptance and reaction it has with the previous generation, so let us begin with the biographies of a few who were elderly by the 1530s.

Christopher St. German, born about 1460, was a noted lawyer and intellectual. In his sixth and seventh decades he began to write about the problems of law and conscience. A deeply Christian man, leading a celibate life, giving his legal services free to those who needed help, St. German forced his household to listen to him read and expound a chapter of the Bible every night.

St. German, who became Master of Requests in 1528, was preoccupied, like many of his contemporaries, with the need for reform and renewal in the Church. Unlike the monk Robert Joseph, St. German saw nothing wrong with attacking the clergy for its failure to fulfill its stated ideals, but he was anti-clerical, not heretical. Conservative Catholic that he was, he wanted the Church to model pious living. The Renaissance papacy was not willing to be that model, and St. German became more and more anti-papal. To his way of thinking, the secular government needed to take control and reform the Church. Sir Thomas More disagreed with him and they carried on a debate in print about papal authority.

St. German's pious concern for reform of the church, crossed with his common law mind, drew him like a moth to a candle toward the royal supremacy. By the 1530s he had become convinced that the papacy was the problem, that canon law had to be tamed by the King, and that Parliament, not the papacy, was the supreme authority in matters of dogma. Of course, he may have had good secular reasons for this persuasion, since Sir Thomas More lost his head for denying the King's supremacy, but it seems likely that he was increasingly certain in conscience that reform would only be possible when the representatives of the people could impose it on the church, using the authority of their king.[5]

Thomas More, born in 1477 or 1478, faced similar choices but reached very different conclusions. He shared St. German's vision of a righteous island commonwealth in which church and state worked together for the good of the citizens. The Devil was in the details. St. German believed that it was essential for the church to come under the authority of Parliament, which would make the clergy good. More thought this was a crazy idea, since priests who were not good were unlikely to become so just because they changed employers. Besides, who would make Parliament good?

More also shared St. German's hope that law and conscience could be fused, the cold formulas of common law warmed by considerations of equity. As Chancellor, More worked for law reform of that kind. But in the end More exalted a conscience obedient to God, over obedience to human law. More could not in conscience agree to Henry's defection from Christian unity, and so he lost his head and became a saint in due time.

Famously, More justified his resistance with an argument for the primacy of conscience. St. German believed that Parliament, functioning as the conscience of the realm, could replace the pope. More was less sanguine, seeing the issue in terms of the communion of the saints. William Roper reports that after his conviction for denying the supremacy More addressed the court. Explaining that Parliament had no more right to overturn the pope's authority than the City of London had to overturn Parliament's, he asserted that the realm had no more right to disobey the pope than a child had to refuse obedience to his father. When he was reminded that all the universities, the bishops and the "best learned men" of the realm had agreed to the Act of supremacy, More retorted:

If the number of bishops and universities be so material . . . then see I little cause . . . why that thing in my conscience should make any change. For I nothing doubt, but that though not in this Realm, yet in Christendom about they be not the least part, that be of my mind therein. But if I should speak of those that be already dead (of whom many be now saints in Heaven) I am very sure it is the far greater part of them, that all the while they lived, thought in this case that way that I think now. And therefore am I not bound (my Lords) to conform my conscience to the council of one realm against the General Council of Christendom.[6]

More's conscience was bound by the tradition of the Church, whose members, living and dead, confirmed the validity of that tradition. His conscience did not stand alone; many before him had confirmed the truth he upheld.[7]

St. German and More had much in common except the stand they chose to make. Their arguments, and their example, certainly impressed the rising young men in the Inns of Court and the Court. More willing to take on board radical ideas, they were impressed, negatively or positively, by the activities and ideas of others as well. The hunt for Lollards, the translations of Tyndale, the stir over Luther's ideas, and the general feeling of disgust about the Renaissance papacy were common experiences, though they had varying results.

The dreams and aspirations of the generation born on either side of 1500 shaped the way in which the Reformation evolved. They believed in reform, and renewal, of the church, but they were at odds about how to carry this out. Moreover, many of them understood that there were opportunities for advancement hidden within the talk of reform. For every saint there were a number of sinners, and many, many who took life as it came.

William Roper was born in 1496 into a legal family. Probably attending Oxford before he entered Lincoln's Inn, he joined the household of Sir Thomas More, eventually marrying his daughter Margaret in 1521. Young Roper was a promising catch as lawyer, but if More had known that his daughter's intended liked Luther, he would have forbidden the marriage. Not long after it was too late, it became clear that Roper was a heretic. He even announced his intention of becoming a Lutheran preacher.

Nicholas Harpsfield, another contemporary biographer of More, tells us that Roper was preoccupied with the fashionable conundrum of faith versus works. Like

FIGURE 1   Sir Thomas More, His Father, His Household and His Descendants, by Rowland Lockey, 1593. © National Portrait Gallery, London.

a younger Luther, and like Thomas More himself at a younger age, Roper spent his time in fasting and prayer until, convinced that he was unworthy of salvation, he fell into despair. But then, in this classic conversion tale, grace came to his rescue. He read Luther's *Babylonian Captivity of the Church* and *The Freedom of a Christian*, both of which pithily reject the idea that salvation can be earned. Roper then realized that he was saved by God's grace, not his own pathetic works.

Full of this new theology, Roper began visiting the German merchants in the Steelyard to learn more about Luther and his teaching. He may even have acquired Luther's German Bible of 1522. Careless about sharing his enthusiasm, Roper's heresy soon reached the ears of the Church. Cardinal Wolsey summoned the young man and his German friends to be examined, and the Germans were forced to recant publicly.

Roper, thanks to Sir Thomas' position, was warned and sent back home, where he had to face More. Harpsfield tells us that More told his daughter Margaret that he could not reach his hard headed son-in-law. "Meg," he said, "I have borne a long time with your husband, and I have reasoned and argued with him in those points of religion, and still given to him my poor fatherly counsel; but I perceive none of this able to call him home; and therefore, Meg, I will no longer argue and dispute with him but clean give him over . . . and pray for him."[8]

Prayer was less than More did for others, since by the middle of the 1520s he was hunting Lutheran heretics with cold persistence, happy to see them burn. By then, Lutherans were seen by responsible men in positions of authority as dangerous. More wrote against them, he pursued them, and he even used his own house in Chelsea as a temporary prison where he interrogated them.

He did nothing so desperate to his son-in-law, but eventually the young man abandoned his Lutheran enthusiasm and came back to the fold. More continued to advance Roper's career, seeing to it that he was elected to Parliament in 1523 and 1529. By the time the Reformation Parliament took up the King's supremacy and the attack on the Church, Roper was standing beside his father-in-law in defense of the faith. Roper and his law partner were listed by Thomas Cromwell as opposed on religious or economic grounds to the bill in restraint of appeals.

Cromwell may have known this because William's brother, Christopher Roper, was a member of Cromwell's household. Despite his resistance to religious reform, and his attempts to create a loophole that would save his father-in-law, William Roper seems not to have suffered personally. He probably served again in the Parliaments of 1536 and 1539. He certainly sat for Rochester in 1545 and 1547, and in all of Mary's Parliaments.

There is no evidence that he acquired any church property, though he was sued in the 1550s by the Company of Cutlers in London for illegally taking the rent of a tenement they claimed to own. The title to the property in Aldersgate Street was confused because its rent had supported an obit — prayers for the dead — until it was forfeited to the Crown during the dissolution of the chantries.[9]

Meanwhile Roper's legal practice throve. Made Protonotary of King's Bench in 1524, he was pricked to be a justice of the peace for Kent in 1526, a position in which he served until 1554, when he became sheriff of Kent. When Queen Mary came to the throne he enthusiastically embraced the return to Catholicism and was duly appointed a commissioner to hunt heretics in the diocese of Canterbury and the home counties.

Throughout the chaotic 1550s Roper remained active in the Court of King's Bench and in Lincoln's Inn, where he served as a governor from 1553 until 1570. He continued in practice and service after Elizabeth took the throne, but, in 1569, he, describing himself as "very aged," took a stand of which Sir Thomas More would have been proud. When summoned to subscribe to the Act of Uniformity in the aftermath of the Northern Rebellion of 1569, he took advantage of a legal loophole and was allowed to post a bond for 200 marks to ensure his good behavior. He could not, he said, subscribe in good conscience.

After that the old man lost his position as a governor of his Inn, though the records of Lincoln's Inn do not indicate why. He resigned his office in the King's Bench to his son Thomas in 1574 and, aged about 78, went into retirement. Perhaps he counseled Thomas as he dodged the halfhearted attempts of the Inn to expel the younger man for recusancy, but old William was left alone by the government until he died in 1578.[10]

A search of his house after his death found mass vestments, and he became one of the founders of the cult of St. Thomas More, but William Roper's navigation of the changes across the century is emblematic of his generation. As a young man he had been attracted to heretical ideas, but he learned how to survive, adapted, conformed, triumphed with Mary, and then ceased conforming. Like so many of his contemporaries, by the time the Elizabethan Settlement came around he was no longer willing to adapt – though we shall never know what he might have done if Elizabeth had been as willing to hound heretics as Mary and Henry had been. For William Roper the highest virtue was obedience. Sir Thomas More had gone to his death in a matter of conscience, but William survived and adapted as much as was necessary, remaining a leader in Lincoln's Inn, an important officer of King's Bench, and respected householder in his parish. Even when he refused to subscribe to the oath of supremacy, he posted a bond guaranteeing his loyalty to the regime.

Roper's life demonstrates one set of choices. His almost exact contemporary John Hooper represents another way people born about 1500 navigated the changes. Hooper made decisions which would lead him to martyrdom.

Born just before 1500, Hooper graduated from Oxford before taking vows as a monk at the Cistercian house of Clive. What happened to his vows is not clear – perhaps he was cast out when his house was dissolved – but he became the chaplain to Sir Thomas Arundell in the late 1530s. Arundell, profiting from his association with Cromwell, went often to Court. In those years Hooper must have been saying mass for Sir Thomas, since Sir Thomas was an open Catholic despite his great profits from monastic lands. "After I arrived at manhood," Hooper recalled in 1546, "I had begun to blaspheme God by impious worship and all manner of idolatry, following the evil ways of my forefathers" as a Catholic priest.[11] By Hooper's own account, it was when Arundell took him to the Court that he first met the writings of Huldrich Zwingli and Heinrich Bullinger. They transformed his life.

His conversion disturbed his employer, and Arundell sent him to Stephen Gardiner, the Bishop of Winchester and a leading conservative apologist for the royal supremacy, for correction. According to John Foxe's account of the interview, Arundell insisted that, no matter the outcome, Gardiner had to send Hooper home again. Gardiner did, but the interview must have demonstrated to Hooper the danger in which he stood. Fearing the Act of Six Articles, he chose exile in Strasbourg over martyrdom. There he met Anna de Tserclas and, in an act that publicly declared his rejection of his monastic vows and priesthood, he married her in 1546. At about the same time he began growing his luxuriant beard, another sign of his commitment to reform. He was no longer a "shaveling" priest. By 1547 he was in Zurich, sitting at the feet of Bullinger.

Hooper's conversion led him to a series of decisions, prompted by his new ideology, which marked him out as a heretic, and made him popular as a leader of Protestants. After Henry VIII died Hooper returned to England, where he was offered the bishopric of Gloucester in Edward's reformed church. He did not accept without reservations, however. A memorialist in Eucharistic theology, he was also a purist. He did not believe that it was right to use any vestige of the Catholic church of Antichrist in Christian services, including costumes associated with priests. Showing his characteristic "indifference to political timing and self preservation," Hooper quibbled with Archbishop Cranmer over clerical dress, starting an international debate in which continental Protestant leaders were invited to join. Hooper only agreed to be consecrated in the episcopal gown he so despised after he had been imprisoned in the Fleet for a month.[12]

As usual, the battle was between the authority of the King, and the authority of conscience. Hooper wanted a pure church; so did Cranmer. But Hooper's church was uncompromising and dependant only on God. Cranmer, as Archbishop, knew that the church was dependant on political power. Both of them knew that those who disagreed with the truth of official theology had to be silenced. Hooper was a determined member of commissions to hunt for heretics, and he undoubtedly approved of the decision to burn Joan Bocher, the "Maid of Kent," for her defiance of approved truth. As Bishop of Gloucester, Hooper accused Thomas Penne of heresy for asserting that the humanity of Christ is everywhere.[13]

Hooper's intolerance of those who believed the wrong thing had a positive side. He believed that he must witness for the truth in the face of persecution. Despite all attempts from enemies and friends to convince him to save himself by fleeing as he had done in the 1540s, he refused to leave England in Mary's reign. He was burnt to death for heresy in 1555. A man who would not compromise, he undoubtedly approved of the punishment even if he knew that the wrong people were being burned.

The generation born around 1515 experienced the Reformation differently. Few of them had the chance to became monks or nuns, though the boys among them might have become priests. They came to consciousness in a time when religious dispute was a natural part of life, in which the authority of the church was deeply discounted and the King's power exalted. By the time they reached their majorities, the deconstruction of the church had begun. So they certainly remembered a world when England was fully, freely Catholic, complete with monks, pilgrimages, and all the other "superstitious" activities "reformed" in the 1530s, but they had little chance to participate in it as adults.

Robert Huick was born in 1515, going up to Merton College, Oxford, where he took his BA in 1529. It was the beginning of a brilliant career as a scholar, physician, and public servant. Elected a fellow of Merton in 1530 and proceeding to MA in 1533, he entered quickly into academic leadership. By the time he was 20 he had served as both first and second dean of Merton and been appointed principal of St.

Alban Hall, next door to Merton College in Merton Street. The Hall was a semi-independent institution whose principals were appointed from among the fellows of Merton.

Huick's promising career at Oxford came to a rude end. Its destruction began with his conversion to the reformed faith. By his own account, it happened when he was about 15, just at the end of his BA. The scales fell from his eyes, he said, and he saw the gospel truth that justification came from faith not observation of the law. It was a good Lutheran insight. This discovery, he claimed, made him zealous to gain other souls for Christ, but it resulted in persecution and shunning. The rest of Oxford was, he said, Pelagian, believing in works not faith, and was enraged with his assertion of solifidianism. He had become so isolated that he saw not one man a month, he bragged.[14]

This claim was made while he was second dean of Merton, so he could not have been that ostracized, but he was criticizing his colleagues for their conservative opinions and for teaching the Medieval schoolmen who, in Huick's view, destroyed the wits of the students. His advanced ideas certainly incensed the leaders of the University. Even though the members of St. Alban Hall asked Cromwell to intervene on his behalf, he lost his principalship, though not his fellowship at Merton.

It was with some bitterness that Huick left Oxford in 1536, after his election as a fellow of the College of Physicians. He migrated to Cambridge where he took his MD in 1538. In terms of a career move, he could not have done better. Rather than remaining in Oxford to explain Galen to undergraduates, he found himself, thanks to his connections, appointed physician in ordinary to Henry VIII. By late in Henry's reign he had become an important figure at court, witnessing the King's will and attending his deathbed. Huick continued as physician extraordinary to Edward VI, physician to Queen Katherine Parr, and to Princess Elizabeth, while taking patients such as William Cecil. He was, in short, deeply embedded in the Protestant side of the Court. Indicative of his status in this period, he was elected to Parliament twice, first in 1547 and again in 1553.

Huick's progressive Protestantism became visible in his personal life when he tried to divorce his wife, Elizabeth Slighfield. Apparently he believed she had committed adultery and that her daughter, Ann, was not his. In a world that did not recognize divorce as a possibility, Huick was asserting his theology by seeking one. The Privy Council, having heard Elizabeth's testimony, believed her husband had falsified the evidence and rejected it. The case was appealed to Archbishop Cranmer, with no known outcome. But his attempt at divorce reminds us that in the evangelical circles in which Huick moved, it was thought that divorce should be permitted.

Huick and all his close friends were Protestants, supporters of the Edwardian Reformation. His colleagues at the College of Physicians were a more varied group, including John Caius, whose conservatism in religion would get him in the same sort of trouble in Cambridge that Huick's Protestantism had caused him in Oxford in the 1530s.[15] Caius chronicled Huick's rise to authority and influence within the College of Physicians. By 1541 Huick had been elected a Censor of the Physicians, along with Augustine de Augustinis, another of the King's physicians. A Venetian, de Augustinis was also a conservative in religion, attempting to flee the realm in 1549 and leaving money in his will for his daughter to become a nun.[16] In 1550 Huick was elected councillor and, in 1551 and 1552, President of the College, before returning to the ranks of its Council. During Mary's reign he held no office in the College, while his Catholic colleague Dr. Caius became President. However, Huick and Caius continued to work together for the good of the Physicians, hunting and suppressing people who were practicing medicine without a license. In 1564 Huick was elected President of the Physicians again, and he remained in the leadership all the rest of his life.[17]

Although his professional life within the College of Physicians continued to flourish under Queen Mary, Huick's political life came to an end. He was dismissed as a royal physician by Mary, undoubtedly because of his close ties to the Edwardian reformers. He resumed the office in 1560 when he returned to Court as Elizabeth's physician.

The Court was, once again, full of his Protestant friends, and he did well. Now that being a Protestant was politically good, the fellows of his old college, Merton, nominated him for Warden. It is not clear why he was not appointed, but he stayed in London and the Court, buying properties and improving them, enriching himself. Oddly, though a physician, he was appointed a judge in the Court of the Marshalsea, with the result that he was elected a member of the Inner Temple.

In his capacity as a learned man, or perhaps simply out of friendship, he was one of the people William Cecil asked for an opinion on whether usury should be totally forbidden in 1571. Huick's answer fitted his Bucerian Protestant outlook. It was liberal, moderate and pragmatic.

The medical doctor observed that a total prohibition would result in greater abuses, a position popular with the reformed theologians on the continent.[18]

Huick died in 1580. His will left everything to his second wife and her daughter, Atalanta, but he also instructed that, if his daughter had no children, his land went to Merton College.[19]

The young man who left Oxford despised for his religion had profited from the power of the evangelical faction in the courts of Henry VIII and Edward VI. He had suffered financially for his religion under Mary, and he had profited for it again under Elizabeth, dying rich and respected. Clearly, he must have reasoned, he had believed the right thing. Moderate Protestant that he was, he was a leader in institutions buffeted by Reformation, working with colleagues of many religious perspectives for common ends.

Of course not everyone had Huick's interest in religion. Many had no conversion experiences and were not much concerned about what was happening to religious traditions. They were more interested in secular success. Even they, however, found that the changes in religion were influencing their lives. Thomas Markham of Ollerton, Nottinghamshire was one such.

Markham was born in 1523, son of Sir John Markham, who fought for Henry Tudor at Bosworth Field. Thomas was raised in an evangelical atmosphere, for his father, according to his old friend Thomas Cranmer, favored the truth of God's word.[20] Thomas benefitted from his father's connections, entering Princess Elizabeth's household in Mary's reign and successfully standing for Parliament in 1553. A soldier in his youth, Thomas was in Berwick commanding a company of 300 men during Mary's last illness. As he reminded Burghley in 1592, he was summoned from Berwick to Brockett Hall, near Hatfield House, to defend Elizabeth if her accession was challenged. He came bearing pledges of support for Elizabeth from all the captains of Berwick.[21]

He did not need to fight for Elizabeth's throne, but she rewarded his loyalty, enrolling him as one of her Gentlemen Pensioners. Known as "Black Markham" for his temper, he quarreled a good deal over property and office. In the 1580s he was involved in a bitter fight with the Earl of Rutland over the fees and profits he took as the Keeper of Sherwood Forest during the earl's minority.

Eventually he left Court altogether and retreated to his country estates. But things were not quiet there. His wife, Mary Griffin, was a Catholic, a "great persuader of weak women to popery," and by the 1590s the national mood was such that she was detected for recusancy. Queen Elizabeth personally prevented her prosecution, saying that Markham was one of her ancient servants, and of good reputation. Markham himself, of course, attended the Church of England, and was trusted enough to act as a commissioner administering the oath of supremacy in 1592, even though his wife and some of their 18 children were Catholic. Markham's sons Griffin and Thomas were suspected of popish treason. By 1594 Markham, by now over 70, was intervening with his old friend Lord Burghley on Griffin's behalf, saying if he was a traitor and deserved to die "let him have it. My humble [prayer?] is that he may be clear yet." Griffin was pardoned.

It was in the midst of this crisis, with his nearest and dearest suspected of traitorous activities, that Thomas Markham was returned to Parliament by Nottingham. Clearly, though his kin were suspect, his honor was such that he himself was not touched by their doings, and he could shield them from their own misdeeds. For a man who seemed to take little interest in religion, the politics of religion forced themselves upon him. He died, senile, in 1607.[22]

A contemporary of Markham, but with a much shorter life span, Thomas Parker, born about 1519, started his career as the clerk of the treasury and auditor of Gloucester Abbey. He probably got the job through his uncle the abbot, William Malvern alias Parker. Because William refused to surrender his Abbey to the King, he was denied a pension and ended up living with his nephew. Ironically, the young

Thomas Parker received a pension as one of the Abbey staff. In this family born for the church another uncle was the chancellor of Salisbury and an important ecclesiastical official in both Hereford and Worcester dioceses.

As the abbey was dismantled, young Parker had to find new employment, transferring his skills to secular administration. After some legal training, he become the clerk of the Crown and justice of the peace for Gloucester in 1544. The income from those jobs allowed him to marry, and they put him in a good position to acquire land, some of which had belonged to Gloucester Abbey. By the 1550s he was a significant enough landowner that he sat for Parliament in 1553.

He died in 1558, leaving his widow and sons respectably provided for. He had made a good thing of the dissolution and the religious changes.[23]

The people born in the mid to late 1530s and early 1540s had a very different experience of English life than their parents. By the time they came to consciousness, much of the traditional world known to their parents and grandparents had been dismantled. They grew up in a time of contesting blacks and whites, in a time Anthony Esler dubbed the "revolutionary middle Tudor decades."[24]

William Roper's son Thomas, born early in 1534, practiced a modified form of virtue. He, like his father, was a lawyer of Lincoln's Inn, and he served in the first Parliament of Queen Mary. In Thomas Roper there is little hint of compromise on religion. In 1557 he married Lucy, the daughter of Sir Anthony Browne and the sister of Anthony Viscount Montague. The Brownes were a devoutly Catholic family, which may explain the connection. In 1565 he, his brother Anthony, and his first cousin were all admitted, on William Roper's petition, to William's chambers at Lincoln's Inn, where Thomas was named the junior Bencher. Like most people in the 1560s, Thomas Roper conducted business as usual, climbing the ladder of professional success. As long as no one demanded his opinion on religion, he did not flaunt it, but he knew what he stood for.

Although it must have been clear to the other Benchers that Thomas, William, and Anthony Roper were Catholics, it was not until 1577 that the Council of the Inn moved against Thomas, who was now Protonothary of King's Bench in his father's stead. But rather than expelling him, they kept offering him opportunities to conform. In November 1577 he was given until the end of the next Easter term. When he did not attend communion he was warned again, in May 1578, and ordered to conform. He did not. In May of 1579 he was told to give his answer "peremptorily, whether he will show himself and so become in life and conversation conformable to the true religion now teached [sic] and preached, nor not."[25] If not, he was to lose his chamber in the Inn. Apparently he then left the Inn — there is no record of an expulsion — though he continued as Protonothary. In the increasingly anti-Catholic climate it is not surprising that his house was searched in 1581. Mass vessels were found, and Thomas and his steward, who was a priest, were imprisoned in the Fleet.

He was released on condition that he attended Anglican services at Orpington church, though it is not clear that he did.[26]

Thomas Roper's concept of religious virtue demanded that he risk advancement and take a stand for his faith. He was not, like his brother-in-law Viscount Montague, imprisoned for hearing mass under Edward, but he was under Elizabeth. In a way, his ideological commitment is representative of his generation's understanding of their relationship to religion. Where their parents had valued obedience to the King as the highest virtue, the most pious children of the 1530s and 1540s knew that the highest virtue was obedience directly to God.

Robert Snagge not only did not remember a fully Catholic world, he hated and feared any relic of that time of superstition. Like many of his generation, his religion was not temperate. One of the first generation for whom there was no experience of pre-Reformation worship, he was an ardent enemy of Catholicism and all it stood for, loudly opposed to any compromise with even its memory. He was an enemy of anything that reminded people of their Catholic past. Born sometime in the early 1540s, he never married, devoting himself to the law and to God. Perhaps he was obsequious in his prayers, but he did not waste much Christian love on humanity. He and God knew what was right.

He entered the Middle Temple as a teenager, appearing in its records several times for "contumacy." A man with a sharp tongue, he did not hold it, and he was so disliked that he was only admitted as a reader when the Privy Council forced the benchers to accept him.

A member of Parliament in 1571 and 1572, his first recorded speech supported a bill that would require people to come to church and take communion, a sure way to smoke out papists. Attempting to modify the bill, his brother, Thomas, argued that the test of orthodoxy should not be the use of the Book of Common Prayer, since many more reformed congregations preferred a sermon. Robert spoke in support of this, adding his special enthusiasm for "the reformation of the universities, of the private schoolmasters in gentlemen's houses, and of the Inns of Court."[27] No wonder his colleagues did not like him!

In the 1572 session, which was obsessed by the treason of the Duke of Norfolk and Mary Queen of Scots, Snagge's intemperate righteousness ran away with him. He wanted Mary dead. "But you will say, spare her for courtesy because she is a king's daughter. But that sparing is dangerous and therefore good to execute her for justice, and then bury her honorably for her parents' sake" he argued, in the teeth of Queen Elizabeth's decision to simply bar her from the succession.[28] Of course, Snagge's commitment to godly government did not take him off committees, and he was as likely to speak about land reclamation or wharves and quays as about religion. In fact, in Parliament he had an opinion on nearly every bill.

His parliamentary activity in support of further Reformation of the church took place when he was about 30. As he aged he frequently had to defend himself against his enemies, insisting he was not a "condemner of his betters." His betters, however, thought he was. Made a justice of the peace for Hertfordshire in 1575, he was removed from the bench in 1587.

By 1599, approaching 60, he was mellowing. When he made his will that year he declared that he believed in the Thirty-Nine Articles as passed by Parliament in 1571 "as the public profession of the church of England (whereof I am a member) and consent therewith therein and according to the creed called the Apostles' Creed, likewise professing in this our church." The young radical had become a elderly Anglican who wished to be buried "according to the order of this church of England." He died in 1605.[29]

Edmund Campion, born in 1540, represents an equally firm intemperance in the opposite direction. Where Robert Snagge hated all things Catholic, Campion committed himself to the destruction of all things Protestant, becoming the first English Jesuit martyr and saint. Snagge's honor was bound to obey his conscience; Campion's was as well. And both men knew one basic fact about religion: it was mutable. They grew up watching religion swaying back and forth as regimes changed and the nation followed the royal whim.

Campion himself represents some of that swaying. Born in London, son of a eminent member of the Grocers' Company, he was marked early as a bright young man. At age thirteen he was chosen to make a Latin address at the entrance of Queen Mary on behalf of the students of London. Later, he was sent to Oxford as one of the Grocers' scholars. When Elizabeth visited Oxford in 1564 Campion was chosen to welcome her.

What sort of upbringing Campion had is not clear. Certainly his father was a Catholic, but we do not know the route the boy followed through the 1550s, though as a Londoner he could hardly have been unaware of the changes that were occurring in the nation. Like most of the boys of his era, he must have known that to succeed one had to conform to whatever regime was in power. And he did. In 1564 he became a Master of Arts at Oxford, swearing, as was required, the oath of supremacy so that he could teach. Encouraged by Bishop Cheyney of Gloucester to believe that there was room for conservatives in the Elizabethan church, Campion was ordained an Anglican deacon.[30]

However, at about the time Campion was ordained rumors began to fly, accusing him of Catholicism. The Grocers became concerned about his conformity, and in 1568 they ordered that he, "being suspected to be of no sound judgement in religion and for clearing of himself herein, the company they thought good he should come and make a sermon a Paul's Cross."[31] If he refused, he would lose their support.

Campion's response to the order was an elaborate set of excuses. He was overawed by the importance of preaching at the Paul's Cross, the national pulpit. Fine, said the Court of Assistants, you can preach at St. Stephen's Walbrook, the

Grocers' parish church. Then Campion argued that as a Proctor of Oxford he was a public person and not free to preach when they wanted him. Moreover, he said, as tutor to many important men's children, he was busy with their affairs. Finally, the Company Assistants had enough of his excuses. They set the date for his sermon for October 17, 1568, and he agreed.[32]

He agreed, but he did not preach, and they voted to take away his money. However, the Lord Mayor of London intervened on Campion's behalf, convincing the company to extend their payments to their old colleague's son another six months before they cut him off, in June 1569.[33] As his money ran out Campion reached a decision. He would leave England for Dublin, to help create the projected University of Dublin.

Accordingly Campion completed his term as Proctor of Oxford, settled his accounts, and left England in August 1569, just before the outbreak of the Revolt of the Northern Earls. After that revolt, and the Pope's bull excommunicating Elizabeth, the middle ground had disappeared for Catholics, even in Ireland. Consequently, Campion, whose sympathies were well known in Dublin, had to move on.

He returned, disguised, to England, where, the story goes, he witnessed the execution of Dr. John Story for the treason of supporting the pope. Strengthened in his resolve by Story's death (baptized to martyrdom with a splash of Story's blood, according to tradition), Campion entered Douai College in France, where he was reconciled to the Catholic Church. In 1573 he became a Jesuit and in 1580 he returned to England, a member of the first Jesuit mission.

In an attempt to make sure that, if he was captured, his true opinions would be available to the public, he wrote his *Decem Rationes*. Widely known as "Campion's Brag," the pamphlet invited anyone to debate him on his ten points. The Queen and the Council, he asserted, were wise, educated, and reasonable, and he was willing to convince them through his sermons. But if they were not willing to be convinced, he promised that many thousands of English people would spend their blood for the salvation of the nation. "And touching our Society [of Jesus] be it known to you that we have made a league . . . cheerfully to carry the cross you shall lay upon us, and never to despair your recovery, while we have a man left to enjoy your Tyburn, or to be racked with your torments, or consumed with your prisons." Clearly Campion had chosen his fate. Captured in July of 1581, Campion got his debates, though under conditions strictly controlled by his enemies. Naturally, they declared victory and Campion was condemned to a traitor's death. He enjoyed Tyburn on December 1, 1581.[34] His example, however, inspired the next generation of Catholic resistors, such as Philip Howard.

The experiences of the generation born around 1540 taught them the mutability of official religion, the need to navigate life carefully, and the necessity of making bold stands consonant with their consciences. The generation born at the end of Mary's reign and the beginning of Elizabeth's reign knew that religious instability only by reputation. They became adults in a world in which religious identities had crystalized. The Council of Trent established certainty for Catholics in 1563; Parliament had finally succeeded in making the Thirty-Nine Articles the law of England, defining Anglicanism, the state religion, in 1571. Puritanism, Presbyterianism, and separatism appeared in the 1570s, too.[35] So these children knew a clearly poly-denominational world. Though their parents may have conformed out of necessity, this new generation was accepting from the beginning. They were the first generation to be raised in a stable Protestant nation, and the gap between their world and the world of their parents produced enormous, creative tension.

Dubbed by Anthony Esler, the "aspiring Elizabethan younger generation," this group included all the leading lights of the English Renaissance. William Shakespeare, Edmund Spenser, Walter Raleigh, Robert Cecil, Robert Devereux, Philip Sidney, Christopher Marlowe, and a host of other major Elizabethans were the children of the 1550s and 1560s.[36]

Grace Sharington married Anthony Mildmay in 1567, when she was fifteen and he was eighteen. Both were raised in families which embraced Protestantism, and Grace Sharington Mildmay left us a detailed description of her pious raising and later life. She lived and died a Protestant, and her memoir, written in the early seventeenth century to educate her granddaughters, is an extended meditation on the operation of God in her life. However, the kind of Protestant she became was probably shaped by her youthful experience. She was an adult before the Church of England, Parliament and the Queen had formally agreed on what English Protestants believed. In that world, her reading and her contacts, with Catholics as well as Protestants, influenced the theological choices she made later. Her belief, for instance, that Catholics could be saved, manifested in her memoir, is consonant with her awareness that so many of those she knew in her youth were Catholics. In a sense, she, like most of her generation, created her own personal theology and made it work for her.

At the core of her raising was a training in godly deportment that differed little from what other girls of her station received. Her governess advised her to do nothing for which her conscience could accuse her, avoiding ribald talk, idle gestures, evil suggestions, and, importantly, people of "subtle spirit, full of words and questions, and of an undermining disposition." Armed against the Devil's wiles, Grace was aware that her reputation could be betrayed by even the most innocent gifts. Reflecting on her father's strictness toward his daughters, she construed it as necessary because parents would answer to God if they neglected the raising of their children. Youngsters must be brought to God and taught to forsake the vanities and follies of the world.[37] As she advised her granddaughter, "hear the word of God attentively and diligently." "Whosoever in the beginning of his life sets this word of God always before his eyes and makes the same his delight and counselor, and examines all that he sees, all that he hears, all that he thinks and all that he loves, wishes or desires by the said word of God, he shall be sure to be preserved in safety."[38]

Grace and Anthony Mildmay had only one child, Mary, born in 1570. We can be sure that Grace attempted to raise her as a godly child. As Grace aged she became more and more certain that only God could be trusted. Her father-in-law, Sir Walter Mildmay, had promised Anthony that he would be his only heir if he married Grace, but Sir Walter split the estate between his two sons when he died in 1589. Anthony's and Grace's attempt to break Sir Walter's will by an act of Parliament failed.[39] Her sister and brother-in-law cheated her out of her inheritance from her father, convincing the old man, the day before he died, to sign a recovery in favor of Grace's sister. Complicated lawsuits against her family followed.[40] Anthony, sent as an ambassador to France 1596–7, proved too inflexible to be a good diplomat. Recalled, he was not paid his expenses by the Queen.[41] In short, life taught one to depend only on God. Guiding one's life by His precepts was the only refuge in a fickle world.

It appears that the religious amalgam Grace Mildmay formed in her youth served her well. If her memoir is to be believed, she used it every day of her life, giving meanings to her tribulations. She practiced what Linda Pollock called "applied rather than theoretical Calvinism." Unable to accept that others, including Catholics, might not be saved, she, who clearly believed she was one of the elect, still believed that most people might be saved if they repented, ceased their wickedness, and turned to God. Like many Protestants, she was unable to accept the black and white simplicity of Calvinist double predestination. Like Catholics who took comfort in the idea that the "not so evil" would enter Heaven after purification in Purgatory, Grace Mildmay believed that most of us are neither so reprobate nor so saintly as to be clearly predestined. So there was hope for us all. She was practicing covenant theology – the idea that God guaranteed salvation if you lived according to God's laws as if you were elected to salvation. It was theology of the sort that English Protestants had learned from William Tyndale in the 1520s.[42]

Certainly, when her husband died in 1617, she cast both his life and hers into a Protestant mold. Seeing in his corpse her corpse, she reminded herself of their reunion at the resurrection. "This my corpse was a man with whom I lived almost fifty years," she wrote, observing through all those years God's favor toward him. He escaped plagues, drowning, and wars. He survived when a lance splinter "ran far into the midst of his forehead," and when he was shot in the head. God's protecting hand hovered over him, and yet he was humble and aware of his own "errors and defects which he found in himself betwixt him and God," earnestly trying to turn his thoughts away from temptations, "which was an assured token of his election and that he was a blessed man unto whom the Lord imputed not his sin." Her own election was demonstrated in that God had preserved her integrity and faithfulness to Anthony, and He always righted her wrongs, as her whole life showed.[43]

Grace Mildmay was a devout woman with a certainty of election, embodying the best parts of Protestant conviction. Thomas Myddelton, a Welshman born in Denbigh in about 1556, displays other sides of the new cultural world. A pious Protestant, he embodied new attitudes toward social morality, exploiting the economic opportunities and attitudes of Elizabeth's age to become a self-made financier and Lord Mayor of London.

A proud member of a Welsh family that held land on both sides of the border, Thomas Myddelton was apprenticed as a merchant. By 1578 he was factor to Ferdinando Poyntz in Flushing, dealing in sugar.[44] Understanding the sugar market, he returned to London in the early 1580s and, as a freeman of the Grocers' Company which controlled sales of spices, he set up on his own as a merchant, establishing his factors at Stade on the Elbe, trading in cloth, sugar and spices. By 1595 he was operating a sugar refinery in London and was a liveryman of the Grocers' Company, which would eventually elect him to its governing Court of Assistants.

His success was undoubtedly aided by a good marriage. In 1585 he married Hester Salstonstall. Her father, Richard, was a merchant in the Low Countries, rising to prominence and wealth in London. By the time of their marriage, Richard Saltonstall was the Governor of the Merchant Adventurers, well placed to help the young man. Sadly, Hester died, two years and two children later.

As was true for many enterprising Tudor men, Myddelton combined his business interests with profitable public service. By 1585 Myddelton had become a deputy to Sir Francis Walsingham in the customs farm, the privatized system of tax collection. In 1592 he became a surveyor of the outports, a job that not only paid well, but put him in contact with all the leading seamen and merchants of the realm. During the long hostilities with Spain, Myddelton invested in the voyages of Drake, Hawkins, and Raleigh, whose seizure of Spanish shipping in the new world made Myddelton even richer. While profiting from privateering, the running sore of the Nine Years War in Ireland brought him new opportunities as a merchant providing victuals for the troops there.

Profits from these activities provided principal for his money lending business. Living in a time when usury, at 10 per cent, was legal for the first time ever, he became a successful financier. Lending money to his neighbors in North Wales brought him blocks of land there by foreclosure, and he bought even more. In 1595 he bought the lordship of Chirk in Denbighshire, which became his son's seat. Not surprisingly, he was elected to represent Merioneth in the Parliament of 1597.

Although he invested heavily in Wales, his primary focus of activity was London. By the time he married his fourth wife in 1603, he was serving as an Alderman and the Sheriff of the City. Lord Mayor in 1613–14, he represented the City in the Parliaments of 1624, 1625, and 1626.

Through all of his activities as a liveryman, money lender, tax collector, member of Parliament and mayor, Myddleton was living his faith. Perhaps his greatest legacy to the Kingdom was his support of Welsh letters and religion. A devout Protestant, he moved in circles who believed that the word of God had to be read by the people. The Welsh people, however, though they had a prayer book in Welsh, had no Bible and little else cheaply available in their own language. Thomas Myddelton, one of Wales' most successful businessmen, became the patron of Welsh authors and translators who were taking the Word of God to the Welsh in print. Myddelton and Rowland Heylyn supported a group of men whose goal was to make religion a living presence in Welsh hearts. Orthodox Protestants, they produced a number of important works, including a Welsh metrical psalter. But most importantly, Myddelton helped bankroll *Y Beibl Bach*, a Welsh Bible that sold for only 5 shillings when it appeared in 1630, the year before Thomas Myddelton died.[45]

The Welsh boy born in the middle of Mary's reign is a model younger Elizabethan. He married deep Protestant conviction with great ambition and financial success. His religious ideals of sober responsibility for his own relationship with God was matched by a sober calculation of profit and an understanding of the new economic world. His conscience could tolerate lending at interest so long as the law allowed it; unlike his father's generation, he assumed that interest rates were a secular matter. The sin of usury was a matter of conscience, not law. As a member of Parliament in 1624 he presumably voted for the new usury law that so secularized the offense that the bishops felt constrained to add a clarifying proviso: "That no words in the law contained shall be construed or expounded to allow the practice of usury in point of religion or conscience."[46]

As another Elizabethan said about usury, its existence depended upon the intent of the lender. Rejecting a moral theology stretching all the way back to St. Jerome, and adapting a new one invented in the middle of the sixteenth century, Walter Howse put it succinctly. When a man lends with the intent to do his neighbor good, there is no sin. So long as the borrower and lender are in charity, and the lender is not forcing impossible terms on the needy borrower, lending is condoned by God – so long as the lender has a "proviso written in the book of his conscience" that he will not molest borrowers who are down on their luck.[47] Presumably, Myddleton would have agreed with the apology written in defense of his colleague "Rich" Richard Sutton. Though a major money lenders, it says, Sutton was not a usurer because he used his wealth to do good. He had good intentions and he fulfilled them by being a conscientious businessman and member of the community.[48] Myddelton's patronage of scholars, service to London, service to the Crown, and service to the Grocers' Company seems to put him into the same category. Using the gifts God gave him, he gave back to God and country in a way consonant with the emerging English Protestant culture.

Others of his contemporaries were more skeptical about the comfortable fit between profit, conscience, and election. Looking at religion as a choice that might be made by an individual guided by conscience, they also could see the choice of religious obedience as a matter of convenience or advantage. In an age stressing outward conformity, they saw religion as real only if it warmed the heart. Consequently, their view of quarreling theologians was dim. A Latin doggerel in Thomas Butte's commonplace book puts it bluntly and sarcastically:

> Sacramental wine does not change the life of the minster,
> As deterioration doesn't deteriorate the deteriorator,
> A better presbyterian makes nothing better.[49]

They were a generation as likely to mock as to be true believers, responding to their parents' enthusiasms with some coldness, seeking their certainties from within rather from without. Their world was a perplexing place where received truths mutated rapidly. Thomas Bastard (1566–1618), in his sonnet "Ad lectorem de Subiecto Operis Sui" called it "a wilderness or mass confuse," lamenting

> Easy it were the earth to portray out,
> Or to draw forth the heavens' purest frame,
> Whose restless course by order whirls about
> Of change and place, and still remain the same.
> But how shall men's, or manner's form appear,
> Which while I write, do change from what they were?[50]

In a generation full of famous examples one is torn between the bitter skepticism and possible atheism of Marlowe and the *peregrinato ad deum* of John Donne, but since no knife ended Donne's career prematurely, he makes a better case study.

Born early in 1572, Donne was younger than Shakespeare, Marlowe, Sidney and Spenser, but only by a few years. Son of Catholic parents, his birth coincided with the first concerted persecutions of Catholics, so he was among the very first English children to be raised with an awareness that they were recusants, religiously unlike the majority and lacking full civil rights. And this awareness was not secondhand. In 1574 Donne's great uncle was hanged, drawn, and quartered for traitorous allegiance to the papacy; two of his uncles became Jesuits. One, his mother's brother Jasper, was imprisoned in the Tower of London in 1584, escaping execution only because, as a former page to the Queen, she allowed him exile instead. The 12-year-old John's mother smuggled messages, and even William Weston, another Jesuit priest, in to see her brother in the Tower. The boy may himself have visited the Tower, and witnessed executions of Catholics.

That same year John was sent to Hart Hall in Oxford to begin his university education. Chosen because it had no chapel and therefore did not make its members attend one, an important consideration for a Catholic, Hart Hall gave him education but not a degree. Since anyone taking a degree had to swear the oath of supremacy, Catholics did not take them. While he was in Oxford, the Hall's catechist was Antonio del Corro, an ex-monk, whose moderate, anti-Calvinist theology stirred visceral hatred in some of the more godly. Whatever else he may have learned from Corro, he must have been made very aware of the divisions within Protestantism. It is believed that he went to Cambridge in the late 1580s, and there, too, he would have seen some spectacular displays of theological intemperance as Perkins, Baro, and their acolytes struggled with one another over the nature of election and other knotty points of the Calvinist theology.

Leaving the universities, Donne went to the law, entering Thavies Inn, a school for equity law, moving to Lincoln's Inn on the common law side in 1592. Twenty years old, he found himself in the lively culture of the Inns, where literary and theatrical tastes were honed as well as law, and where more fleshly pleasures abounded. It was there that he began to write poetry, and where he became notable as a ladies man. It was also while he was in Lincoln's Inn that his brother Henry was caught harboring a priest. Charged with felony, Henry died of plague in Newgate prison.

By now Donne was wealthy, and he may have used some of that wealth to travel. There is speculation that he spent time in Spain, which may account for his knowledge of Spanish. It may also be that living in a Catholic country for a period disturbed the young recusant's certainty about his religion. A nation where everyone was Catholic must have presented a different face than the Catholicism of the embattled English recusants.

Certainly by the mid-1590s Donne was seriously exploring his relationship with religion. Possibly still a Catholic, he was interrogating what religion was or ought to be, wrestling with his Catholic upbringing. In 1610 he recalled how, "I used no inordinate haste nor precipitation in binding my conscience to any local religion." He made no determination until he had, he continued, "surveyed and digested the whole body of divinity controverted between ours [Anglican] and the Roman Church." The satires and elegies he wrote during this period show his deep appreciation of the irony and hypocrisy visible in all denominations.

The result of Donne's survey was conformity or conversion to the Anglican church. It is impossible to say when he made his decision to conform, but it was sometime near his participation in the Earl of Essex's successful attack on Cadiz. Donne enlisted in that expedition in 1596, sailing with Essex again on the Islands Expedition, which failed to seize the Spanish treasure fleet. On that second voyage he became acquainted with Thomas Egerton, son of Lord Keeper Sir Thomas Egerton. On his return Donne entered Egerton's service, taken by all biographers as proof that he had conformed, despite his personal motto "ante muerto que mudado" ("sooner dead than altered").

Alteration of religion paid off in many ways, including a seat in Parliament in 1601, and he was rising in the world, when he did a stupid thing. He courted Ann More, the sixteen-year-old niece of Egerton's wife, who was living with them. The couple married, without permission, in February 1602. Ann's father was enraged, and Egerton felt that his servant had violated his trust. Dismissed by the Lord Keeper, Donne was imprisoned while his father-in-law sued to get the marriage dissolved. The union, however, was legal and Donne was eventually released and reconciled with Sir George More. Unfortunately, Egerton would not take him back, and his career was in ruins.

Cast out of favor and into country seclusion, Donne spent several years writing poetry, studying civil and canon law, and cultivating patrons. It was then that he wrote most of his *Divine Poems*, including his meditation on the operation of grace

> Batter My heart, three person'd God; for you
> As yet but knock, breathe, shine, and seek to mend;
> That I may rise, and stand, o'erthrow me, and bend
> Your force, to break, blow, burn and make me new.
> I, like an usurpt town, t'another due,
> Labour to admit you, but Oh, to no end.
> Reason, your viceroy in me, me should defend,
> But is catpiv'd and proves weak or untrue.
> Yet dearly I love you, and would be loved fain,
> But am betroth'd unto your enemy:
> Divorce me, untie or break that knot again,
> Take me to you, imprison me, for I
> Except you enthrall me, never shall be free,
> Nor ever chaste, except you ravish me.[51]

Clearly, the man who wrote that had come to a felt understanding God's love and his own inadequacy that was not at all Catholic, and not rational either, suggesting that his search for the hill of Truth had ended a very personal event.

With the accession of James I, Donne's opportunities improved. Eventually, on January 23, 1615, with the King's urging, he chose to be ordained as an Anglican minister. In the following March the King pressured Cambridge into awarding him the degree of Doctor of Divinity, making it clear that this minister of two months was on the fast track for advancement. The business of the doctorate underscored the resentment felt against Donne's rapid climb up the ladder of royal patronage. In a university and church bounded by established courses of advancement, Donne had jumped the queue. As John Chamberlain reported in a letter from Cambridge on March 30, 1615, Donne "purchased himself a great deal of envy, that a man of his sort should seem *per saltem* [at a leap] to intercept . . . so many more worthy and ancient divines."[52] Donne was appointed the Divinity Reader for Lincoln's Inn in 1617, where he began his brilliant preaching career. By 1622 he was well enough entrenched in the Court to be appointed Dean of St. Paul's.

By the time he died in 1631 Donne had obtained a kind of Anglican sainthood.[53] It was not an ending that would have pleased his parents, his teachers, his siblings, or many of his college friends, but it was a brilliant career which rested on a clear understanding of how the politics of religion worked in the early seventeenth century. For Donne believed religion was an interior experience, and he understood that there was a market for religion like everything else. Clearly, he did not see the two in contradiction, and he knew the power of the Supreme Governor of the Church in ecclesiastical politics. He was a religious man of the post-Reformation era. Used to religious diversity and a church subservient to a nationalist ideal, he made it work for him.

Neither Grace Mildmay nor John Donne understood the religious world that produced people like the monk Robert Joseph. For them, religion was about personal, internal conformity with God's will more than participation in the community of Christians. They were a product of a national experience which taught each generation a further lesson about the insubstantiality of religious institutions, about the corrupting fanaticism of those who claimed to speak in God's name, and about how much religion of all sorts was a product of political happenstance. By late in Elizabeth's reign they had learned to live in a multivalent religious world. The pretense that everyone could be brought to one truth under one true church had dissolved in the face of multiple religious possibilities. Increasingly, true religion was measured by either patriotic conformity, or the political act of separation. But that mutable political world only conscience could be trusted as a guide for the soul.

The politics of Reformation were lived by everyone. They could not be avoided, for they impacted every institution and penetrated the world views of those living the experience. As each generation accepted previous changes as natural and reacted to new challenges, the nation slowly acquired a post-Reformation culture. Based on Protestantism, that culture was an amalgam, adaptation and refashioning of many existing habits, but the end product was a very different set of life choices for people in 1610 than there had been in 1510.

Individual choices were shaping post-Reformation culture because individuals acted them out within the context of institutions. "No man is an island, entire of itself" wrote John Donne in middle age, making a point historians must remember. All histories are congregations of biographies, and all biographers track their subjects through public spaces. The adaptations of the Reformation generations, as they came together in parish churches, guildhalls, town halls, colleges, and all the other places people meet in consensus and conflict, become evident in the histories of their institutions.

3

Families and Reformations

"I may . . . persuade myself," young Richard Hooker told his congregation in the Temple Church one morning in 1585, "that thousands of our fathers in former times, living and dying within her [the Catholic Church's] walls, have found mercy at the hands of God." Horrified, the second minister of the Temple Church, Walter Travers, preached a sermon of refutation that same afternoon. The thought that any Catholic could escape hellfire upset him terribly. He feared tolerance, even of dead Catholics, would lead people back to Satan.

Hooker's position was a comforting one for all those who remembered their parents and neighbors who had died confessing faith in Christ as the chrism was applied. Unless, they reasoned, the departed had been priests and other teachers of error, they were not much more likely to be in Hell than backsliding Protestants. It was not a doctrine liked by those who wished to condemn all who had supported Catholicism in the past. But most people could accept that dying ignorantly, sure of one's Catholic faith, was not the fault of the defunct. As Hooker noted, quoting Sir Thomas More's defense of works, it is easy "even for men of great capacity and judgment to mistake things written or spoken." And so he concluded "We must therefore be contented both to pardon others and to crave that others may pardon us for such things."[1]

The blow of the Reformation cracked families, introducing divisive reversals of authority and contradictory values. They had to find ways to cope with the fissures. Families did not explode under the pressure. They reinvented their folklore, remade their memorials, rewrote their wills, ignored their religious differences, and sought ways to minimize the tension within and withstand the pressure from without. In the process they tended toward neutral ground, private treaties of internal toleration that allowed the bonds of love and duty to paper over the chasms of ideology.

These private treaties of tolerance began to harden into habit in the later years of Elizabeth's reign, when what Hooker had dared to say was a common concern. In the 1580s nearly every Protestant in England had Catholic grandparents, if not parents, creating self-contradiction in a religion which taught that parents were to be honored and obeyed. Even if they were certain that Catholics must all be burning in Hell, bonds of affection and duty made it nearly impossible for people to abandon their progenitors and kin as damned. As the son says to his mother in *A Conference Betwixt a Mother a Devout Recusant and Her Sonne a Zealous Protestant* of 1599, "your firm and fervent love to me, dear mother, gives me encouragement to speak boldly unto you what I am . . . within terms of duty and reverence ever due unto you." His love and duty prompts him to attempt her conversion to Protestantism.[2]

The Reformation demanded that one resign loved ones to Hell — beloved grandparents, dear siblings, and, often, one's own children. Christ commanded his followers to give up father and mother for his sake, and to let the dead bury the dead, as theologians were happy to repeat, enjoining people to follow their consciences. However, to obey conscience often meant rebellion against parental authority, separation from one's family, and removal from the culture of one's youth, placing one's own judgement above the authority of everyone but God.

How did a family deal with these rebellions as each generation, in its turn, found its values rejected and watched some of its precious kin disappear into the maw of Hell, led on by the will-o'-the-wisp of conscience? And once people had learned to accept this, what kind of society emerged? Needless to say, there are many different responses to the problem but, humans, emotionally unable to live as theologians, tend toward compromise. In families, if nowhere else, people had to learn to accept a multi-denominational world in which each individual was recognized to have some choice in how he or she related to God.

The trouble began with changed religious allegiances that took a multiplicity of forms, ranging from the frightening burst of spiritual certainty that blinded St. Paul, through the intellectual conversion that convinced the head, to the emotional warmth that convinced the heart, to the pragmatic conformity that convinced the ego and kept the purse full, to the unthinking acceptance of a world unlike that of one's parents. Everyone in England who became Protestant experienced one of these forms, and each form presented a different problem for those above and below them in age.

The people most likely to be attracted to new doctrines were youngsters. Inquisitive and rebellious, they were challenging their elders as they found their own identities. Ironically, those same youngsters grew into parents and grandparents, watching their radical ideas become accepted norms beyond which their children tried to push. This meant that the cultural changes of the sixteenth century sank in slowly, generation by generation, and that all the changes were negotiated between the values of the elders and the youth. What seemed strange and new to one generation seemed natural to the next, but young and old had to live together.

This chapter asks how the culture of personal and family life changed in response to the great crisis of values brought on by the Reformation in England. Creating neutral private spaces, in which conformity and deviance in religion were accepted as individual choices, families developed strategies for coping that prevented disintegration while shaping group identity.

Inverted Obedience

The family was where training in obedience to authority began, with each child possessed of parents or parent surrogates who expected and taught obedience. In the family home, and in the extended family of a master, a child was brought up to serve and obey, instructed in religion, and turned into an economically viable person. Wives, servants and children were in tutelage, a state which assumed that their superiors knew better than they on all subjects. But the cultural changes of the sixteenth century damaged that neat model of patriarchal authority by inserting an appeal to God in conscience that could overturn the rulings of one's superiors.

Archbishop Whitgift, preaching the Accession Day sermon at St. Paul's in celebration of the Queen's Elizabeth's ascent to the throne, tried to convince his listeners that obedience to the Queen was absolutely necessary, ordained by God. But he knew there would be objections, and he himself had to admit their justice. The magistrate's orders bind "in conscience" and must be obeyed on pain of damnation. Unless, he excepted, the magistrate commands anything against the will of God. Then "*Melius est obedire Deo quam hominibus*": i.e. "It is better to obey God than men."[3]

But this theology damaged traditional conceptions of family hierarchy and responsibility. It taught children to prefer God to their parents, wives to dispute with their ungodly husbands, and God's servants to demand the death of Queens and the overthrow of magistrates who failed to obey God's will. As many people in authority recognized, these ideas were dangerous.

Reformation, of the kind the evangelical reformers hoped to instill, was supposed to begin in the heart. There God's loving grace worked to produce faith and comfort, transforming those whose hearts were awakened, empowering them to act with the certainty of faith. But people acting out of faith and conviction often trampled human conventions, with disruptive and embarrassing consequences.

Writing to his mother from his rooms in the Inner Temple in about 1536, 19-year-old Robert Plumpton instructed his mother in religion. "I am bound to write to you, yea and you were not my mother, because it hath pleased God . . . to send me some understanding of scriptures," an understanding that demanded an evangelical fervor toward everyone. "It is my duty to instruct you," he told her, in the rule left by Christ, recorded in the Bible. "Wherefore, I would desire you for the love of God, that you would read the New Testament, which is the true Gospel of God . . ." He did not, he insisted, seek to teach her heresy, but to show her the "clear light of God's doctrine." To that end, he sent her the small edition of Tyndale's translation of the New Testament, urging her to read the "introducement" to find the marvelous things hidden therein.

With puppy presumption, Plumpton concluded that his mother was lucky to have lived long enough to see the return of God's word, "for the gospel of Christ was never so truly preached as it is now." Continuing, he reminded her of the covenant made in baptism and the necessity of having God's law written on her heart. In one paragraph he beautifully paraphrases Tyndale's "Prologue to the Epistle of Paul to the Romans," which is itself a translation of Luther's prologue to the same book. There he found the essence of Protestant faith, the knowledge of the law of God,

understanding it spiritually as Christ expounded it, Matthew v, vj, & vij chapters, so that the root and life of all laws is this: love thy lord God with all thy heart, all thy soul, all thy might, and all thy power, and thy neighbor as thyself, for Christ's sake; and love only is the fulfilling of the law . . . and that whatsoever we do and not of that love, that same fulfils not the law in the sight of God . . .[4]

How his mother, whom he describes as fervent about God's laws, responded to his letters we do not know. They reached her about the time the Pilgrimage of Grace began to swirl around their Yorkshire home. It is possible that Elizabeth Plumpton recoiled with horror from her son's flirtation with Lutheranism. At any rate, his parents saw to it that he married into a family that was and remained devoutly Catholic.

Robert Plumpton's temerity in lecturing his mother grew from his certainty that his elders were raised in a time of religious darkness. It was a common feeling among English people who discovered Protestantism in its early years. As a young man John Hooper, the future Edwardian Bishop of Gloucester, had sought to obey God by becoming a Cistercian monk, but after the dissolution of his monastery, he converted to Protestantism. This horrified his father, who remained a devout Catholic. He once wrote Bullinger that his father so opposed his Protestantism that the old man promised him to become a "cruel tyrant" in the future if he did not return to Catholicism. In 1550 Hooper reported that his father was still living in ignorance of the true religion.[5]

Whether John Hooper's father ever was a cruel tyrant, it must have been hard, and baffling, for his family when John, having become a bishop in the reformed Edwardian church, was burnt to death for heresy. Had he obeyed his father he would not have endured such an end.

John Hooper made conscience his guide, but he assumed that God spoke through conscience and had to be obeyed. Fathers and Queens could command him to ignore the conviction of his conscience, but he could not obey without risking his soul, even though God had, in other places, commanded him to obey his father and the magistrates. As Sir Francis Hastings told a correspondent, identified only as "cousin

Ann S_____" in 1574, obedience to family was dangerous to the soul. There were, he told her, many worldly persuasions that would pry her soul away from God, and the greatest of these was her family. Therefore, he wrote, "Take heed . . . how you give ear to popish persuasions . . . I know they will say to you: your father, your mother, all your friends and kindred are good Catholics and in professing this religion you must needs condemn them and all your forefathers which were wise and learned . . ." to them she must answer: "each one is saved by his own faith and not by the faith of another." Although her enemies would tell her that if she embraces God she forsakes family, she should remember that Christ taught that those who will not forsake father and mother for His sake will not have eternal life.[6]

Early in 1553 William Baldwin, in his satirical novel *Beware the Cat*, gave voice to the same inversion. Listening to the cats gossip, the reader hears Mouse-Slayer tell a story which, she says, occurred "in the time when preachers had leave to speak against the mass, but it was not forbidden." "My dame . . . and her husband," she says, "were both old, and therefore hard to be turned from their rooted belief which they had in the Mass, which caused divers young folk, chiefly their sons . . . to be the more earnest to persuade them." Now, it happened that the old lady went suddenly blind. Sending for her parish priest, she was told that her blindness was caused by God, who was punishing her for listening to heretics who denied transubstantiation. Repenting, she received the Eucharist and her vision was restored by sight of the communion "cake." She thanked the priest exceedingly, and he charged her

that she should tell to no young folks how she was holp, for his bishop had throughout the diocese forbidden them to say or sing any Mass, but commanded her that secretly unto old honest men and women she should at all times most devoutly rehearse it. And by reason of this miracle, many are so confirmed in that belief that, although by common law all Masses upon penalty were since forbidden, divers have them privily and nightly said in the chambers until this day.[7]

Clearly, Baldwin's cats knew that masses were for the old, not the young, who were opposed to their parents' faiths.

To abandon one's family for the faith was a weighty matter, and, in the hierarchical world of sixteenth-century England, it required the certainty that came from knowing with heart and head that one was following God.

Of course, if a man was following God, his family was expected to follow him. As John Knox put it, paraphrasing St. Paul, "brethren, you are ordained of God to rule your own houses in his true fear, and according to his word. Within your houses, I say, in some cases, you are bishops and kings; your wife, children, servants and family are your bishopric and charge."[8] Thus a man whose conscience was awakened to faith was expected to take his family with him. But what if his family did not want to go? What if family members had convictions contrary to those of the patriarch? Could a woman have a free conscience? As Knox so famously put it, a woman could have no authority over a man, and she must be guided by men, even if she is single, because St. Paul commanded women to keep silent in the church. And yet the doctrine of priesthood of the believer seemed to free women and children from spiritual obedience to men, if those men did not obey God.[9]

Ironically, the gendered language of obedience to God equated female attendance at mass with adultery, but the "man" betrayed was God and the monarch, not the husband, though his honor was deeply impugned if his wife refused to obey him in matters of religion. Marian religious prisoners often wrote their wives demanding that they refuse to attend mass, commanding them as husbands to obey God. And yet women were, of necessity, credited with the ability to obey God in their consciences if their husbands failed to command them to it.[10]

In some cases this forced a direct reversal of the hierarchy. Bishop Hooper, imprisoned in the Fleet, awaiting execution for heresy, wrote a letter of advice concerning a woman whose husband was troubling her for her Protestantism. Hooper walked the fine line between counseling obedience as commanded by Paul, and rebellion as demanded by God. The wife was to convert her husband if she could. If she could not, she was to entreat him to allow her freedom of conscience and not force her to attend mass. If he would not agree, but used her lovingly, she was to stay with him, even though he might turn her in as a heretic. But if she was too weak to face execution, then "rather than to break company and marriage with God and her, conjoined by the precious blood of Christ, she must convey herself into some such place as idolatry may be avoided. For if the husband love the wife, or the wife more the husband, more than Christ, he or she be not meet for Christ." If the wife felt she had to depart rather than disobey God, she was to associate herself with honest, virtuous and godly company, to demonstrate her godly intentions.[11]

In 1593 John Penry, awaiting execution for publishing a defense of separatism attempting to prove that his idea of reformation was not inimical to the nation, instructed his spouse on her behavior after his death: she ought to remarry after his execution, but "take heed to your choice that first he with whom you marry be of the same holy faith and profession with you, next that he be meet to be your head, even such a one as you shall think meet to govern you as an head and to rule you as a lord, and in this choice look not to wealth or estimation in the world, yet rather choose many blessings . . . but only respect the fear of God and the meetness of the person."[12] In short, choose God, and a husband to match.

By the time Penry was executed it was possible to argue that a recusant wife was a danger to civil order. A wife, whose womanly weakness led her into recusancy, argued John Leggat in 1599, demonstrated that her husband could not rule at home, making it impossible for him to rule "abroad." And so, by the same logic, ignorant, weak women, Satan's instrument since the Fall, refusing to use God's religion appointed by the Queen, threatened the foundations of the entire kingdom.[13] And yet, the wife's conscience was to be directed by the gospel.

Young people, even male youngsters, were under the same tutelage as wives and were expected to obey their parents in all things. But here, too, the monopoly on conscience demanded by sixteenth-century religion sanctioned disobedience in God's name. Rebellious youth found this a useful doctrine, and, as Susan Brigden has shown in her seminal article on "Youth in the Reformation," they were more likely than most to find the liberty of the gospel exciting, especially when combined with an iconoclastic riot.[14] Declaring one's Protestantism in the 1530s, or one's Catholicism in the 1590s, was a sure way to declare youthful independence.

John Foxe tells many stories of the splits occurring in families because of the forwardness of the youth for the gospel. Julius Palmer's mother was so upset with her son's heterodoxy she threw him out of her house, refused to see him again, and ordered him to no longer recognize her as his mother. Cutting him from her will, she declared "thy father bequeathed nought for heretics: faggots I have to burn thee."[15]

Could God, who commanded "honor thy father and thy mother," and insisted that magistrates be obeyed, overturn his ordained hierarchy with haphazard gifts of spiritual conviction? And if He did, what then? What if father, mother, grandfather, grandmother, Queen and bishop − all those God taught you to obey − insisted you were wrong? Did you dishonor yourself if you obeyed them rather than God? The son in Leggat's dialogue between a recusant mother and her Protestant son confronts this directly, pointing out that conversion, and the certainty that goes with it, is the result of divine grace operating in the converted person. "Did ever any whom we read of in the scripture," he asked, "feeling the piercing power of God's spirit smiting upon the rock of their hidden heart [say] they would yield after three months, or six months?" "No, no." In criticizing his mother he was not being critical of her; he was doing what God willed him to do, as an instrument of divine grace, but it was about her, not him. "Your self be judge and answer yourself," he told her, since only conscience could be her guide.[16] Thus, disobedience to human authorities was never true disobedience if inspired by God. The disobedient child or subject might actually be the instrument of conversion chosen to do God's work − a sort of Judas Iscariot, without whom Christ would not have been betrayed so he could die for humanity's sins.

As the concept of personal religious choice penetrated society, concepts of honor changed to include the idea that living one's personal life according to one's personal religious values was highly honorable. As Felicity Heal has pointed out, the newer concepts of honor could, by the late sixteenth century, be wholly internalized, owing nothing to external affirmations. To be "godly" was to be honorable.[17] So long as you knew you were acting honorably, and God knew it, you were honorable. This internalization contributed, naturally, to a further isolation of an individual's honor from the honor of the family.

Family Memory

Often the differences between generations are not so much in what they say they believe, as in how they talk about it. William Holcott, who describes himself as "God's meanest minister and simplest servant (yea the vilest and wickedest worm of the western world and island of England)," made his will when he was "about age sixty," in 1573. Born about 1513, Holcott had experienced the entire Reformation as a cleric, holding the parish of Buckland in Berkshire at the time of his death.

Clearly a Protestant, believing in the priesthood of the believer and rejecting the intercession of saints, he nonetheless chose to describe Christ as "my continual chantry priest." A strange choice of words for a Protestant, yet, for a man who was nearly forty when prayers for the dead were first forbidden, they conveyed exactly his abandonment of purgatory and acceptance of Christ as his savior. To Tom Love, his heir, such a choice of words must have seemed odd indeed. Love had been baptized by Holcott and confirmed by Bishop John Jewel sometime in the 1560s. With only an historical knowledge of chantries as one of the superstitions practiced in the dark times of papistry, Love would never think to talk of Christ as his "chantry priest."[18]

The slow loss of memory that accompanied the loss of the material evidence and availability of older forms of religious expression meant that within two generations people no longer spoke "old Catholic." The liturgical forms had become alien, the responses and prayers had been forgotten, and the events had dimmed, even for those who were inclined to prefer them. To the young they were alien.

In 1607 20-year-old John Ridgeway recalled how he was taught the sign of the cross by his guardian,

which, although I did not know the virtue of it, nor why I made it, yet I know that I observed it as diligently as I could, especially when I went to bed; and when I went out I perceived that women on meeting did so and I thought that if those women should be witches, they might likewise be magicians (which in those parts are greatly pestered), and this thought used frequently to fill me with fear.[19]

Ridgeway's confusion is not surprising. Government officials and Protestant preachers had worked hard to be sure that youngsters saw such Catholic ritual actions in a negative light. Their iconoclastic campaigns were designed to obliterate the images of the old church, and to eradicate popular understanding of the old habits. The cross, in all its forms, was the subject of learned dismissals. In 1566 Mr. Harris of

New College told the audience at Paul's Cross making the sign of the cross worked no magic, telling how it failed to prevent the suicidal depression of a young man who left Oxford for Rome, where he threw himself into a river.[20] No wonder a boy of the 1590s saw it as old womens' superstition.

But this enthusiasm for rewriting and obliterating the past left gaps in personal, familial, and national narratives. How could John Ridgeway understand the grandmothers of his Devon village who made the sign of the cross? The late Elizabethan and Jacobean enthusiasm for antiquarianism was, in many ways, about recovering versions of the past that could patch the holes left by Reformation.

These holes were not just in religious practices; they were in all forms of daily life which had been connected with the church in the "old days." In 1595 John Martin of Clare, Suffolk, was called by a commission of the Duchy of Lancaster as a witness in a case concerning the property of an almshouse. Aged about 75, Martin was there because he embodied the parish memory. He could recall, he said, a board, hanging in the chancel of his parish church, on which were inscribed the list of lands belonging to the parish. Though it was removed during the dissolution of the chantries under Edward VI, he could still recall some of its content, since he had heard it read often from the time he was born, about 1520, until it was taken out.[21] Functioning as a mnemonic device for the parish, this board kept alive a world of pious intentions along with the literal memory of property owned. Martin's aged memory was one of the last links to that time when donors exacted prayers from the parish in return for their property.

The reading of the board in Clare church stabilized the memories of even the illiterate, while oral history was busy remembering the past in new ways. A character in a dialogue says in 1608, " 'We old men are old chronicles . . . our speeches, like leaves turned over and over, discover wonders long since passed.' "[22] But what he does not say is that memory is a strange and faulty thing, prating unconscious of the editing, lacunae, and manipulation that shape it. Propagandists understand this intuitively, and in Reformation England the invention of new memory was a national industry, and a personal strategy for making sense of tales told by old folk around the fire. Seeing the memories of their elders through their own eyes, people remembered the past in ways they could understand it, in ways that reenforced their own values. And they confused "remembered" with "read" and "experienced" with "heard of."

John Aubrey, busy saving the memories of the past in the seventeenth century, once remarked that " 'before women were readers, the history was handed down from mother to daughter, ' "when they sat up late by the fire telling tales " 'of the old time.' "[23] But that was "before women could read." The culture of the post-Reformation world was, as Aubrey knew, producing more and more readers, contaminating what he believed to be a pure source of history. In fact, the source was never pure. As Adam Fox has shown, much of what passed for folk memory in early modern England was shaped by printed accounts, whose contents were transmuted into folklore. This transference was one of the ways in which post-Reformation generations, saturated with sermons and increasingly literate, acquired a version of history that explained the superstition and darkness that had existed before their enlightened time. Popular knowledge went from the page, to the ear, to the folk memory, and then back again to the collecting antiquarian's page. Memories were often inventions of the propagandists.

Family folklore was subjected to a different sort of editing. Obviously, tales told about the history of the family around its hearth were not taken from books. But as they were retold, they were recast into new molds. A sort of "political correctness" edited and re-moralized the tales. For instance, Sir William Wentworth liked to remember his family's history, recording the providences his family had enjoyed. In 1607 he told the story of his own conception, in 1561.

Sir William was a Protestant, so he edited it for Protestant consumption. By 1561, he relates, his father and mother had "only" four daughters in eleven years, but not a son. Then it pleased God to visit the elder Sir William with a burning fever, during which, while he was lying in what was now, he told his son, the dining room, an apparition of a "well favored gentlewoman of a middle age in apparel and countenance decent and very demur" appeared. "Wentworth," she said, "I come from God," calling herself "God's pity." She was there to tell him he would live many more years (he died in 1588) and have a son. Putting her hand into his bed, she anointed his privates and said "when thou art well, go to the well at St. Anne of Buxton and there wash thyself and thank God." According to the prediction, he recovered, bathed at the well of St. Anne, and begot a son. The younger Sir William said his father and mother both liked to tell this story.[24]

Strikingly, this was not the sort of miracle that Protestants expected to enjoy. The intercessions of saints were not vouchsafed them. Consequently, Sir William did not conclude, as his father, mother and grandmother probably did, that St. Anne had answered their prayers and given them a male heir. Just who edited the story is unclear, since his parents may, by the time he was old enough to hear it, have dropped references to a saint, but it remains an important example of how memory changed to fit changing times. Some events needed explanations that were more appropriate to the age.

This mutation and emendation of memory went on at all levels and in all sorts of institutions. Family folklore, however, was special, in that it was so localized. Sir William was pleased to repeat his father's satisfaction that no one in their family ever made a living as a priest or a lawyer, but not all families had such clear consciences when it came to their ancestors. Every family tree was full of people who had lived in times of superstition, duped by the Devil and Antichrist into following the damnable Catholic religion. The Elizabethan Protestant enjoyed election to salvation, but what of his or her father and mother, grandparents, kin, neighbors and all the rest? Protestant family chronicles are strikingly quiet about ancestors who were devout Catholics.

The Elizabethan Catholic had another sort of problem. Families which had remained loyal to the old religion were increasingly excluded from public life as suspicions of their allegiances deepened. This exclusion created an identity crisis for people whose social rank indicated that they ought to be defending and governing the nation. One response to this disjunction between their social rank and their current impotence was to create a version of family history that glorified their isolation as proof of their virtue. Portraying their families as martyrs to the truth of Christ, they wore their decline as proof of Christian virtue. Nostalgic for a better time, they held themselves up as examples of people resisting the decay of all that was good. This conception of virtue and honor, wrapped up in family history, was a powerful family folklore that helped bind the generations together, explaining past suffering and imposing continuing duty.

Mervyn James, writing of local history in Durham at this time, has described this nostalgia as "sense of transience, nourished by religious, political and social change . . . the past rendered more poignant by contrast with the decay of traditional values which some could perceive around them and the supposed stable permanence which antiquity had achieved."[25] All of this feeling was packed into family histories like that of Sir Thomas Shirley. Shirley prepared a huge genealogical roll and wrote a genealogical history of his family, together with a massive compendium of heraldry and family history entitled "The Catholicke Armorist."

Recounting the history of his family, he highlighted their sacrifices. His father, George, and his brother, Sir Henry, had both practiced occasional conformity, attending Anglican services to protect the family's property. Yet they, despite appearances and compromises, remained loyal to the faith. Each died, according to Sir Thomas, in the bosom of the Roman church. Other members were less circumspect. Sir Thomas's uncle died in Flanders fighting against the Dutch Protestants and their English allies. His aunt Elizabeth joined a nunnery at Louvain. His mother, Frances, daughter of Henry Lord Berkeley, and his stepmother, Dorothy, widow of Sir Henry Unton, were paragons of Catholic devotion. Sir Thomas' mother, Lady Frances, fatally ill in 1595, when he was five, begged her husband to be sure their children were brought up in the Catholic faith. Sir Thomas himself suffered financial loss and imprisonment for that faith.

Told this way, with the commitment to the faith the core family value, Shirley's story proved them to be of the lineage of true knights of Christ.[26]

Similarly, family stories became a way of extolling the virtue of ancestors and keeping the living on the Catholic path. When Sir Anthony Fitzherbert, Justice of the Common Pleas, a commissioner for the dissolution of monasteries, and for the trials of Sir Thomas More and Bishop John Fisher, was dying in May 1538, he delivered a warning to his family that was still quoted in the seventeenth century. In his last moments he ordered his sons never to buy, accept as a gift, or in anyway use lands and goods taken from the church. His sons and their relatives, they claimed, strictly observed his command, patiently suffering exile and other inconveniences because of their Catholic faith.[27] Clearly, Sir Anthony was not an opponent of the royal supremacy, and he died before England became Protestant. His children, however, when faced with a Protestant church, treasured their patriarch's commandment as a part of their justification for their recusancy.

In the Holles family a similar tale was told about church property, but with a superstitious thrill. As recalled by Gervase Holles in the middle of the seventeenth century, the family had escaped bad luck when Denzel Holles died in 1590, before completing his new house. Denzel had intended to build it out of stone salvaged from the "sacrilegiously demolished" church of St. Mary, pulled down in 1586 by the citizens of Grimsby. Death prevented him, saving the family from the fate of those who used the stone in their houses. The Hattcliffe and Mussenden families used the stone and brought a curse down on themselves, so that "none of the name being now left in Lincolnshire but such as are descended from bastards."[28]

For the Holles, the identification with pious ancestors was not important, since they were out of communion with them. They were, in fact, embarrassing unless they were martyrs for the Protestant cause. The silence over religion in their family histories is not, therefore surprising – grandfathers' ignorance, superstition, and service to Antichrist were not something to brag about. They preferred to remember the times when their ancestors had been true to the faith.

James Whitelocke, composing his *Liber Famelicus* in the early seventeenth century, tells only one anecdote about his family's experiences with religious tension, but it was important to remember. His own father, Richard, a merchant dealing in Bordeaux wines, died in France in 1570, only five years after James was born. The most important story he knew about his father was how, on his last trip to Bordeaux, he fell into a pleurisy. Sick for three weeks before he died, Richard Whitelocke refused the sacrament of extreme unction and so, because he would not participate in "such popish ceremonies," he was excommunicated. Canon law refused excommunicates burial in consecrated ground, and he was denied a grave. Outraged, English merchants in Bordeaux loaded their guns and escorted Richard's corpse to an honorable burial in an olive grove.

Whitelocke's record of his father's death and burial used the tropes of evil Catholics and godly Englishmen to drive home the moral that he and his descendants were sprung from a righteous Protestant who testified to his faith on his deathbed.[29]

Of course, not all remembering was positive. John Smith of Nibley wrote his history of the Berkeley family in order to display to young George Berkeley the dangers of acting as his godless parents acted. Reminding him to obey the Lord before all else, he showed George that his frivolous and feckless father and mother were unworthy of imitation![30]

Though young George Berkeley was warned to keep God's law before him, Smith of Nibley's record of the family he had served for so many years pays no attention to the family's religious history. For this conforming, if sinning, family, religious change was of little importance. As Smith told it, the most important things for them to remember were the lawsuits and property acquisitions made by the family. Clearly, the business of the family was getting and preserving property, managing property, and fighting over property. This focus on property became especially important because it was neutral ground. In families in which there was religious division property could provide a common focus. The Hastings family is a fine example of this.

Henry Hastings, the third earl of Huntingdon, was branded the "The Puritan Earl" by Claire Cross in her biography of him. Henry, Lord President of the North, was a Puritan, but it is not safe to assume that all his family shared his enthusiasm. The mother of the 'Puritan Earl' was Catherine Pole, the daughter of Henry Pole, Lord Montague. Thus, she was the niece of Reginald Pole, Cardinal and papal legate for the restoration of England to Catholic obedience. Catherine Pole Hastings' sister, Winifred, married Sir Thomas Hastings, so that the "Puritan Earl" had Cardinal Pole for a relative twice over. His Uncle Edward was a notable papist, too, which was a good thing when Mary came to the throne, since his father, Francis, the 2nd earl, was closely associated with the Dudley family and nearly lost his head in the Jane Grey fiasco. Henry, the 3rd earl, married Katherine Dudley, the sister of Robert Dudley, earl of Leicester, known for his support of the more puritanical.

Brother Francis agreed with Henry's theology, as his letters eloquently attest, but it does not appear that brothers George and Walter were hot Protestants. Certainly George's wife, Dorothy Porte, came from a family that was well known for its Catholic ties. Her sister was the mother of John Gerard the Jesuit, and her father was a staunch Marian Catholic. As adults the Hastings boys went their own theological ways, but they remained family, and in communication, until they died.

As it turned out, Henry and his brother Francis, partly reared in Edward VI's court, were the most Protestant in their later years. George and Walter were much less vocal about their religion. Little Walter, in whom his God Father, Cardinal Pole, took a special interest, received much attention from the Cardinal.[31]

George was known to be sympathetic to his Catholic relatives, the Gerards, but he did allow his brother the earl to sponsor the education of his son, Francis, in Basle, where he studied Calvinist theology. Camden says that the boys, though divided by religion, got along just fine.[32]

They also got on with their cousin Lord Hastings of Loughborough, even though he, and their Pole cousin Arthur, were arrested for plotting a Catholic overthrow of Queen Elizabeth in 1561. Hastings of Loughborough was encouraging Arthur Pole to marry the Earl of Northumberland's sister, part of a plan to promote a Catholic succession and proclaim Mary Queen of Scots Queen of England. Employing

FIGURE 2   Henry Hastings, 3rd Earl of Huntingdon, by unknown artist, 1574. © National Portrait Gallery, London.

sorcerers to forecast Elizabeth's death, Pole was sentenced to death for treason, but Elizabeth reprieved him.[33]

To get along with their kin, the Hastings family accepted that the family business was not religion. It was mutual support, power, and property. At only one point is it clear from their letters that the issue of religion intruded itself into family business. On December 14, 1595 Henry, the 3rd earl of Huntingdon died, leaving his title to his brother George. Shortly after, Sir Edward Hastings told Sir Francis of their brother George's treatment of Henry's preachers (Camden says Henry wasted his estate favoring ministers[34]) and his likely attitude toward "the church" – meaning the reformed church. Sir Edward said that George

hath begun at the very entry in such goodly manner as not only myself but all the godly preachers and others are of my mind for he is very desirous to hear the word preached and to that end doth most earnestly entreat the preachers to come unto him and such as already hath been with his company he hath used most honorably . . . and for himself I am this far a witness his lordship in my hearing did deliver with tears that except the lord in mercy would look upon him and send the grace of his holy spirit to give him he was altogether unable to perform those duties that would be expected of him, and truly in my conscience I think he did speak it from the bottom of his heart, and hitherto he doth continue most comfortable to us all that wish well to the church. . . .[35]

The deathbed of the 3rd earl is famous for the presence of preachers bearing charts of predestinarian comfort. George, clearly, was not of that ilk, but at least he was going to treat his brothers and their cause with gentleness.

The Hastings boys may well have learned their ability to work around religious barriers from their parents, who were of the first generation to confront the necessity of religious flexibility.

George Hastings' wife Dorothy came from a family that consistently acted as good Catholics and conformable subjects of the crown, as the wills of her grandfather and father, both named John Porte, demonstrate.

The Portes were a legal family. Sir John Porte the elder rose to be a justice in King's Bench under Henry VIII. In 1528 John became frightened for his life. The sweating sickness was in his house and he, his wife, his son and daughter, and many of his servants were ill, causing him to turn his thoughts to last things. The will he wrote then was a model of late Medieval piety. He left his soul to "our most blessed lady Saint Mary, Saint John the Evangelist and all the holy company of heaven to be means for me to our Lord Jhesu" and instructed that his body be buried in the chancel of the church. He ordered his executors to hire a priest to pray for his soul for 20 years, and he left money to a number of monasteries upon condition that they "yearly forever the Tuesday in the vth week of lent devoutly sing and say for my soul and my wife's, our fathers' and mothers', and for such persons' souls as my father in his life yearly used to have an obit for, and for all our ancestor souls, good doers' souls, an obit with *placebo* and *Dirige* everyone. . . ." He also left money for his Oxford college, Brasenose, and made bequests to the Prior of Repton and the prioress of Nuneaton.[36]

Luckily, the sweat did not take John Porte in 1528. In the 1530s he was busy as a justice and a commissioner imposing the Henrician reforms, trying Sir Thomas More and Bishop John Fisher, and dissolving the monasteries. He took advantage of the dissolution to acquire Dale Abbey, a number of monastic advowsons, Repton Priory and the manor, advowson, and rectory of Etwall. Perhaps God was angry at his greed, for two weeks after he signed the deeds he sickened and died while on assize at Worcester.[37]

The will he wrote on March 6, 1540 is short on religious sentiment. It begins by giving Henry VIII his full title of "in earth supreme head of the Church of England immediately under God." John Porte left his soul only to almighty God. Making bequests to family members and to his curate, he simply asked that they find a priest to sing for his soul for one year after his death.[38] A month later Sir John's wife Margery died. Her will, like her husband's, is remarkably reserved about her faith. Leaving her soul to the Virgin Mary, she simply asked her executors to "order for the wealth of my soul by their discretions . . .," requesting burial in Etwall church with her husband.[39]

One might surmise, from the differences between the wills of 1528 and 1540, that John Porte had lost some of his old-time religion. His son, John Porte (hereinafter known as John Porte II) knew better. When we look at his will, we can see that, as far as his conscience was concerned, his father's 1528 will was still binding. He declares:

I will that my fathers last will . . . shall be observed and fulfilled and that not only, but also all other his wills heretofore made as far as either conscience or reason will requite and that my executors peruse all my fathers said wills as well as the last and so to fulfill them as is a fore rehearsed as they will answer afore God and in the promises to discharge their consciences and mine.

So his son believed the first testament embodied his father's real intention, not the probated will of 1540.

Made on 9 March 1556/7, John Porte II's will is a classic of Marian piety. He talks of "mass or divine service" and expresses his trust in Christ, but he is not to be saved by Christ alone. He also expects "the intercession of his holy and blessed mother Mary and of all the holy saints in heaven to have the fellowship of his holy Angels and the fruition of his godly majesty."

There follows an orgy of pious giving, much of it modeled on his father's first will, but bigger. He wants a chantry and almshouse founded at Etwall, and a school at Repton. He commissions prayers for himself and for his relatives' souls; he repairs roads, he builds walls to keep the swine out of the churchyard, he gives doweries to three score maidens, he sends copes and vestments to the churches where he owns advowsons, he makes a gift to Brasenose College, and he grants leases for life for a rose. Fashionably, he ordered that a fine marble tomb be raised in honor of himself, his father, and their wives. Of course, he leaves nothing to monasteries, since they were dissolved – in some cases the monasteries named in his father's will were now his personal property.[40]

This is a Catholic will. John Porte II wanted all the bedesmen he could get, and he was willing to pay. It worked. His will was carried out by his executors. He is still named as Founder on the web site of Repton School, which undoubtedly remembers him on founders day, and of the web site of the village of Etwall, where his tomb, his almshouse, and his wall are still to be seen.[41]

But this will is not just Catholic, it is transitional. No one making a will in 1557 could be certain that it would be enforceable. Mary and Philip might or might not have a child, and, since every monarch for the last thirty years had changed the religion, you never knew what was coming. John Porte II's will reflects that in his interest in a fine marble tomb and in his extensive gifts to the poor. Moreover, he wanted to be sure things were legally binding. In asking for the creation of Repton school he instructs his executors "without delay . . . to establish by the king and queens highness license and other lawful assurances [the property] to the said school forever." In a Weberian manner, frustrated Catholic instincts were being channeled into gifts which perpetuated the giver's name without being directly linked to prayers. If chantries were dissolved again, Repton School would not go with them. Nor would his almshouse, since the inhabitants were not directly enjoined to pray for his soul, even if it was implied they should.

By the time Dorothy Porte Hastings, John Porte II's daughter, died, this process was well advanced. On January 26, 1606, Dorothy, mindful that death was near, wrote what was, compared to the multi-paged statements of faith of her Hastings brothers-in-law, a simple declaration. She knows, she says, she deserves perdition with all hypocrites in Hell, but God has seen fit to save her "with the merit of Christ his death and passion . . . by gods mercy bestowed upon me to blot out all mine offenses. . . ."

The Dowager Countess of Huntingdon did not have much wealth she could dispose of, but she did make grants to the poor of Ashby de la Zouch and Parkington, much as her father had done 48 years before.[42] Of course, her grants to the poor did not imply the expectation of prayer for her soul, but the continuation of bequests to the poor may have elided the differences in their intentions.[43]

These three members of the Porte family represent the stages of a family's transition to Protestantism. Dorothy was most certainly raised a Catholic, and she was surrounded by Catholic relatives of one kind or another, but she was also surrounded by Puritan relatives of one kind or another. Her will is hardly that of a Puritan, but it can pass in Protestant circles. Perhaps she had been a hypocrite about religion, but by the third generation, her generation, the family had, like most, made the transit from Medieval Catholic to some flavor of Protestant.

But it did take three generations. The Reformations that occurred happened across the length of lives, slowly, as people found ways to get along in families that were increasingly complex religiously.

Ties of Kinship

Tudors took kinship very seriously, since it operated as a primary means of organizing social prestige and place in the community, as well as a basis for social mobilization.[44] Kinship imposed duties and expectations on individuals that crossed many boundaries. The ways in which family connection and experience might influence a member's standing and positions were numerous. On one level kinship implied a generalized duty to those who claimed you as kin – a pyramidal set of claims with many smaller folk claiming the backing of the families on the top of the social structure. On another level, the emotional ties to kin demanded responses. In all cases, the important issue of family solidarity and advancement made it impossible to ignore relatives.

Obviously, the introduction of religious distinctions between kin did not dissolve the reciprocal duties involved in blood and marriage relationships. For example, Thomas Copley converted to Catholicism in 1563, leaving for continental exile in 1566. Nonetheless, he felt free to call upon William Cecil for help, since he was Mildred Cecil's cousin. The friendly response of Lord Burghley was couched entirely in terms of marital kinship. Burghley wrote Copley in 1574:

I was also the more inclined to conceive well of you because I knew you were of blood and kindred to my wife so as your children and mine by her were to be knit in love and acquaintance by blood. And indeed as I have good cause to love my wife well, so have I always taken comfort in loving her kindred, showing to them as I might all good friendship in such causes as were offered to me . . .[45]

Burghley promised to defend him against the ardently Protestant Lord Howard of Effingham because they were kin, despite their differences in religion

One thing that changed in the years after the Reformation was the way in which some families thought about potential mates. In mid-century religion does not seem to be a marital issue. There is overwhelming evidence indicating that marriage connections were still being arranged with power, profit, and connection in mind, rather than religion. The child marriages documented in the Chester Consistory

Court are an extreme example of this state of mind, but it was obvious among all classes. People entered into marriage without, apparently, considering the religion of the intended. All this is hardly surprising, since, lacking a crystal ball, people could not know for certain that a marriage was crossing an ideological boundary.

Had Francis Alford been thinking about the implications of marrying a Catholic, he might not have wed Agnes de Augustinis in 1562. The widow of Augustine de Augustinis, she is a mysterious figure who had a great deal of impact on his life, for better and for worse. By 1562 Alford was 32; and she was probably older, for she had borne three children by 1551.

It is not known when Agnes married her first husband, but by 1530 the Italian was the personal physician of Cardinal Wolsey and, by the late 1530s to Henry VIII, rising in the court with the patronage of Thomas Cromwell and Lord Sandys. In Henry's later years Augustinis did well, receiving grants of land in the mid-1540s — though he may have been in debt, since he quickly sold many of them.[46]

By December of 1546 Augustinis was back in Venice, his hometown, perhaps looking after the property there that was later willed to his daughter.[47] He obviously returned to England but thought better of it. In the spring of 1549 he tried to "depart to Flanders," but a Yeoman of the Guard caught him before he could leave.[48] This escape attempt, so tantalizingly close to the time of the rebellions against the religious change, cannot be linked clearly to any cause. We do not know when the Venetian died, though he made his will in Lucca in April 1551. It was enrolled in the Prerogative Court of Canterbury in 1561, leaving his "dilecta uxore" Agnes 500 marks and 1500 gold ducats, as well as her own dowry.

The will is interesting because it allows us a glimpse of the family Francis Alford inherited when he married. The two sons, Alexander and Julius, were left equal portions of the Doctor's considerable property. The only daughter, Livia, was given a difficult bequest. If she wished, through the inspiration of God, to become a nun, she was to receive 300 ducats. If she wished to marry he provided her with a dowery of 1500 ducats, but only if she married in Italy. The bequest was to be paid in Padua.[49] When, in the 1560s, Livia was betrothed to one "T.M. gent," she and her fiancé faced the daunting task of traveling to Italy in order to marry and secure the bequest. Unable to find a chaperone for her daughter's journey, Agnes and Francis petitioned Queen Elizabeth to revoke their license to marry beyond the seas, promising to find some other legal means to provide her with her dowry.[50] Clearly, Livia did not become a nun, but, equally clearly, she was raised a Catholic.

Meanwhile, Augustine's and Agnes' son Julius lost his mind. After an inquisition before the Lord Mayor of London in January of 1566, Julius was declared insane and his property was granted to his stepfather, under the supervision of the Court of Wards, a profitable windfall — though it never stopped the complaints of poverty that fill Alford's papers.[51]

The mid-1560s saw the birth of Francis' and Agnes' only son, who would predecease them in 1580. A letter survives that illustrates the power of Francis' affection for the boy. He entreated two physicians to attend the child: "I will not say to you as the woman said to great Physician *dic verbum et sanabitur filius meus*, but I will rather say that if you will employ all the cunning you have, my son cannot be saved, yet loth he should want any help that learning or remedy might give him by the means of his poor father . . ."[52]

In 1560 his family welcomed a nephew, Edward, the son of his brother Roger Alford, into the world. Roger was a close and trusted servant of William Cecil all of his life, rising to be a Teller of the Receipt of the Exchequer, and his will expressed his desire that Edward serve Lord Burghley, too. Roger was almost certainly a committed Protestant, described by his bishop in 1564 as "earnest in religion."[53] Both Roger and his son Edward would be members of Parliament. Roger died in 1580, leaving his brother Francis to care for his sister-in-law. Either Edward or Roger's stepson William attempted to cut her out of their father's will, causing Francis much grief.[54]

Francis' nephew William married the recusant daughter of Sir John Bourne. Thus, in his brother's family Francis faced a range of religious interest stretching from earnest Protestant to recusant Catholic.

After his brother Roger died, Francis was rumored to have sold part of his brother's property for the "finding of an obit," but he denied this. The rumor is fascinating, in that such a death memorial had definite papist overtones and suggests once again his possible Catholic connection.[55] (However, it may also simply mean that he wished to construct a tomb, since the word "obit" was still in general use for memorials.)

His own wife was Francis Alford's closest Catholic connection. In April of 1582 William Fleetwood, the Recorder of London and another eminent parliamentarian, wrote Lord Burghley of the arraignment of the wife of the Steward of Gray's Inn for "hearing a mass in Shrovetide in the house of the wife of Francis Alford in Salisbury Court, at which mass was Mrs. Alford herself and one Roberts a gentleman and one Hyde who is Mrs. Alford's man. The Seminary priest was one Deane." Deane and Hyde were not prosecuted because they turned states' evidence, while Secretary Walsingham dealt gently with his parliamentary colleague's wife. "Mistress Alford was spared because Mr Frances is bound for her and she promises to go to the church and this is by Mr Secretary's order."[56]

Francis Alford had, as a member of Parliament, taken the Oath of Supremacy, and his letters show him to be, at least outwardly, a supporter of the Elizabethan Settlement, if an enemy of Puritans. He spoke frequently in Parliament about religious issues, to his cost, since Elizabeth was convinced that he supported Mary Queen of Scots. In fact, he was an ardent supporter of due process for those suspected of Catholicism. Undoubtedly, his reaction to recusancy legislation was shaped by his own family. His wife was entertaining seminary priests in his home.

Perhaps his stepchildren, one of his nephews and one niece by marriage were recusants too, and Francis Alford's profession of a civil lawyer encouraged him to support the forms of the old church courts, even if he was not a Catholic.

What would it have been like to be the son of Francis and Agnes Alford? He would have been well aware of the possibility of religious choice, torn between conflicting duties to his parents. He could choose conformity, recusancy, or puritanical reform. All were being modeled for him in his immediate family.

In these family contexts we can often see a microcosm of the Reformation process as people chose their positions.

Look at what happened in the family of Sir Nicholas Bacon (1510–79). Born, by his own description, on Childermas (December 28), 1510, he was converted to Protestantism while a student in Cambridge in the late 1520s. Though a Protestant, Sir Nicholas, an enthusiast for stoic philosophy, sharing with many of his generation a fear of rapid religious change that made him a *politique*. Although he was thoroughly Protestant, he was very worried about people whose faith carried them beyond the law.

Marrying twice, Nicholas had five sons by his two wives. Three were born to Jane Ferneley and two to Anne Cooke. Little is known of Jane's religion, but Anne, famously well educated, was a committed Puritan. Spread far apart in age and experience, Nicholas' five boys were religiously diverse. Jane's three, born in the 1540s, rejected their father's moderation, opting for one extreme for their generation, Puritanism. Anne's two sons, born so long after their eldest half brother that he might have been their father, placing them in a new generation, became skeptics, critical of religious enthusiasm of all sorts.

Number one was also named Nicholas (ca. 1540–1624). He was a devout friend of Puritanism in his home county of Suffolk, using his wealth and power there to support ministers, some of whom gratefully dedicated books to him. His will summed up his philosophy: "Christ, none but Christ only! Go out my soul, go out! . . . I pray God to bless my children and deliver the kingdom from popery."

The second son was Nathaniel Bacon of Stiffkey, Norfolk (1547–1622). A "zealous favorer of the preachers of the word," he was a leading Puritan in Norfolk and a known critic of bishops.

Number three was Edward Bacon (1548–1618). As a young man he was sent to the continent to get his languages, and he lived for a time in the household of Theodore Beza. The experience in Geneva must have made a deep impression, for he became a strong supporter of the Puritan cause in Suffolk.

Number four was Anthony Bacon (1558–1601). Thanks, perhaps, to his mother Anne, translator of Jewel's *Apology* and an ardent Protestant, Anthony was a conventional Protestant when he went abroad in the 1570s, living, like his elder brother Edward, in Beza's home in Geneva. Later his travels on the continent induced in him so much toleration of Catholics that he actually lived with a recusant for a time. Suspected of papistry and accused of sodomy in France, his mother once denounced him as "a traitor to God and his country." Ironically, he did eventually return to England and hold a seat in Parliament, only to be drawn into the circle of the Earl of Essex.

The fifth Bacon son was Francis (1561–1626). The famous Sir Francis was much less committed to religion than some of his brothers. In fact one might suspect that his religious philosophy was a reaction to the enthusiasms of his mother and older siblings. In his writings he actually argued that atheism is more conducive to human progress than is religion, asserting the power of human reason over revealed religion. What his Puritan mother thought of that can only be imagined!

Sir Francis' nephew, Edmund Bacon (ca. 1570–1649), shared his intellectual enthusiasms more than his father Nicholas' Puritanism. Edmund was a reclusive scholar who spent his fortune studying science and literature. His philosophical correspondence is voluminous, but he says so little about religion in it that his religious position is unclear.[57]

Within the Bacon family circle there were many minds on religion. Father Sir Nicholas was, in late sixteenth-century terms, a moderate who believed in civil order as much as religious duty. Wife Anne was an enthusiastic and intolerant Puritan. The sons of wife Jane shared Anne's predilection for Calvinist theology, while Anne's sons did not. One was deeply suspected of favoring popery and the other was a famous skeptic. Grandson Edmund, only nine years younger than Francis, shared his scholarly distrust of religious enthusiasm.

The boys had often shared rooms at the Inns of Court and followed one another to Cambridge and the continent, but they chose conflicting religious courses. It is notable that the last two sons and the grandson, all born a decade or two after the last of the first three, did not embrace Puritanism, preferring tolerance and intellectual distance over their elders' commitment. Clearly the children of the 1560s had very different ideas about religion than those of the 1540s.

Children of the 1580s and 1590s experienced a very different religious milieu. In 1600 Henry Lanman, responding to the questions of the Jesuits interviewing him for admission to their college, said of his family, "I am the eldest of four sons, and the only Catholic. I have four sisters, three of whom are married, but only the eldest is a Catholic, and her husband, whose name is Berwick, and a gentleman, has been lately received into the Catholic church. The rest, with my father, are schismatics, as are my relations I believe on both sides."[58]

Henry Lanman's account of his family's religious diversity is a perfect demonstration of the way in which late Elizabethan youngsters lived with, were related to, and did business with, the "heretics" and "schismatics" amongst them, just as the heretics and schismatics were related to and doing business with the papists in their midst.

In the end, this poly-theological world which so deeply worried true believers became habitual for most people. Lacking zeal, they sank slowly, gently into habitual Anglicanism. Father Augustine Baker, born in Wales in 1575, tried to explain his parents' generation's experience of religion. In his *Memoir* he talks of how they, though raised Catholics, went to the Anglican service and noticed little change, except in the language of worship. Slowly, over time, they became, he says, neutrals in religion, neither Catholic nor Protestant, ignorantly conforming without zeal or knowledge.

This neutrality had an effect on the way they raised their children. Lacking zeal, "they gave no education at all . . . as to any religion to their children; but regarded only in them a good moral extern carriage, to which through nature they were even of their own selves well disposed. But what their children's belief or practice should be, in matter of religion, they heeded not."[59]

Baker saw his parents' neutrality as a problem. Perhaps his father and mother saw it as their only choice in a world that could no longer expect an entire family to share a religious consensus.

Marriage and Honor

Baker neatly explains how many families must have dealt with the religious changes. They ignored them. But by late in the century, kinship connections were, in some places and in some families, being replaced by sectarian connections which changed the marriage pool. Catholics were practicing endogamy when they could, and some Protestants were inclined to do the same. As the Cambridge theologian William Perkins explained it, one of the first "accidents" or variables of marriage is "parity or equality in regard to Christian religion, for in marriage there is a special care to be had that believers be matched with believers."[60]

Tudor parents had always sought to match their children properly according to wealth, station and other considerations. Now religion was added to the list. If a marriage was to prosper, the couple needed to agree in faith.

We seldom get to hear conversations about the choice of a mate outside of the formal negotiations and contracts, but in the case of Mrs. Elizabeth Palmer the evidence survived. Her correspondence with her brother-in-law, Richard Stephens of the Middle Temple, details negotiations on her behalf for a marriage with Sir William Bowes. A widow, in 1589 Mrs. Palmer was seeking an advantageous match. Bowes, according to Stephens, was a good prospect. A northerner who owned lead mines, he "haunted" the preaching in London, and was godly, upright, wise, and learned in Hebrew, Chaldean, Greek and Latin. "What should I say?" wrote Stephens, "He seems to be a good man."

Negotiations continued. Mrs. Palmer met Sir William and they began discussing a marriage contract. Things became difficult when he insisted that, if they had a son, the son should inherit all, while she insisted that her son by her first marriage should share in the inheritance. It took effort on the part of her friends to keep the match alive, but finally Stephens reported that Bowes "in confidence of her godliness" would take her. She and Stephens were not confident of Bowes' godliness, however, and the lawyer pledged to sift Bowes soundness of judgment in "religion and sanctification."

Stephens arranged a conversation between Bowes and some ministers. They reported him to be unsound in his opinions about justification by faith and church government. When he told Bowes this, Bowes demanded another test, agreeing to an interview with Walter Travers, godly preacher of the Temple Church, and three other divines. In the end, Bowes, reasonably, became exasperated with their probing and stomped out.

And so Stephens told his sister-in-law that he did not think it was a good match. Her mother wrote to the same effect, and Mrs. Palmer sent back Bowes' tokens. Bowes, feeling slandered, insisted that his godliness be tested by some gentlemen and justices in Sussex, so he could purge himself of their slurs on his godly reputation.[61]

John Penry, awaiting execution in 1593, wrote his daughters Deliverance, Comfort, Safety, and Surehope a letter of advice. They, he assumed, would choose husbands, with the advice of their mother, that were compatible with their religious consciences. They were to have nothing to do "with those assemblies and meetings where the ordinances and motions of AntiChrist's kingdom are retained" – the Anglican Church. And so, naturally, their husbands were to pass the religious purity test lest they force their wives into a relationship with Antichrist.[62]

Late Elizabethan recusant families often had the same attitude. Instructed by their priests to "come out" and withdraw from Protestant society, their marriage pool was limited. The varieties of separatists have a similar problem, practicing endogamy in order to contain the dangers of exogamy. Members of the Family of Love often had to move long distances or marry people much younger or older than themselves in order to stay within the group.[63] Naturally, children who chose to marry outside the religious affinity created trouble in the family, disobeying parental authority and breaking the bond of religious community.

That these attempts to limit the marriage pool by tests of theological purity were rare suggests that most families, though cognizant of possible conflicts, were putting other interests first. In keeping a family intact, considerations of property and honor were as important as religion.

The Jesuit William Weston tells a story that captures the importance of family honor, neatly. Sometime in the late 1580s Weston was in the home of an unidentified sheriff on the invitation of the sheriff's son-in-law, who was contemplating conversion to Catholicism. While he was talking with a large group, word came that an old priest was holding a religious discussion in another room. They were suspicious of a trap. Justifiably, as it turned out, for the sheriff's daughter-in-law had laid a snare to catch the Jesuit.

Weston's host, thinking fast, appealed for protection to his father-in-law, dining with guests in another room, even though "the man was a heretic and was probably commissioned *ex officio* to hunt down Catholics." The sheriff, saying that it "would be unbecoming if a treacherous action were to take place in his own house under his very eyes and to the discomfiture of his son-in-law," chastised his daughter-in-law and ordered Weston released.[64]

The action of the sheriff in this story illustrates how families weathered ideological tensions. Placing family honor first allowed him to keep his family together in the face of the religious animosity among his kin. Across the three or four generations it took for the Reformation to settle, family members learned to ignore their religious differences, concentrating on those things in which they had common interests. As the individual's ability, if not right, to make choices based on conscience came to be accepted, families became accustomed to the idea that significant religious variance within themselves was possible and even natural. To function as family they had to give religion a lesser place, stressing instead morality, loyalty to conscience, and patriotism as proper objects of virtue. As these newer values emerged, new roles within the kin group came with them, so that the family became, more than ever, about promoting family honor, property, and power. Within that structure there was room for individual conscience in religion.

In 1604 Sir William Wentworth advised his son how to deal with religion in public. He ought, he said, "rather be in conversation religious, than speak earnestly against the Catholics." Perhaps thinking of his in-laws and his own parents, he described Catholics as "learned and wise men" holding all the same fundamental beliefs as Protestants. "Only ambition, pride and covetousness and want of charity do cause this hateful contention."[65]

A Protestant who spoke against recusancy in Parliament while raising his son to be a moderate Calvinist, Sir William was the third generation of a family which, like all English families, was weathering the great cultural divide known as the Reformation. To reach the point at which he could give his son such advice, he had to come to terms with his own parents' Catholic faith, retell the family history in ways that supported his own Protestant faith, and develop a personal philosophy that allowed him to deal with theological difference. He was teaching his son the lessons he had learned in the process, creating a family dynamic that made religion a side issue. Neither praying for his parents' souls nor expecting his son to pray for his, he told his boy what he knew about how to live in the world – and that included avoiding religious disputes.

Wentworth, born four years after John Porte II's death, told a very different family story than that recorded on Porte's tomb. Such a perpetual chantry in stone for his extended family was no longer imaginable.

4

Dissolutions and Opportunities

In 1541 the town of Liverpool assessed the laity of the community five marks to hire a clerk to play the organ and sing plain song and prick song, beautifying their religious services. A decade later the Portmoot of Liverpool, reacting to the Edwardian campaign to cleanse the churches, ordered "that the church goods shall be called for and put in a place together to the town's use, and all the commons of the town may be privy to the same." That same meeting cut off the wages of their clerk, who had fled to Spain. Forced by events, the leaders of Liverpool had moved from investing in their church to saving their investment as best they could.[1]

The Reformation presented institutions of every type with two problems. First, they were forced to make decisions, in response to the Reformation, that involved their corporate incomes and identities. Secondly, the decisions they made reflected their other problem, finding ways in which they as organizations could negotiate the growing ideological differences between members while achieving their organizational ends. The adaptive choices they made recreated them in a Protestant form.

Although some institutions felt greater pressures than others, there was not one that escaped the impacts of the Reformation. Parishes, cities, towns, guilds, companies, colleges, schools, hospitals, cathedrals, fraternities, and all others changed their practices, their vocabularies, and their ways of relating internally as circumstances demanded. Demographic and economic changes would have stressed them anyway, but the Reformation speeded up and deepened their distress.

In the realm of spiritual solidarity the death of purgatory presented serious problems for the existence of community. Every institution served a dual purpose in the sense that it served both the living and the dead, linking them together in a chain of mutual support. Every community offered prayers for founders and benefactors, and all sorts of institutions managed endowed prayers and charities in the interest of departed members. The community of the institution mirrored the community of the saints, promising to pray for the souls of its departed brethren. As late medieval religion expanded these duties to the dead, institutional officers played

FIGURE 3 Foundation deed of the Chapel of West Brentford,
Middlesex, with miniatures of St Mary and St Saviour, 1529. Public
Record Office, E314/148.

a greater and greater role in maintaining them. Duties to the dead joined the round
of communal worship, processions, rogations, and feasts with which communities
cemented their identities.

Even those who delighted in the death of the old religion could not have foreseen
the changes coming to institutions as the full force of the Reformation sank in. Beat
Kümin has identified five areas of socioeconomic impact in the parishes, areas shared
with most institutions. First, the status, number, and purpose of the clergy changed

markedly. Second, the size and allocation of church resources altered dramatically. Third, the distribution of ecclesiastical patronage passed from the Church into the hands of the Crown and secular landlords. Fourth, the provision of education, once intimately connected with the church, passed into lay hands. Fifth, the organization of poor relief altered in important ways, passing from the Church to local and national governments, while the nature of private charity changed.[2] To these a sixth could be added. The amount of money spent on ecclesiastical services declined precipitously. How institutions dealt with these impacts depended on their mission and management, but the limiting of ecclesiastical power and importance demanded a response.

Importantly, choices they made began the creation of a new set of cultural norms which altered religious sub-texts of institutional life, substituting secular interests for religious community in most institutions. This substitution was idiosyncratic, depending on the institution, its relation to other powers, and its secular purpose. Consequently, there were many styles of response, determined in large part by local interests, allowing the Reformation to play itself out in many different forms. It was this ability of local institutions to tailor responses that permitted the English Reformation to sink slowly into the culture rather than bursting the dam of civility, sparking religious civil wars like those raging abroad.

Like individuals and families, institutions created *ad hoc* strategies in responding to see-sawing religious policies. Their choices were limited, since communities generally did not have the strength or the will to resist, but they minimized the impacts and protected local resources as much as they could. It is also clear that many organizations asked themselves how they could profit from the changes produced by Reformation. Each could resist, cooperate, or play for advantage. Most chose to cooperate and resist at once, adapting to the new circumstances in ways that attempted to co-opt them for local purposes.

Institutional leaders' responses reshaped the role and function of their institutions. They gave old habits new explanations and purposes, while narrowing their functions. No longer concerned with the dead as well as the living, no longer constrained to enforce the will of God, no longer investing in spiritual services, secular institutions recognized their secular roles as primary.

But these changes did not come all at once. Old religious habits died the death of a thousand cuts, as the customs of the older generation were removed by the Crown's flaying knife. As Robert Whiting noted in his study of southwest England in the Reformation, traditional practices dwindled slowly but steadily in the era between 1530 and 1570. This lingering agony was caused by a complex of small decisions taken for local reasons. "There is abundant evidence," he writes, "of the importance of essentially non spiritual considerations, ranging from xenophobia and a sense of political obligation to economic interest and a fear of physical punishment," in accounting for these responses.[3]

The first places in which the Reformation changes were felt were the parishes and the monasteries. The parishes became an ideological battle ground in the mid 1530s as Cromwell and his agents sought to eradicate superstition as they understood it. These attempts to interfere with custom were local and piecemeal, however, since each parish had different habits and institutions. Many probably did not bother responding at all. The dissolution of the monasteries and shrines, then the chantries, colleges and hospitals, had a much broader impact in both negative and positive ways.

Cleverly, the process of reform became linked to the self-interest of the powerful in every community, uniting the virtue of obedience with the opportunity for profit. The interests of some groups were served even as the religious devotions of others were disrupted. People could always be found to abet the reforms as profitable, spiritually, or fiscally. Given the local nature of all institutions, it is hardly surprising that each one did it its own way, within the constraints of the law. Nor is it surprising that the profits of the powerful made people cynical about the process, which taught that stripping the church of its wealth was the way to get ahead in the world.

Ecclesiastical Institutions

We have to understand property law to understand the Reformation. Property law hedged the English Reformation in, limiting the scope of the destruction and reconstruction by protecting the rights of the lay owners and users of ecclesiastical property, setting the parameters for institutional responses and acting as a sea anchor to stabilize the nation.

The Reformation's impact on the church was impeded by the fact that English law treated many "livings" as personal property. This convenient legal myth made it possible for monks to surrender monasteries in exchange for pensions, but it also kept ideologically hostile clerics in institutions that were officially reformed. This same legal reality prevented bishops from reforming their prebendaries or replacing parish priests.

This retarded all of the religious reforms – Henrician, Edwardian, Marian and Elizabethan – by preventing rapid restructuring of religious institutions. The result was, on the one hand, that no thorough religious change could be suddenly imposed on the land and patrons could choose clergy to their liking. On the other, it permitted ecclesiastical personnel to find some *modus vivendi*.

The law concerning property in church livings is highly complicated and little studied, but it is clear that it decelerated the Reformation. It was so difficult to remove a conforming incumbent from his living that it was often easier to await the grim reaper than to sue to do it. Although bishops were the spiritual authorities over their clergy, they had great difficulty shaping their work force. Lay impropriators owned many advowsons to churches, giving them the right to nominate the incumbent upon a vacancy. Alternatively, they could sell or grant the right of nomination to some other party. The bishop had to institute the nominee, having little right to resist a nomination so long as the nominee met the educational requirements for institution. This placed the lay patrons between the bishops and the clergy, and they, acting out of self-interest, pressure from the parish, or any other motive, could resist attempts to remove a priest or appoint one the bishop deemed suitable.[4]

The royal supremacy did not change this, as Bishop Barlow of Bath and Wells learned in 1550. He had deprived his Dean, John Goodman. Goodman counter sued. Bishop Barlow appealed to the Privy Council, which ordered the Justices to stay Goodman's case, but they refused, declaring that they had sworn to allow no restraint of the law. Then they issued their ruling: "A spiritual office surrendered to the King, notwithstanding the new erection of the same by any Act of Parliament, remains still a spiritual office as it was before." Therefore Goodman had the same property in his office as he had before the Royal Supremacy and could not be deprived. Not to be thwarted, the Privy Council imprisoned Goodman for disobedience.[5]

As Goodman's case suggests, livings and advowsons were forms of property which could be defended in common law, often beginning with a writ of *Quare Impedit*. Therefore, common law courts could prohibit actions in the church courts concerning church livings.

In the post-dissolutions era the search for "concealed lands" – property which should have come to the Crown at the dissolutions, but which had been "concealed" from it – forced patrons and incumbents to defend and explain their right to use their properties. These cases give us a look at how property in church livings was traded and managed.

Early in Edward's reign John Hunt was forced to defend his possession of the free chapel of St. Leger in Wymondsham against a claim that it was forfeit to the Crown. In his replication Hunt explained that Richard Brewer, a priest, held the chapel as part of his demesne, in free hold for life. Brewer, the incumbent, then leased it to Hunt. The lease, made in 1542, was for 55 years. The agreed rent was a penny a year. Although the lease would have extinguished itself on Brewer's death, he was not dead, he was in Oxford teaching Hebrew. It was Hunt's contention that the free chapel was Brewer's personal property, as incumbent, and that he did not owe the King arrearages on his rent.[6]

In another case of concealed lands, Frances Palmes explained how Sepulchres Chapel, within York Minster, belonged to the church of Otley, Yorkshire. Sir Thomas Magnus was the Master of the Chapel and had the right to all its tithes and commodities as part of his office. In 1544 he rented the chapel to Robert Redman for thirty years, at an annual rent of £41. Frances Palmes entered the picture as executor for Dame Elizabeth Jonson, the assignee of Robert Redman. Thus Palmes had the right to all the tithes and other revenues generated by the chapel. He was, in effect, the third person to control it since 1544. The issue, here again, was whether the property had been annexed to the Crown by the dissolution of the chantries, but no one was challenging Palmes right to the revenue. The question was to whom he owed the rent. Even if he owed it to the Crown, he still had a right to the revenues of the chapel.[7]

The common law cared about the rights of patrons of livings first and foremost, since the right to present also meant that the patron actually owned the church and its tithes. The right of presentation, as a property right, was well guarded. Oxford and Cambridge colleges, for instance, owned (and still own) large numbers of them, carefully defending against the attempts of bishops to institute men of their own choosing. Incumbents might, therefore, be paid rather than receiving the tithes for the term of their incumbency. This allowed the patrons to hire and fire as they wished. In the dissolutions the existence of these hired priests protected the tithes and other property of a chapel from seizure, since only the salary paid to the priest was used for superstitious purposes.[8] The Warden and fellows of All Souls, for instance, were the owners of the parsonage of Alderbury, Wiltshire. Their appointment of priests there was done "of their mere devotion," and the priest appointed was "at all times removable at their pleasure, and not perpetual." Thus the parson of Alderbury was a creature of the College, beyond the reach of the bishop.[9]

The question of who had the right to give a priest, or minister, a church was also the subject of litigation. This often arose because the patron of a living could grant or sell the right of nomination to a third party, who then might claim the right to present again. In 1570 a complicated case of this was recorded by Justice Dyer.

The first Elizabethan Bishop of Lincoln had instituted William Malin to the prebend of Biggleswade in Lincoln Cathedral. Soon, the Bishop's right to institute Malin was challenged by one Cranwell, who insisted that Thomas Watson, the Marian bishop of Lincoln, had granted him Biggleswade in reversion – that is, that it was promised to him the next time it was vacant. Faced with the suit the Bishop claimed that he was only doing what the patrons of the living told him to do. Malin had been instituted on the presentation of the Earl of Leicester and Sir William Cecil, who had the right of nomination from the present bishop. When John Man, the Warden of Merton College and owner of the living died in 1569, they presented Malin, the headmaster of Eton.

In the end the Bishop said he did not care who held it, so long as his ultimate ownership of the living was confirmed, and so Malin kept it. It appears, moreover, that Cranwell's claim to the living in reversion was not good because Bishop Watson was dead, nullifying the contract.[10]

Bishop Parkhurst, the first Elizabethan bishop of Norwich, ran into the problem of property in church livings when he tried to present one held by the aged recusant Dr. Willoughby to someone else. His attempt provoked a rebuke from the Queen. Didn't Parkhurst know that Willoughby had been physician to Ann Boleyn? Didn't he understand that he was an old man? Parkhurst defended himself by arguing that Willoughby had refused to subscribe to the articles of religion, effectively depriving himself. Nonetheless, he was forced to require the new incumbent in the living to pay Willoughby "such a stipend yearly has he hath hitherto enjoyed." Thus, even in 1572, Parkhurst was forced to recognize the property rights of a man who had refused to subscribe to the articles of religion, who was, perhaps, too old to provide cure of souls, and who practiced medicine rather than being an active clergyman.[11]

One suspects that Parkhurst might have agreed with the authors of the admonitions to Parliament who so loudly denounced "Advowsons, patronages, impropriations, and bishops' authorities." Patrons and bishops, they insisted, auctioned off benefices, "thrusting" pastors on parishes without the parishioners counsel or consent, causing mischief. Of course they proposed that congregations elect their ministers, which would never do in an episcopal system, but they could all share the certainty that private property in church livings was a stumbling block to reform.[12]

Just how large a stumbling block becomes apparent when we understand how many livings were in the hands of lay impropriators. Bishop Cox of Ely summed it up when he said "my diocese is very miserable, for almost all is impropriated." In Ely the Cambridge Colleges owned many of the churches, and many of the rest belonged to land stripped from the monasteries and transferred to laymen. In all, 62 percent of the Ely benefices had their tithes taken by a lay person or institution, leaving very little to pay for spiritual services. This was higher than the national average, estimated at 43 percent in 1603, but in all dioceses impropriations forced the bishops into an endless battle with non-resident and pluralist clergy and their patrons.[13] Nor could they expect much sympathy from the Crown, since many of those impropriated livings belonged to it and were used to pay for the services of men like John Man, the Warden of Merton College, ambassador to Spain. As a result, very few clergy were appointed by the bishops. In Coventry and Lichfield, Bishop Bentham nominated only 5 of 147 ministers instituted in his diocese between 1560 and 1570.[14]

By the end of the reign the bishops estimated that of the 9,284 livings in England, 3,845 were impropriated. Worse, when impropriation was combined with leased tithes and grants of patronage, five-sixths of the benefices in the country were in lay hands, and the grip of the laymen was strengthening.[15]

Clearly, property rights mocked the enthusiasm for reform, moderating the swings of the religious pendulum by damping its movements. Control of nominations, property disputes, livings with their incomes sucked out, and political interference, hampered bishops of all theological dispositions in their attempts at change.

On the parochial level the impropriation of benefices worsened the poverty of many livings. Even without sharing their tithes with a patron, many benefices were simply too poor to support a clergyman – especially a married one. The ideal Protestant minister had a degree, a wife and family, and he was in short supply until late in Elizabeth's reign.

All of this meant that many parishes had irregular services at best. Before the Reformation this was a problem, and it was worsened by the Protestant insistence that clergy be educated. Ordinations had collapsed in the 1540s and did not recover until the 1570s, when a clerical career began to look more enticing.[16] In the meantime, the seesaws of religion took their toll on the clergy. In the 1540s some men married as a matter of evangelical principle, costing them their benefices. In Edward's reign some committed Catholics were deprived. In Mary's reign a campaign to rid the church of married clergy forced some out, though many gave up their wives – at least on paper.[17] Others became exiles for religion. In 1559 the first Elizabethan visitation tried to find the Marian clergy who were unwilling to conform. It did not find many, but some were removed, and some went into exile. By 1560 the shortage had reached crisis proportions, and, even worse, the morale of the clergy who remained was poor. Those who survived by changing their spots on a regular basis must have developed a flexible attitude toward ideology and a less than zealous commitment to any particular church settlement.

Many of the senior early Elizabethan parish clergy were men like Anthony Blake, the Vicar of Doncaster. In Edward VI's reign he took a wife and moved her into the vicarage. Deprived by the Marian authorities for marrying, he appealed to Cardinal Pole who absolved him and gave him Whiston, a parish near Doncaster. Soon complaints were heard that he was frequently seen with his wife in Doncaster. When Mary died he resumed his living at Doncaster and kept his living at Whiston, reuniting with his wife and becoming a committed pluralist. Though he may have been a Protestant, he, like so many others, proved to be a Nicodemite[18] at best, a mere time server at worst.[19]

Early in Elizabeth's reign the bishops appointed readers to fill the vacancies in the parishes, but they, being neither priests nor preachers, were a stop gap, simply reading the prayer book and homilies. What parish religion looked like when there was no incumbent remains a mystery, but neither sacraments nor reformed preaching could occur in the absence of an ordained man.

Of course property rights in church livings predated the Reformation, and clerical leaders were highly conscious of the problem – even if they were part of its cause. In the canons of 1529 they attempted to impose some discipline on pluralities, the ownership of multiple church livings, to ensure better spiritual services.[20]

As part of the same program of reform the Crown recognized that spiritual services depended on the presence of clergy in the parishes, and that spiritual possessions, as possessions, could be regulated by statute. Lay disgust at ecclesiastical pluralism and greed is obvious in the Act's preamble. For the "virtuous increase and maintenance of divine service, . . . [and] the increase of devotion and good opinion of the laity toward the spiritual persons," the clergy were forbidden to purchase leases to ecclesiastical property. Those who had them were forced to sell them to the lay person of their choice. And in the future, it said, no clergymen could hold more than four benefices, worth in total no more than £8 – unless they received a dispensation. But dispensations were plentiful, since ecclesiastics working for the royal family, privy councillors, archbishops, knights of the garter, widows of certain ranks, and many others were exempted.[21]

This statute made it harder for clergy to be pluralists, which was good, but it also ensured that the control of ecclesiastical property was concentrated in lay hands, since there was no limit on how many leases a layman might own.

In the 1550s clerical leaders once more tried to solve the problems of presentation, pluralities, non-residence, and neglect. In the reform of the ecclesiastical laws drawn up by Cranmer's select team in 1552 these problems were targeted. But the House of Lords balked and defeated the new regulation, in part because they made it heretical to be Catholic, and, perhaps, because any tightening of rules concerning advowsons threatened their property rights.[22]

Cardinal Pole tried again in 1556. His Legatine Constitutions ordered that no grants of the right of presentation, advowson, or nomination to benefices were to be allowed. He ordered this under papal authority, so it probably was not binding in common law, and it was quickly overturned by the Elizabethan Settlement.[23]

In Convocation in 1563 the bishops proposed new regulations that would allow them to deal with the problem, but they were never introduced into Parliament. In that same session William Cecil proposed a bill for uniting parishes to increase the size of their livings, but it was defeated by those who felt that it threatened the property of patrons. In 1566 Elizabeth prevented the so-called alphabetical bills from being debated, so the reforms were left hanging. Finally, in 1571, legislation was passed that gave the bishops marginally more control over benefices. For the first time, it was possible for a bishop to deprive an incumbent who refused to take the oath of supremacy.[24] At last it might be possible to be remove Catholic incumbents from the cure of souls. But that did not solve the problem of the ill-educated, the lazy, or the inept. They could keep their livings.

In the same Parliament there was an attack on those who leased their benefices for long periods, refused to pay for their upkeep, and alienated their assets permanently through fraudulent deeds. The finger was pointed especially at colleges, deans, chapters, parsons, and vicars – the personnel of the church – who, it was contended, were looting it. The Act limited the length of leases to 21 years or three lives. Some of its force was lost, however, when it specifically excluded those colleges whose statutes allowed them to make longer leases.[25]

The third statute of 1571 concerning ecclesiastical livings was the most important for reforming the ways in incumbents could grant away their property. Aimed at preventing ministers from transferring church property to other uses, it made it clear that grants were good only for the length of the incumbency, and that the incumbency was defined by residence.[26] However, it specifically exempts impropriated property, so that the lay patron was still doing what he liked with it.

The impropriation of benefices had a serious impact. In the royal manor of Havering in Essex, for instance, the living was owned by New College, Oxford, which had, since the late fifteenth century, installed its own graduates there. No one expected the vicars they appointed to be resident, but, nonetheless, they were paid the small tithes of the southern part of the parish and given the use of the vicarage of Hornchurch. It was a modest living. The great tithes of the parish went directly to the College, which usually leased them to a layman along with the rectory manor.

The absentee vicars were expected to hire a curate to take daily charge of St. Andrew's in Hornchurch, and to appoint a chaplain to look after the church of St. Edward in Romford. That chaplain received the small tithes form northern Havering. The third church in the manor was the chapel at Havering-atte-Bower, which was only occasionally supplied with a priest.

Before the dissolution of the chantries, the inhabitants of the manor solved the lack of clerical services from their vicar by hiring four priests of their own, through their religious fraternities and chantry. One of these priests was a preacher, who gave sermons at Romford and in neighboring churches, while another ran a school for poor children. They raised the funds to pay for these services, like parishes all over the country, by renting out land and stock, all of which was taken by the King's surveyors in 1547, terminating the priests' services.

Their vicars were mostly absentees. The last ordained priest to hold the living at Havering, Richard White, was instituted in 1538. After 1552 he was practically never in the parish, though he was vicar until 1570. Thus the people of Havering were practically bereft of spiritual services during the crucial middle years of the century. The parish had become substantially Protestant by the end of the 1560s, because the job of schoolmaster, vacated by the ejected priest, fell to a man who became an outspoken Puritan.

If for much of Elizabeth's reign Havering's souls had no one looking after them, the vacuum allowed them to sort out the confusion in their own way. In Romford a strong Puritan strain emerged in the church community, fed by the most powerful families in the neighborhood. These families appointed their own chaplains and, in the 1590s, acquired the right of nomination from New College, volunteering to pay enough to keep someone resident. They wanted, and got, a Puritan. Hornchurch, on the other hand, became a refuge for those who preferred the use of the surplice, sprinkling at baptism, the sign of the cross, and no preaching.

The rural free chapel at Havering-atte-Bower became a haven for Catholics. From 1565 until 1580 there was no curate there, just a lay reader who could not offer communion. Then, in 1589, Romford dumped its drunken rector Richard Atkis on the free chapel, where he remained as curate until his death in 1608, aged 80. Completely ineffective, he was forbidden to preach. In practice, those in the manor who wanted sermons were going to Romford; those preferring a prayer book service went to Hornchurch, and others, shunning both, went to the clandestine catechizing of the radical schoolmaster or met privately on Sunday to study the scripture. And they ignored the Catholics who avoided communion by going to the free chapel. The manor had sorted itself out.[27]

Lest it be assumed that the problems created by impropriations and nominations only affected the parishes, it should be noted that even in Canterbury Cathedral, archbishops Cranmer, Pole and Parker had to contend with prebendaries and deans who did not share their religion. Cranmer had Dr. Nicholas Wotton imposed on him as Dean by the King in 1541. Of no certain religious views, Wotton was a pluralist, holding the deanship of York as well as of Canterbury. Of the first twelve prebendaries at Canterbury six were former monks, and four of those left Catholic wills, one of which, written in 1565 by Robert Searles, was proved in 1570. In mid-century Canterbury was a Protestant cathedral "only by a kind of legal fiction and under duress."[28]

We can hear Archbishop Cranmer's anger over his inability to appoint prebendaries committed to godly life in his complaints that they loved idleness and "belly cheer," and his frustration that they had their houses in the precincts for life. He wanted the King and Parliament to make change the property law, making possible to "reform them" if they misused their prebends, but the Crown did nothing.[29]

Canterbury seems to have re-instituted Catholic worship out of affection when Mary took the throne, and members of the chapter enthusiastically helped burn heretics, including colleagues, but it took a condemnation for heresy to get a man out of his prebend. And then the Elizabethan Settlement reversed things, handing Archbishop Parker a see largely controlled by avowed Catholics. Like Cranmer, he complained bitterly against the people being put in as prebendaries. At one point a serving man was being foisted upon the church, and at another there was an attempt, blocked by the Archbishop, to give a child a prebend.[30]

The compromise between the archbishops and prebendaries of Canterbury seems to have been to concentrate on administrative detail and money, ignoring potentially difficult theological issues. The later Elizabethan prebendaries were preoccupied by their own interests, collective and individual.

The result at Canterbury was summed up by Patrick Collinson when he remarked that

Such undertones of religious strife can hardly have been dissipated overnight. Yet the Canterbury historian, as he advances into the reign of Elizabeth, has the impression of dying echoes of confessional thunder and finds that the story becomes progressively less ideological. Indeed, a story, as such, becomes more difficult to construct, as the history of the Cathedral turns from a narrative of events into the anatomy of an institution.[31]

Canterbury's turn away from ideology toward management was not just a turn away from religious conflict, though it must be seen as that. It was also a turn toward managerial solutions for structural problems. Reform was only possible in a church that had some control over its property, and the laity were not willing to grant it much.

But even where the clergy had control of livings they often used them in ways that weakened the church. William Sheils' work on the rectory estates of the archbishopric of York shows that the archbishops often leased ecclesiastical properties to their relatives, weakening the church, while creating new families among the gentry of Yorkshire and Nottinghamshire.[32]

The post-Reformation church continued to be plagued by the problem of impropriations. Archbishop Whitgift complained bitterly about it, but very little was done about it after the legislation of 1571. The inefficiency it created was one of the prices the laity were happy to pay, since it was so beneficial to them.[33]For the institution of the church, it meant that change was difficult to institute and enforce. Although visitations could do spot checks for conformity, they had little power over the quality of the clergy. This, of course, meant that many parishes suffered from poor spiritual services.

In 1586 people who desired a reformed clergy assembled a "View of the State of the Church," listing the positions, names, incomes, and attributes of rectors and vicars across the land. After asking "what his conversation is," they asked two other questions: Who made him a minister? and Who is the patron? They knew that the quality of the clergy was related to the patron's nominations. Thus when Mr. Waddam Tanner presented a man "lately a serving man and simple fellow," who never preached, to look after a thousand souls, he was not advancing the cause of religion in Cornwall. And what good did the 700 people in Wen derive from their pluralist vicar, appointed in the long ago reign of Henry VIII? He was decried as "a massman, a grazier, ignorant, his curates unlearned. A great taker of bargains, non resident in both charges."[34]

There was one virtue to the system that made private property of church livings. Frustrating as it was to those who wanted to see the church properly reformed and the people educated, the power of the impropriators helped slow reform to a safer pace. The inability to discipline its personnel easily and effectively forced the church to wait upon the passing of the old incumbents. As the old priests died, men truly Protestant filtered into the dioceses, so that even if they were no more upright than their predecessors, they were Protestant in their sentiments and messages.

Dissolutions

Scrupulous attention to legality was the price paid by Henry VIII for Parliamentary sanction of the nationalization of the church. Statutes operate within legal structures and the Common Law has always been about property, so it is not surprising that Reformation statutes paid close attention to the property involved. Naturally, most Reformation histories are more interested in the religious intentions of the statutes, and there is no doubt that Thomas Cromwell conceived the closing of the monasteries as a blow against what he considered superstition and abuse. But their dissolutions involved elaborate legal maneuvers, legitimatizing property seizures without frightening the people of England with the prospect that the King could take corporations at will. The result was a legally defined operation that worked according to established law as determined by Parliament.

Anyone who had purchased the right to use property belonging to the dissolved religious institution had his or her rights in the property protected. The only exceptions were the abbots who had "owned" the monasteries and the patrons who had given property to them.[35] Legally, it was necessary to treat abbots and abbesses as if they owned personally the houses they ruled, permitting them to exchange property with the Crown. Thus the current ecclesiastical possessors of the usufructs of ecclesiastical properties were treated as if they owned them in fee simple. It was this legal fiction that allowed the dissolutions to occur. Abbots and abbesses, monks and nuns were considered to represent corporations which had the legal ability to alienate their real estate in exchange for things of like value. When each member of a community signed the act of surrender it was, legally, a property exchange that was occurring, not a seizure.

It was this recognition of the rights of the religious to the temporalities of their institutions that guaranteed the pensions of the ex-religious and, a few years later, the ex-chantry priests. They had not, in this fiction, been deprived of their property. They had traded it for an annuity.

The principle was established first by a series of acts of surrender, confirmed by Parliament, that directly traded land. Then, after the Pilgrimage of Grace, Henry discovered a more efficient way to do it. At Furness in Lancashire the abbot, charged with supporting the rebels, voluntarily deeded the Abbey to the King, establishing the principle that a monastic house was the personal property of those who lived there. Accordingly, the inhabitants could grant it away freely if they so chose.

This was established by the Act for Dissolution of Abbeys, whose preamble pretended that the abbots, priors, prioresses and abbesses just might feel like surrendering their houses to the King, "of their own free and voluntary minds good wills and assents, without constraint or coaction or compulsion of any manner of person or persons."It was done "by the due order and course of the common laws of this realm," too. What they freely alienated included their monasteries "and all their sites, circuits and precincts of the same, and all and singular their manors, lordships, granges, mises, lands, tenements, meadows, pastures, rents, revocations, services, woods, tithes, pensions, portions, churches, chapels, advowsons, patronages, annuities, rights, entries, conditions, commons, leet courts, liberties, privileges and franchises appertaining."[36] The Act took one exhausting paragraph to do that. There followed fifteen provisoes and "general savings" to guarantee that the property rights of laity would not be disturbed.

By the time the dissolutions were finished, Henry's new Court of Augmentations owed £4,463 6s 8d a year in pensions to the ex-religious.[37] The values of the pensions were based on their positions in their houses — abbesses and abbots were well paid — and the actual wealth of the institution. In keeping with the principle of exchange of properties, the pensions were calculated as a share of the value of the monastery. These annuities were property, they could be sold, and they continued to be paid until the last monks and nuns died.

Of course the law might have been used to resist the dissolution of the monasteries, but the nature of monastic foundations meant that there were few who had a vested interest in protecting them. Most monasteries had been founded by families and individuals who were anxious to have prayers said for their souls. But by 1535 most monasteries had no local patron willing to defend the prayers offered there. Most patrons were too long dead, and the living had little interest in maintaining obits for people of whom they had no memory. The endowed, cloistered monasteries stood for an antiquated form of spiritual life, which consumed resources without providing benefits of the kind desired by the contemporary pious folk, whose tastes had changed. They preferred orders who worked in the world, preaching and serving, as the many new sixteenth-century orders, such as the Theatines and Jesuits demonstrated.

Moreover, the advowsons of religious houses were heritable and alienable, and had long since passed out of the families that founded them. As the rich got richer, these properties passed up the food chains. Thanks to entails, escheats, and heiresses, the advowsons and patronage of many monasteries had passed to the Crown and upper nobility, disconnecting the patronage from the localities.[38]

In those cases where the patronage was still held by one who took a personal interest in the house, there was often a reaction. Patrons sought, if not to save the foundation, to recover the property for other uses. Thomas Howard, the Duke of Norfolk, tried to convert Thetford Priory into a secular college, arguing that, since it was the burial place of his ancestors, it should be maintained. He failed to save the monks, but he did get the priory to use as his family chapel.[39] Thomas West, Lord de la Ware, had a similar concern about Boxgrove Priory in Sussex, near his home at Halnaker. As soon as he heard that small monasteries were to be dissolved, he wrote to Cromwell asking that Boxgrove be spared. He was, he said, its founder, and "there lieth many of my ancestors and also my wife's mother." It housed his parish church, too, and he had built a chapel in it for his own burial. If it was to be suppressed, he begged that he would be granted the property, or at least that it remain "unspoiled." He offered to buy the church ornaments, the crops, cattle, farm implements, demesne lands and four parsonages belonging to the priory. With Cromwell's help he was able to acquire the chattels, and he paid £10 for the church. But he was only able to get a 50-year lease on the demesne lands. This story has an ironic ending. In 1539 Henry VIII let it be known that he wanted de la Ware's house at Halnaker and de la Ware, in political trouble, was forced to give up his home and his lease on the priory to the King, in exchange for a nunnery and eight manors in Hampshire.[40]

These cases and others demonstrate that patrons were interested, when they existed, in what happened to the monasteries, but there were not many around. The fact that some founders and patrons tried to repossess monasteries rather than allow them to be seized by the Crown, must have accounted for the provision in the acts of dissolution that specifically exempted patrons from directly claiming the property.

If few patrons stepped forward to defend monasticism, as opposed to protecting the family vault, there was, in some places, violence in defense of the monasteries and traditional religion. The most notable instance of this is the Pilgrimage of Grace, when perhaps 30,000 men took the field in defense of local autonomy, saints' days, and the monasteries.

The rebels in Lincolnshire demanded that no more abbeys be suppressed. The Pilgrimage of Grace in Yorkshire made three demands about the monasteries in their Pontefract articles: that the suppressed ones be restored, that the Franciscans Observant be revived, and that Lee and Layton, the royal surveyors who had built the case for dissolution by reporting moral laxity in the monasteries of Yorkshire, be punished for what the rebels believed were their lies. The rebels reopened some of the closed houses, and some abbots and monks responded enthusiastically. At Sawley the Abbot and brothers immediately resumed the religious life, allowing their house to be used a communication center by the rebels. Four other convents were involved in the revolt, and the abbots of some of the larger houses were implicated as well. In the aftermath a number of abbots were executed and their houses forfeited. Jervaulx, Kirkstead, Whalley, and Bridlington were seized and closed.

Of course, the Pilgrimage of Grace was followed by violent suppression. No one alive at the time could have been unaware of the price paid by the rebels, and when the second round of monastic dissolutions occurred in 1540 there was scarcely a peep heard in complaint. By then many knew of the profits to be made through dissolution, and the faith of many more had been shaken to such an extent that they no longer respected monasticism. Even men who might have led resistance to the changes of the late 1530s had been either cowed or convinced.

John Porte senior, whose 1526 will is a perfect example of late Medieval piety with its bequests for obits and gifts to the Prior of Repton, to the prioress of Nuneaton, and to the monasteries of Beauvale, Chester, Burton, Croxden, Tutbury, Repton, and Trentham "beseeching them to sing or say an obit for my soul and all Christian souls and to pray for me."[41] When the dissolution of the monasteries began, however, Porte was appointed a commissioner to oversee their destruction in his locale. Conveniently, he was able to secure monastic property directly from the Prior of Repton, just before he dissolved the Priory.[42] In the following year he bought Dale Abbey. Finally, out of the possessions of Beauvale Priory and Welbeck Abbey he acquired the manor of Etwall itself from the crown, together with the advowson and rectory of the church there. He had become the patron of his own parish church.

Whatever he felt about religion, Porte had recognized that the dissolution presented an opportunity to improve his family wealth and taken it. Best of all, he had taken it while demonstrating that most valued Tudor virtue, obedience to his king.

Men like Justice Sir John Porte understood the law, and, no matter what they thought about religion, they knew an opportunity when they saw it. They may have regretted the dissolutions, but they did their duty and they reaped their profits, making it acceptable to look greedily at the church's property. More people were ready to take part in the spoil, and fewer were shocked by it.

Ethan Shagan's account of the plundering of Hailes Abbey by its former servants and neighbors proves that this attitude was spread through all classes. After the Abbot exposed the famous "Holy Blood of Hailes," a vial of Christ's blood, as a fraud, the Abbey was surrendered to the Crown. Then the opportunists moved in. Night after night the locals stole lead, glass and other valuables, filling their villages with the loot. The pillage was an open secret. Some of the thieves were evangelicals, but some were clearly traditionalists who believed, as one said, "Catch as catch can." Whatever the Abbey may have meant to them even a few years before, it was reduced to its constituent elements, stripped of its sacred nature by royal commissioners, preachers, and cooperating local leaders. Under these circumstances, Shagan observes, "the patterns of community religiosity which had depended upon the abbey would have to adapt or disappear."[43]

The experience of the dissolution of the monasteries had set the stage for the dissolution of the chantries that came next, making the choices clearer. Direct resistance was futile, money was to be made, and power could be had.

Thus, when the chantries were dissolved petitions, begging letters, lies and legal hair splitting were deployed to either keep or acquire properties that individuals and communities wished for themselves. In this case, the properties involved had, for the most part, small value, and the local parishioners were generally the donors and recipients of the donations.

The first act dissolving the chantries and colleges was passed by Henry VIII's last Parliament in 1545. It was a response to the desperate need for revenue to finance the war with Scotland, not an attack on Purgatory *per se*. Its justification, however, was moral outrage at the way in which the properties and revenues of colleges, free chapels, chantries, hospital, fraternities, brotherhoods, guilds and stipendiary priests were being abused by their founders and patrons. These secular persons, claims the Act, were converting the property to purposes other than those intended when their foundations were licensed by the Crown. In a strange twist of logic, the Act declared that, since the properties were being abused, all those institutions paying First Fruits and Tenths to the Crown were dissolved and forfeited to the King's use.[44]

The provisoes of the Act tell another story, since they carefully guarantee that the King can give this property away, and that it will not be subject to the tax of First Fruits and Tenths that had been owed on it when it was dedicated for religious purposes. Moreover, anyone owed income from the properties was guaranteed that payments would continue, and the personal properties of wardens, masters, and chantry priests were protected.[45]

The Act was right in one particular. The incomes of chantries, guilds, hospitals and colleges were already being diverted. The King himself had begun it, since the 1540 Act for the dissolution of monasteries had granted the Crown colleges and hospitals which "hereafter shall happen to be dissolved." Between 1539 and 1545 Crown dissolved some sixty foundations. Towns, seeing the possibilities, or perhaps the handwriting on the wall, joined in. York, for instance, secured a private act of Parliament that allowed it to suppress seven of the its nine chantries and all of the obits the city had supported. Similar things happened in Canterbury, Colchester, and Lincoln. In Richmond in Yorkshire the burgesses took the property of six chantries, two chapels and ten obits, paying the priests out of the town's revenues to continue the prayers.[46] The management of chantry property was expected to yield a surplus that cities like York invested in rental properties for the good of the corporation. In the York memoranda book someone asked and answered the question "how the 500 marks [for Howme's chantry] were spent for the benefit of the commonalty," explaining that the City earned six marks per annum, after expenses, from tenements purchased with the gift.[47] Under such circumstances, the only clear reason for these early dissolutions is to secure the endowments for the city before they were taken by the Crown.[48] Although religious sentiment favored the continuation of prayers for the dead, fiscal prudence argued that voluntary extinction of the chantries was preferable to seizure.

In cases like these, the aldermen were acting with the interests of their communities to the fore. Whether they believed that souls must be prayed for, they were well aware that the King would take the property if they did not preempt him. Families, fearing the same thing, sometimes abolished the prayers for their nearest kin. In Cullompton, Devon, John Trotte's own sons dissolved his almshouse, founded about 1523, expelled the bedesmen, and took the property back in 1544.[49] These voluntary dissolutions are excellent examples of the way some people protected the interests of their communities.

The preamble of the 1545 Chantries Act suggests that this response was known in other circumstances as well. Donors attempted to preserve their gifts for purposes consonant with their intentions and the welfare of their souls, rather than allowing Henry to seize their property. It was precisely because of this that the second act dissolving chantries, in 1547, said that anything used for superstitious purposes within the last five years was forfeit.[50] The drafters were attempting to defeat the efforts of individuals and communities to keep properties they believed ought to remain in their possession.

Although that loophole was closed, it was possible to defeat the intent of any Act by appealing directly to the King, which is what Oxford and Cambridge did. Under the terms of the Act all colleges, schools and hospitals were forfeit, not just colleges that functioned as chantries. Surveyors were sent throughout the realm to identify properties to be annexed, and special commissioners were appointed to appraise the two universities. Matthew Parker, the vice chancellor of Cambridge, was joined by William May, the President of Queens' and John Redman, Master of Trinity, in preparing the assessment of Cambridge. A similar team was appointed for Oxford.

In February 1548 Parker and May attended the King at Hampton Court to deliver their report. It is a brilliant piece of statistical obfuscation. It values Cambridge University and the colleges and carefully sorts out their income and expenses, making distinctions between various expenses to show how much is spent on ministers and sermons, alms to the poor, maintaining chapels, paying the fellows and servants, and a host of other things. Against these they set the incomes of the foundations. In every case the expenses exceeded the income. In the case of Clare Hall, for instance, the expenses were £30 16s more than its revenue of £163 3s 2d. The University's expenses were £355 16s 2d greater than its annual income of £3,901 3s 6d.[51] The numbers proved that Cambridge University and all of its colleges could not afford to operate.

Not surprisingly, Oxford was in the same position. There, each college looked much like Merton, which had an income of £397 8s 11d and expenses of £424 7s 3d, leaving it in deficit £26 18s 3d.[52]

Clearly, the universities were making soup from stones. Or so Parker and May told the King. In a memorandum of their conversation with Henry, Parker recalled that His Majesty, after looking over the engrossed accounts of the Cambridge colleges, said admiringly, "that he thought he had not in his realm so many persons so honestly maintained in living, by so little land and rent." But then he asked the obvious question. What did it mean that the colleges expended more yearly than their revenues? "We answered," said Parker, "that it rose partly of fines for leases and indentures of the farmers renewing their leases, partly of wood sales," the occasional revenues which were not part of fixed rents from their properties.

whereupon he [the King] said to the lords, that pity it were these lands should be altered to make them worse; (at which words some were grieved, for that they disappointed *lupos quosdam hiantes* [certain gaping wolves]). In fine, we sued to the King's majesty . . . that he would favour us in the continuance of our possessions such as they were, and that no man by his grace's letters should require to permute with us to give us worse. He made answer and smiled . . . and bad us hold [keep] our own. . . . With which words we were well armed, and so departed.[53]

Matthew Parker was Dean of the College at Stoke, as well as vice-chancellor of Cambridge, and he saved it from dissolution using the same techniques. Appealing to Queen Katherine Parr, he argued that, since the College was located adjacent to lands she held, it provided a number of useful services, from educating her tenants' children to giving hospitality to her officers when they visited her holdings. Alms, hospitality, and free education were all joined to the preaching of God's word, and so, he argued, it should be allowed to continue. Katherine apparently agreed, for Stoke escaped the first dissolution. It would not be so lucky in the second.[54]

But not everyone was as informed, or as skilled, as the few who succeeded in putting the property to different uses before the seizure, or avoiding it using political skill. Many properties fell to the Crown. However, the first Act dissolving chantries did not apply to those privately held, since they did not pay First Fruits and Tenths. The second Act seized those that were left.

The 1545 dissolution of the chantries, colleges, hospitals and free schools paying First Fruits and Tenths had been a revenue measure. The King needed more money, and he found a vulnerable class of property to take in order to get the money. It was not aimed at abolishing Purgatory and prayers for the dead. The nationalization of a little property did not make Henry VIII a Protestant, though evangelicals and greedy courtiers were delighted to see him seizing and closing more religious foundations.

When, after Henry's death, the evangelicals came to predominate in the govern-ment, the chantries were attacked for theological reasons. The Crown still needed the revenue for its war with Scotland, but the Act was forthright in its disgust at the superstitions practiced in the chantries, and about its intention to destroy them, turning their revenues to better uses, such as supporting grammar schools, helping the poor, and providing for the universities. To which end, all the chantries, free chapels and colleges in existence five years before that Act were annexed by the King for redistribution. In addition, the King was to have and enjoy the lands and goods of all fraternities, brotherhoods and guilds in perpetuity.[55]

The Act mandated that commissioners be appointed to survey all the lands and other properties belonging to all these foundations. The surveyors were to cover the entire country preparing lists of property to be annexed by the Court of Augmenta-tions. They were empowered to reassign the lands to support schools and parish churches, a power that sometimes led to abuses.[56]

Responses to Dissolution

As it dawned on communities that the King was taking properties that had been given and managed for the local good, some chose to resist. In 1548 the people of Seamer, Yorkshire, met the commissioners for chantries with violence. Lighting a beacon to call the country to arms, as many as three thousand attacked them. Seizing Matthew White and four others associated with the dissolution, they carried them into a nearby wood and murdered them. As they should have expected, the leaders of the mob were executed.[57] This, however, was a rare choice. Most places submitted with meekness, attempting to protect their "superstitious" properties through law and politics, and, in the end, incorporating the new owners of the properties into the fabric of their lives. The dissolutions demonstrated the new role the Crown could play in even the smallest villages.

In Wales passive resistance and legal foot dragging were used by some of the parishioners of Llanfaredd [Llanvarethe] and Llanelwedd in Radnorshire to keep the ox teams they bought to support masses. It is a complicated story, but it appears that in about 1541 one of the bells in the parish church broke. After deliberation, the parish sold the broken bell and invested the money in yearlings, to be trained as ox teams. When they were big enough, these teams were rented out, earning money to pay a priest or two to say mass at a chapel of ease about a mile from their parish church. The churchwardens at the time managed the rentals.[58]

A similar arrangement was made in the parish of Llanelwedd nearby, where a dozen oxen, a cow, and twenty lambs were part of the stock supporting a priest.

In 1547 the King's surveyor, John Basset, touring the parishes, was told by the churchwardens about the oxen.[59] Declaring the livestock to be forfeit to the Crown,

Bassett appointed Rees ap Gwilliam to seize and keep the animals in the King's name, but the churchwardens of the two parishes refused to hand them over. Ap Gwilliam was forced to bring suit in the Court of Augmentation against the people he knew were concealing the beasts.[60]

In the ensuing exchange of informations and replications the parishioners of Llanelwedd claimed that "May last was twelve month" (before the survey of the chantries) that they, concluding that the income from the oxen was insufficient to support two priests, had sold all their animals but two oxen and twenty lambs, dividing the profit amongst themselves "as they might lawfully do." Not only did they no longer have the oxen, they insisted that if they had them, they did not fall under the Act because they did not support a superstitious activity.[61]

Oddly, the parishioners of Llanfaredd now claimed that the oxen they held were bought to support the repair of their church, not to pay for superstitious masses. It was, they said, about "May last was twelve months" (before the survey of the chantries) when they concluded that the oxen would not produce enough revenue to fix the church and sold them to members of the parish.[62]

The legal holding action fought by the parishioners seems to have worked. Whatever the justice of the case, by January of 1551 John Bassett admitted defeat. He told the judges in the Court of Augmentations that the oxen were gone, bought by other men, and he asked them not to hold his deputy ap Gwilliam responsible for delivering them.[63]

In Montgomery a similar strategy was pursued by parishioners. The surveyor complained that the livestock employed by the parishes of Llandussill, Berio, Newtone, Maghenlleth, Bettus and Churchestocke were being kept from the King. The people there "being obstinate and disordered," "alleging that their ancestors were the first givers and gatherers of the said cattle and by such pretense having embezzled and already sold divers parcels of the said stock did and yet do refuse either to deliver those same or to make account therefore."[64]

In Godmanchester, Huntingdonshire, the bailiffs of the town ordered that all the deeds belonging to two of their six guilds be burned and their possessions concealed from the royal commissioners. Two more of their guilds were leased to members of the royal household. The bailiff's campaign to save the property was repeated in many places, a form of passive resistance that demonstrated their savvy. As J. J. Scarisbrick remarks about these sorts of creative responses to the dissolutions, "this was just the sort of thing at which late-medieval English men and women had become extremely adept: enfeoffments, fictitious conveyances and conceal-ments. . . ."[65]

In Wiltshire the resistance to the removal of the altars and superstitious fixtures in Highworth parish met with a different sort of resistance. The churchwardens were carrying out the King's order when the farmer of the vicarage, John Boller, protested. "Wherefore do you pull down these altars?" he demanded, "A dog commanded you to do this and thou hast no more authority to do this than has a dog . . ." This incident quickly became a prominent part of a local quarrel between the Warnefords and the Hungerfords, but it is striking that, when the case came before the Star Chamber, Boller claimed that he did not care about the altars; he cared about the stone. As the farmer of the vicarage he claimed a right to the salvage.[66]

For every loss there was a gain for someone, or some institution, and some of the people who benefitted from the dissolutions took seriously the idea that the property should be redistributed in the interest of a better commonwealth. Sir Walter Mildmay, one of the judges of the Court of Augmentations, was in the perfect position to profit from this new wash of property onto the market, and he did. But he was also a man who believed in education. In Chelmsford the dissolution of a chantry had extinguished the livings of two schoolmasters. Mildmay, his brother Thomas, who was an auditor in the Augmentations, and another Augmentations judge, Robert Keilway, re-founded the school in 1551, endowing it with the incomes of several chantries. Thomas Mildmay then gave it a home, granting it the former friary at Moulsham.[67]

This pattern was followed in many places, especially since the commissioners were given the power to transfer property to such good purposes. Any good local leader understood this and made use of it, if he could. In Cambridgeshire John Cotton and other landlords in Landwade successfully petitioned the Augmentations office to provide an annuity for their parish priest. In the time of "superstition," they said, the parsonage of Landwade had been appropriated by the farmer of the parsonage of Exening, Suffolk. The farmer was the Abbot of Battle, who in exchange for the tithes from Landwade, had paid the prior of Fordham an annual pension of £56s 8d to find a priest for the parish. When the Gilbertine house at Fordham was dissolved on September 1, 1538, the support for the priest disappeared. The Dean and Chapter of Canterbury were collecting the tithe, but they had been released from paying the pension by letters patent of Henry VIII. John Cotton, seeing in the dissolution of the chantries an opportunity, managed to convince Edward VI's Court of Augmentations to resume the payments so the parishioners did not have to find the cost themselves.[68]

The kind of astute local leadership that could divert the stream of revenue back into local hands did not exist everywhere, and much of the property went to individuals who were less than scrupulous about its use. This had the potential to create deep rifts within communities – in the Llanfaredd case some locals tried to buy the oxen from the Court while others of the parish tried to conceal them – and it could victimize those least able to defend themselves. Although the law said that the new owners of ecclesiastical properties had to continue paying the pensions owed by former foundations, they were easily forgotten in the great shuffle of real estate. Elderly people employed as bedesmen in hospitals were especially vulnerable.

In Toddington, Bedfordshire, the old men in the Hospital of St. John the Baptist petitioned Henry VIII for help. They were resident in a chantry founded by John Broughton, where one priest and three poor men were to pray for Broughton's soul and the souls of the monarchs. Broughton had endowed the Hospital with lands from the "late" monastery of Dartford and a manor in Kent, which he gave to the monastery of Childerlangley before it was dissolved. The prior of Childerlangley was supposed to pay the bedesmen five pounds a year from the gift. But then Childerlangley itself was dissolved. Its possession then passed into the hands of a bishop, who just happened to be the former prior of Childerlangley. Somehow the pensions were forgotten in the confusion. By the time the petitioners complained, they were owed £25, "which is unto us . . . our utter undoing, for as God knoweth we are impotent aged persons having nothing else to live upon save only this our pension . . ." Forced to depend upon their neighbors' charity to live, they begged the King for mercy.[69]

It was this sort of thing which was on the minds of communities as the hospitals, chantries and colleges were dissolved across the 1540s. Given the losses incurred, there had to be ways to mitigate and turn to advantage the impacts of the dissolutions.

Towns felt the dissolutions more keenly than other institutions, and enjoyed the greatest opportunities. Although the closing of the monasteries had deeply affected some towns, such as Cerne Abbas or Reading, where their primary customer and employer disappeared, or Peterborough, where the Dean and Chapter of the cathedral were given all the powers formerly possessed by the Abbot, all towns had to confront the problems and opportunities raised by the seizure of chantries, schools, religious guilds and colleges.

The seizure of large, wealthy foundations distressed the towns in which they were located, giving them a good reason to complain. Southwell Minster, for instance, had 63 priests and clerks and an income exceeding £1,000 a year, making it a very important source of business and power in Nottingham. Morever, such intercessory institutions often had multiple roles, giving a lot of people, some of them very important people, a serious stake in them. The same endowment often paid a priest, funded and housed a school, and provided poor relief. With the loss of such an endowment the community had to seek other ways to educate the young and relieve the impotent. Unable, and sometimes ideologically unwilling, to prevent the dissolution, community leaders attempted to salvage what they could.[70]

These attempts took a number of forms. Direct purchase of properties was the most obvious, but one that few towns could immediately afford, though many bought them over time. In Bristol, for instance, the Crown took £4,258 17s 6d in property, much more than even the third city of the realm could afford. However, as Tittler tells us, by "judicious planning and persistent attention to possibilities for other purchases, it had substantial success in both acquiring other properties and in managing them effectively thereafter." By 1548 Bristol had spent £1,829 17s 10d acquiring the Carmelite and Franciscan priories, Gaunt's Hospital, the properties of the Hospitallers of St. John, the Chapel on the Bridge, and other holdings.[71]

The strategic brilliance of Bristol's moves becomes apparent when the political implications of the dissolution purchases are considered. Not only did the city reserve for itself considerable revenue, it also took control of the spiritual peculiars within the City. Now the writ of the Mayor ran everywhere, and the City was under a single ecclesiastical authority, the Bishop of Bristol, whose see had been erected on the lands of St. Augustine Abbey. The functions of the two religious guilds that survived the dissolution had been altered, too, so that their resources were now devoted solely to relief of the poor. For the merchant oligarches who ran Bristol, this must have been a satisfactory conclusion, leaving them with much greater power in the City.[72]

In many places, wealthy men and women came to the rescue. Buying the ecclesiastical properties, they returned them to their communities, as gifts, as legacies, or as sales. Richard Pate set an example. Born in Cheltenham, he married the widow of the mayor of Gloucester and took up residence there. A lawyer, Pate's first civic duty in Gloucester was as a commissioner for the dissolution of the chantries in 1547, remaining intimately involved with it for the rest of his life, representing it four times in Parliament. The nephew and namesake of the Marian Bishop of Worcester, he rejected his uncle's faith. Speculating in monastic lands, he was noted as "an ancient professor of the gospel." Whatever his personal faith, Richard Pate used his wealth to help his neighbors. He established the school and hospital in Cheltenham that bear his name. He bought the property and possessions of the Guild of the Blessed Virgin Mary in Chipping Sudbury and resold them to the borough for the same amount he paid. And he conveyed almost all the chantry land he acquired in Gloucester, yielding more than £100 in annual rental income, to the City. He did all this before he died. In his will he left money to help Gloucester's poor, relieve its prisoners, and repair its buildings.[73]

In Exeter wealthy citizens helped in a different, yet profitable, way. The lands the town wanted were acquired by Sir John Williams and Henry Norryce. In 1549, thirteen members of the Chamber of Exeter promised to go sureties for the City to buy them for £1,460 2s 3d, to be paid over three years. The annual rent expected from the purchase was approaching £95 a year, so they paid a discounted price of 16 years' purchase. Then, to raise the cash, the Chamber sold £76 worth of the rentals to thirty-two citizens. Although Exeter had bought the properties at 16 years' purchase, they sold them at 20, with the knowledge of the purchasers. In short, thanks to the willingness of the wealthy citizens to help, Exeter secured for itself, without spending a penny, £17 of annual income. At the same time, a number of citizens of Exeter benefitted from the dissolution.[74]

As these cases illustrate, if a town was lucky, or skilled, private individuals or the Crown could be convinced to rededicate dissolved properties to good uses. Pre-

Reformation endowments, which often included provisions for repairing bridges, caring for the poor, helping prisoners, and maintaining schools, could be acquired by the community and put to the same use. And for some towns and individuals, there were political benefits as well.

Robert Tittler has worked out the implications of the dissolutions on the towns in detail, finding five areas of impact and opportunity. First, the dissolutions brought onto the open market an unprecedented amount of urban property, both immediately and over the next half century as the Crown released it. Second, local authorities, seeing the needs and opportunities, moved to secure these properties that had belonged to the church, making them very mindful of their legal positions. This led to the third impact, an increased demand for incorporation and other legal safeguards to protect their new properties. The fourth effect arose from the changed balance of power in the towns. Properties not directly acquired by the towns were picked up by lay people, who became forces to be reckoned with in local politics, increasing the tendency toward oligarchy noted by many scholars of Elizabeth's reign. The last effect was an increasing enthusiasm for Protestantism on the part of this new urban elite, whose wealth rested upon the seized properties.[75]

Certainly, the Crown had further empowered the communities who got the property, as well as enriching a group of influential men who supported schism for the simple reason that the Supreme Head guaranteed their new wealth. When Mary set about restoring Catholicism, her program nearly foundered on the rock of secularized ecclesiastical properties. Parliament would restore Catholic doctrine, but it would not tolerate the return of the church lands. Legal advice to Mary in 1554 indicated that she simply could not give the property back. Not only because the lands had become the foundation of the fortunes of many, who provided the services upon which the Crown depended, but also because the lands in question were recognized in law as the hereditary possessions of their owners. The Crown did not dare overthrow these families by taking the land. Moreover, the Crown was the guarantor of all property rights in the nation. Seizing the property would convince the nation that the Crown could not be trusted to ensure safe possession of anything. Nor could the Crown afford to buy the properties. Consequently, the adviser suggested, it should be argued that since, in canon law, it was admissible to alienate church property to ransom hostages from the infidel, the lands taken from the Church by the English Crown should be seen as ransom paid to liberate the English from the clutches of heretics.[76]

As that adviser understood, Mary's government could not force the return of secularized church property. Allowing people to keep it was the *sine qua non* for the return to Rome. By the same token, when Elizabeth came to the throne concerns over property drew support for the royal supremacy from odd quarters. Richard, Lord Rich, for instance, supported Elizabeth's supremacy. Despite his own enthusiastic conservatism under Mary, who had appointed him to her privy council, Rich had enriched himself as Chancellor of the Court of Augmentations, presiding over the dissolution of the monasteries and chantries. A consistent sycophant in his earlier years, Rich turned pious in his old age. After burning Protestants in Essex for Mary, he found, at last, enough courage to vote against the Elizabethan Act of Uniformity. However, he voted for the supremacy. Its passage allowed him to recover more than £1,600 worth of monastic property he had been forced to give to Queen Mary. Moreover, he managed to convert his newly created chantry in Felstead into a grammar school rather than losing it to the Crown, as he would have under the terms of the Elizabethan Act against the "overplus" of chantry lands.[77]

As Il Schifanoya reported to Venice, in 1559, the third dissolution was supported enthusiastically in the House of Commons. He did not think, however, that Elizabeth would benefit from the dissolution, since "they all make demands of her, some for a piece of land, some for a garden, some for a house, and some for the fee simple of estates for their residence; . . . nor can she refuse . . . There is no doubt of the Bill passing, as it favors personal interests."[78] Indeed, there were so many property interests served by the Elizabethan Settlement of religion that it created a mini land rush.[79]

Besides those towns who took advantage of the dissolution to acquire properties within their borders, there were those who saw the end of monastic power as political liberation. Reading, for example, was controlled by the Abbot of the powerful royal monastery there. Although the leading men of the town had succeeded in creating a Guild Merchant in the early sixteenth century, the Abbot appointed the mayor. Moreover, the livings of the three Reading parishes belonged to the monastery, allowing the churchwardens little control over the incumbents. Naturally, there was a great tension between the monks and the town, so that the lay leaders of the community quickly allied themselves with Cromwell. Although the small group of powerful men who dominated Reading did not agree about religion, they did agree that they hated the Abbey, and many served on the jury that sent the last Abbot to die for denying the royal supremacy. Dissolution meant, for them, self-government, in the sense that the King became their lord, rather than the abbot. In 1542 they were granted a charter by the Crown and, in 1560, Reading became an incorporated borough.

The principle that guided the mayors and churchwardens of Reading was that the power invested in them by the community had to be used for the "good and profit of the parish." This common-law principle, together with local custom, became the shelter in which they could hide as the vagaries of royal policy swept over the community. They could respond to threats to parish goods, and protect themselves, by asserting their devotion to law and local custom. When Mayor John Bourne made his will in late 1558, he expressed his Catholicism and his pragmatic desire to help his parish. He left books and a cope to St. Mary's church, "upon condition that God's service be there maintained as it now is and if that service do otherwise alter then I will it to be sold" and the profit given to the parish's poor.

But to protect Reading these leaders, no matter what they felt personally, had to show themselves to be loyal subjects of the person wearing the crown, protecting themselves and the town from retribution and easing their search for incorporation. This sometimes left them in a morally ambiguous position. William Edmundes, a known Protestant, felt he had to take action against a fellow Protestant who expressed disloyal opinions about Queen Mary because he was a sworn servant of the Crown. "I am her Majesty's officer . . . I may not conceal it [the treasonable utterance], neither will I," he said. Given Edmundes' attitude, it is not surprising that John Saunders, a burgess since 1546, was expelled from the guild for slandering the government in 1553. The town's leaders would not tolerate behaviors which brought the community into disrepute with the Crown.

Ironically, though they eagerly participated in destroying the monastery, the dissolution impoverished Reading. Free of the abbot, Bourne, Edmundes and their colleagues found themselves living in reduced circumstances.[80]

Towns and parishes were expected to be inclusive of their residents. There were other institutions that had much more specialized missions, but they, too, had choices to make in the midst of the dissolutions. The livery companies and trade guilds, like universities and inns of court, had all formed around religious practices and all prayed for their departed colleagues at their annual feasts. They too set to work to find the silver lining. It was a lining that was easy to discover, since so many people were benefitting by the dissolutions.

Take, for instance, the Drapers' Company of London. As a city guild it had, over time, accumulated a long list of duties to the dead. Supported by endowed lands, these duties left the Company officers managing property that yielded poor returns, costing time and money. At the same time, the property was an endowment to use, so they could not easily sell it. The dissolution of the chantries came to the Drapers' as a blessing in disguise.

Setting aside the question of whether they feared for their immortal souls if the prayers stopped, looking at the problem as one of management in an inflation tortured age, the dissolution of the chantries got the Company out of a hole that was growing deeper and deeper.

The Drapers' Company administered property valued by the Crown Commissioners at £557s per annum in rent. This property supported "superstitious" prayers for the departed, but it was intimately bound up with bequests to the poor. These bequests involved managing the endowed property and the alms houses. The Company paid priests, clerks, bedesmen, and all the other people it took to run a chantry.

These bequests in return for prayers were often small, yet they required administration. Lady Baily left lands to provide 20 d worth of bread money for the poor of St. Michael, Paternoster Row, on every Sunday. Sir John Richards and his widow left £145 for charitable grants to poor drapers. In 1534 William Prudd bequeathed land within the City worth 40s for his alms, requiring that coals be provided to poor householders in St. Laurence Poulteney Parish and St. Mary Abchurch parish. In 1518, Sir John Milbourne built 13 almshouses for poor members of the company, and left lands to support them. He died in 1534, leaving the Company to choose and oversee the poor, who were expected to serve as bedesmen under the governance of a priest.[81]

Bequests were treated as business propositions by the City companies. In May 1556 the Grocers were offered a house or £40 in exchange for an obit for "Parson Jennings." They rejected the offer on the grounds that it would not be profitable to the Company.[82] On the same principle the Merchant Tailors refused William Roper's offer of a tenement from whose rent £4 a year was to be given to poor prisoners. A committee of the Company inspected it, reported that it was ruinous and likely to fall down, and rejected the offer. However, the Parish Clerks' Company, which lost its endowments in the dissolutions because their Company was considered *de facto* superstitious, accepted Roper's tenements.[83]

Thus for the Drapers' the loss of their superstitious endowments did little direct harm to the Company's revenues, while relieving it of the duty of administering the bequests.

But they had not lost the property permanently. The Drapers, like all the City companies, were invited to buy back the property they had lost to the Crown when the chantries were dissolved. Augustine Hinde and Richard Turke, two London Aldermen, and William Blackwell, the common clerk of London, bought all £18,744 11s 2d worth of "superstitious" property of the livery companies and the City from the Court of Augmentations. In turn, they sold it back to the companies that had originally owned it.[84] The syndicate offered the Drapers their £55 7s worth of annual rents at 20 years' purchase, or £1,114 0s 2d. After getting some corrections made in the record, the Drapers got it down to £1,082 6s and closed the deal. They then sold £706 13s 4d of the newly acquired property to members of the Company, finding the remainder of the price in their own revenues.

The Pewterers, after paying the amount spent on "superstitious" activities to the Crown for one year, bought all their rents back from Hinde, Turke and Blackwell.[85] It is unclear what they paid to reacquire rents, worth £15 4s, but they did not sell any of the properties to finance the transaction.[86] Their books indicate that they simply continued business as usual, except that they no longer had to apply any of the annual rent to pay for masses. The obit for Laurence Ashlyn, managed by the Pewterers for the former Master of the Company, was supported by the rent from

13 small tenements in Gregory Alley outside Cripplegate. Yielding £5 10s a year, the Pewterers paid from that amount the following expenses, using the remainder for the repair of the tenements and the charges of the Company:

Priest and clerk	3s 8d
Peals at mass	4d
wax	8d
poor people in alms	2s 6d
Master of our Co.	6d
every warden	4d
to 2 that were masters	2d
Beadle of the Co.	4d
Bread and drink	1s 0d
Total	9s 6d

These expenses declined precipitously after the dissolution of the chantries and the imposition of Protestant worship. In 1548/9 the charge for Laurence Ashlyn's obit (though not called an obit in the account book that year) was only 2s 10d. In accord with the will, they still paid alms to the poor worth 2s 6d and 4d to the beadle of the Company for distributing them. The remaining 7s remained in the Company's hands, helping to pay the cost of buying back the obit from the Crown.[87]

From the fiscal point of view, the return of Catholicism was a double insult. The Pewterers had bought back their own property from the Crown in 1550; in 1554 they prudently returned to observing the obit as prescribed by Ashlyn's will, at the full cost.[88] When Protestantism returned, in 1559, the cost of Ashlyn's obit (still called an obit) fell again to 2s 10d.[89] As the dust of the Elizabethan Settlement cleared, the Pewterers began thinking of Ashlyn's obit as a bequest to the Company. Notably, in 1561 the clerk had written "Mr Ashlyns obit" and then crossed out "obit" and inserted "bequest."[90] As happened elsewhere, the Company continued paying for those parts of the obit which were not "superstitious." In 1563 they gave a dinner in Ashlyn's memory. Although they no longer paid for priests, clerks, wax, or peals of bells, they gave the usual 2s 6d to the poor, paid the Master 6d, the two Wardens 8d, the beadle 4d, and spent 5s 10d on dinner. By 1565 they were convinced that a meal for the Assistants of the Company, not the mass, was what Ashlyn had intended in his gift, so the entry reads "spent at a dinner ... according to his [Ashlyn's] will" 5s 10d.[91] The Master and the two Wardens were now being paid to go to dinner with the Assistants at the Castle in Fish Street, rather than praying for the soul of Laurence Ashlyn in the church of St. Mary Abchurch. By 1571 this dinner was remembered as the old custom.[92]

In this case, the extra income might have been used to increase the alms payment. After all, the rate of inflation in the 1550s had halved the value of the 2s 6d given to the thirty poor men and women in Ashlyn's will. But it was not. However, the Company did not ignore the will altogether, since they spent on the feast what would have been spent on the mass. They simply converted one form of memorial expense into another.[93]

The Pewterers were not alone in their approach to their "superstitious" property. The pattern of repurchasing and continuing everything but the mass is common. The companies, colleges, towns and cities were all caught between the legal and emotional need to honor the wills of the departed donors and the legal and prudent need to obey the king or queen of the moment.

As Queen Mary truthfully put it, in a letter to Oxford just a month after her accession, the statutes and foundations "have been much altered, broken, and almost utterly subverted, whereby not only the last wills of many good men have been broken, and many wise politic and godly ordinances confirmed by Parliaments and by sundry our progenitors foully, and irreverently condemned, but the consciences of many honest men, which by their oaths were bound to the observation of the said statutes and foundations have been much encumbered."[94]

Of course, Protestants could argue that she was ordering them to break the Edwardian rules and statutes just as much as Edward VI had, but she caught the tenor of the times.

Merton College, one of Oxford's oldest foundations, exemplifies Mary's concern. It had acquired many endowments that ensured masses for the souls of the donors. However, Merton began ignoring the bequests long before the dissolution, unless the donor was recently deceased and had living friends and relatives. Merton's exquisite system of accounts allows us to see what was done, and at what cost.

By 1547 Merton had on its books bequests for 31 obits, other than that of the founder, 25 of which were received before 1543. The oldest gift, after that of Walter de Merton, was established by Ela, Countess of Warwick, in 1295. In exchange for 20 marks the Warden and fellows agreed to buy property to support an annual mass for her soul and the souls of all Christians. After it was sung, the Warden, fellows, and chaplains who had attended were paid to have a drink in her honor.[95]

In 1471 Henry Sever, a former Warden of the College, willed Merton a tenement in Fleet Street and a house in West Tilbury, in exchange for a yearly obit for himself. For obits for Mercy Carew he gave them the profits of St. Alban Hall, a residence next door to the College.[96] The Carew family held the farm of Holywell Manor, which belonged to Merton.

Thomas Kempe, the Bishop of London, gave the College 600 marks and a great gilt cross in March 1490. The College was to use the money to buy land to support a "liberata" or allowance to the warden and fellows, and to pay for the obsequies and solemn requiem on Kempe's death anniversary each year. They promised to use the Sarum rite in his memorial, and to pray for the soul of his brother John Kempe, Cardinal and Archbishop of Canterbury. Thomas Kempe may have been generous, but he was not naive. His agreement with the College insisted that the terms of the contract be read annually before the fellows to remind them of their promise in perpetuity. Solemnly promising to observe their pact, they admitted the Bishop as a brother and special benefactor of the College, to benefit from all prayers, vigils, and other pious works of the fellowship.[97]

Seven years later Thomas Lee, a former fellow and a descendant of the founder, promised silver plate and £30 in cash, two thirds of which was to go to poor scholars and the College chest, or general fund. For this, the Warden and fellows promised that an obit would be held on the anniversary of his death every year for 40 years and 4d would be donated annually to the *praeco mortuorum* of Oxford.[98]

In 1510 Bishop Fitzjames of London, another former Warden, struck an agreement with the College. In return for five marks rent from the manor of Knoll, the fellows promised to find an "honest chaplain" to celebrate a mass daily on his behalf. On the anniversary of his death each year 26s 8d was to be spent out of the rent in his memory. Each chaplain (there were 3) was to have 4d; each of the two clerks received 4d; the bellringers got 8d; 8d was spent on wax, and the balance was divided equally between the warden, fellows, and bachelors.[99]

In fraternal solidarity, Ralph Hamsterley agreed with the College in 1514 that he should have his exequies solemnly celebrated on the day after those of Bishop Fitzjames, under the same terms. Another 26s 8d was to be distributed.[100] A fellow from 1476 until 1484, Hamsterly became master of University College, but was buried back at Merton. After Hamsterley died in 1518 more money was added to the bequest, so a priest was appointed to pray for him at the altar of St. Catherine in the College's church of St. John.[101]

In theory, then, the chaplains and fellows would have been busy praying for the souls of all these people, in accordance with their solemn pledges. The College account books, however, suggest that it did not happen in quite that way. The accounts show that the obsequies for most donors were sporadically performed. The more recent the gift, the more likely the services were to be celebrated, so that Countess Ela's obsequies were observed in 1522, 1523 and 1524, but not again until 1556–9. It should be noted, however, that the payments to each of the fellows for a drink in her honor were religiously made each year, as if they had all attended her mass.

Thomas Sever had obsequies in 1501, 1508, and 1512–15, with a gap until 1527, after which they continued without a break until 1539. The year 1540 was skipped, in 1541 they held his memorial, and then they remembered only in 1543, 1546, 1547, and 1548. One mass was said for him in Mary's reign. Mercy Carew, for the sake of whose soul Sever had given St. Alban Hall to the College, had sporadic remembrance. In 1501 there was an obsequy held for her; the next was in 1509, followed by 1510, 1511, 1515, and 1525; then 1543, 1546, 1547, and 1557.

Despite their solemn promises of annual masses, Kempe's obsequies were recorded as said only once in the sixteenth century, in 1539. Thomas Lee, for whom they promised to pray every year from 1502, when he died, until 1542, had a regular mass until 1516, after which they were said only in 1522, 1523, 1524, and 1548.

Bishop Fitzjames was one of the lucky ones. He received his annual due on schedule until 1543, when there was an interruption until 1547. Naturally, it stopped during the Edwardian years, but he was prayed for in the period 1556–9. His friend Hamsterley did not fare so well. Hamsterley funded a priest for his chantry, and between 1518 and 1532 there was an annual appointment. But then the record is silent about appointments to Hamsterley's chantry until 1558, when William Atkins became his chantry priest.[102] Atkins prayed for his soul for the first time in years, but he did not have long to last as a chantry priest, since the prayers were stopped again in 1559.

Overall a pattern emerges that suggests that Merton was not terribly interested in praying on behalf of the dead. The payments show that the Warden and fellows were most likely to remember the promises made by their predecessors if a visitation was threatened, or there was a good political reason to demonstrate commitment to the old religion, or perhaps, if there were people in the College who remembered and cared about the deceased. Generally, the obits had been kept with some regularity until 1516. After that, the sudden enthusiasm for obits in Mary's reign was only matched by the period 1522–4 and 1536–9, although the conservative mid-1540s did see an increase in activity On the other hand, the fellows showed a commendable zeal in collecting the "liberata" left to them by donors. Even when there were no masses said for Countess Ela, every fellow received his appointed three shillings a year from her fund – even after the Reformation had abolished any pretense that prayers were being said for her.[103]

Is this slackness evidence of religious changes in the College, mere laziness, or bad bookkeeping? We may never know, though when one looks at the wardens a pattern emerges. The first return to pious duty, falling between 1521 and 1524, coincides exactly with the wardenship of Roland Philipps. Philipps may have insisted that the College statutes be observed.[104] The burst of obits in the middle of the 1540s falls in the first couple of years of Thomas Reynolds' wardenship, but, unlike Philipps, Reynolds went on being warden until deprived by the Visitor, Matthew Parker, in 1559. A noted conservative, Reynolds may be responsible for the sharp increase in obits between 1556 and 1558, though falling, as it does, in the height of the Marian persecution of Protestants, it may have been prudent to observe obits, no matter who was warden.

Changed wardens cannot account for the flurry of obits circa 1536–7, but it was a disturbed time in Oxford, and there were religious divisions in the College. Among the fellows were men of pronounced views. Of the twenty-four men shown in the Register as of the fellowship, three were elected before 1522. These seniors were joined by six more between 1522 and 1524, and another seven were elected between

1527 and 1529. Three were chosen in 1531, and five in 1532. In general, this suggests that the character to the college had changed dramatically in the late 1520s, and that by 1535 only half the fellows had been there more than six years. Among the "elders" were a number of young men who would later align themselves with the conservatives. Walter Buckler, elected in 1522, Richard Smith, elected in 1527, and John Ramridge, elected in 1527 may have sided with those who favored traditional forms. But John Parkhurst and Robert Huick, both chosen in 1529 are notable examples of men who did not.

Parkhurst became a bishop under Elizabeth, and Huick dramatically and vocally converted to Protestantism. Proclaiming his certainty of salvation by faith not works, he complained that his colleagues were shunning him. In 1532 Huick was expelled from the principalship of St. Alban Hall for his religious views, and he left the College in 1536.[105] Parkhurst left in 1538, as did Ramridge, who would die in religious exile in 1559.[106] It is very hard to know how this mix of men affected the religious life of the College, but Parkhurst, at least, made his student John Jewel compare the biblical translations of Tyndale and Coverdale, suggesting that some of the students were getting an evangelical education.[107]

This was probably offensive to men like Richard Smith, who, in the early 1530s, was preaching in support of the doctrine of Purgatory and condemning the Lutheran doctrine of *Sola Fide*, maintaining the necessity of the work of fasting as an Apostolical ordinance. Smith went on to become Regius Professor of Divinity at Oxford, until he was deprived in 1548.[108]

Whatever the fellowship's religious divisions, and no matter why Merton neglected its obits unless under pressure, its chapel responded, like every other parish (Merton's chapel, St. John's, was also a parish church), to external demands for change. Undoubtedly the changes were greeted with a variety of reactions in the little community of the College and the parish, but the fellows recognized that the cost of the Reformation had to be borne. Oxford and Cambridge colleges were lucky, in the sense that they were allowed to keep their "superstitious" endowments, and that dissolved religious foundations were often handed to the colleges. In 1548 the visitors to the two were charged to convert monies spent in obsequies and feasts, choristers, chantries or other daily ecclesiastical services, to the support of scholars in literature and philosophy, and to convert all endowed chantries into a exhibitions for scholars.[109] This mitigated some of the worst effects of the dissolutions, turning them to the colleges' advantage by releasing money to support scholars in fields other than theology, and men who were not ordained. In Merton's case it meant that the Hamsterley chantry became an exhibition to which no one was elected between 1548 and 1556, leaving the income in the hands of the College for other purposes, such as paying for the changes in the chapel.

At Merton, the first sign of the Edwardian purge was the purchase of the royal injunctions and the homilies, along with a chair for the reader of the homilies,

in 1547/8. At the same time carpenters came into the chapel to remove offending images, and a painter was paid 18d for blotting out offending pictures. After
that, new hymn books and psalters, in English, were purchased for Merton's
chapel.[110]

In 1549 the Kingdom was ordered to begin using the new Book of Common
Prayer on June 9. Accordingly, the chapel bought two copies (suggesting that they
were to be used only by celebrants), and all the minor altars were removed. Only
the main ones, belonging to St. John and the Virgin, were left standing.[111]

In the 1549–50 fiscal year the walls of the church were whitewashed, as were the
windows, presumably to cover the stained glass. Humphrey Burneforde, the sub
warden in charge of the chapel in 1550/51 destroyed the last two altars. Then he
paid Henry Bolton the carpenter 9s for a communion table to replace the high altar.
The holy water stoups were taken out too, so that by 1551 the church had no
idolatrous images, no altars, and no visible stained glass. It may have retained its
rood screen, but presumably its statues were removed, so that the chapel completely
conformed to the model of a reformed Protestant place of worship.[112]

All of these changes cost money, but there were pluses as well as minuses in the
ledger. The cost of maintaining the chapel fell dramatically. There were no more
pictures and statues to maintain, altars to adorn, and tapers to burn. Thus the chapel
expenses, which often were £30 or more a year in the 1520s, were halved by the
early 1550s. But this state of affairs reversed itself when Philip and Mary were on
the throne.

In 1556/7 the chapel expenses jumped back to pre-Edwardian levels as the
apparatus of Catholic worship was restored. A new holy-water stoup was placed by
the north door and a new pyx and holy-water bucket were acquired; canopies,
candelabras, altar cloths and other dressings for the new high altar, a frame for the
sepulchre at Easter, new copes and vestments, incense, and a painted image of Christ
were bought. In the following fiscal year, Henry Bolton the carpenter installed an
image of nine apostles on the high altar, along with a new image of St. John. Bolton,
who had dismantled the chapel in the Edwardian purge, must have found this ironic.
All of this activity meant that the chapel costs, excluding the stipends for chaplains,
organists, clerks and cleaners, jumped to £26 4s 11½d".

The spike in costs for the Merton chapel in 1557/8 was followed by a drastic fall.
On St. John's Day 1559 Protestantism returned to England and the process of
restoration was reversed. The altar was removed on August 18, the new communion
table was installed on September 2, and on September 23 new psalters were
purchased.[113] Consequently, the chapel expenses were only £6 in 1559–60, just over
£7 in 1560–1, and about £4 in 1563/4.[114]

Revenues fell drastically too, for the chapel now depended almost entirely on
tithes rather than the fees and offerings that accompanied obits and major feasts. In
the last year of Mary's reign the chapel had the following extra income:

Christmas offering	1s 4d
Purification of the Virgin offering	2s 5d
Easter offering	14s 9d
St. John the Baptist offering	7s 2d
wax for obits	2s 0d
Churching of Mrs. Gilbert	2d
funeral offerings	10s 0d
	£1 17s 10d

The custom of offering at all four feasts had been maintained in the chapel throughout Edward VI's reign, but in 1559/60 there was no income in the chapel except £65s transferred by the first bursar.[115] Even the tithes that should have been paid do not show on the account. Corpus Christi College, for whom St. John's Church in Merton was the parish church, did not pay the expected 6s 8d. Eventually some missing tithes were resumed, and the custom emerged of offering at Easter only, an offering that yielded only seven or eight shillings in the mid-1560s. One other effect of the changes brought on by the Elizabethan Reformation was a reduction in staff in the chapel. In 1564 the Warden complained that although he was required by statute to feed four chaplains at his table, they had no purpose. After consulting the visitor about how the statutes of the college were to be read, it was agreed that the number could be reduced, since the end of "mass business and the like" made some of them redundant.[116]

These gyrations in Merton's chapel left fiscal traces of the wild swings in religion in the nation but, of course, the fellows lived through all of them. The failure to collect any tithes or offerings at all in 1559/60 may tell us much about the state of mind at the end of the 1550s – frustration, exhaustion, and disillusionment was the natural outcome of the swings. And the members of Merton's little society must have known that some were about to lose their places in College because they were on the wrong side of the ideological line. The Marian persecutions had left very deep wounds. But if we look at the ways in which Merton managed its chapel we see a consistent pattern of conformity, within which the fellowship attempted to maximize its opportunities. They followed the letter of the law, and they took advantage of its loopholes. Their occasional celebration of requiems shows the same pattern. No matter what religion was to individual members of the College, the society had come through the dissolutions fiscally intact, and better off. Their expenses were down, but they kept the properties that produced most of the revenues. They had converted their chantry priest into an exhibitioner, and they continued to pay themselves the "liberata forinseca," the bonuses given the fellows for praying for the souls of people like Countess Ela. In short, the Reformation produced greater income and lighter duties. To their credit they spent some of the income on preachers and students, but the money was now discretionary. The College had survived. It remained to be seen whether the fellowship, shattered by the religious conflicts, could be repaired.

Repairing and rebuilding institutions and communities was the primary job of leaders of extra-ecclesiastical institutions the 1560s and 1570s. The years of the dissolutions had forced redefinition on everyone, teaching the lesson that it was safest to concentrate only on the issues on which people, despite their conflicting ideologies, could agree. Ironically, the church itself, caught in the web of property law, could not respond to changing times as easily as lay corporations.

Taken together, the legal treatment of ecclesiastical property made the Reformation possible, in the sense that secular interests were protected and rewarded. This, in turn, increased lay control over the church, giving the laity a larger stake in the royal supremacy. Consequently, the transfer of property and power changed the face of local government, rearranged the power structure, and left many, many parishes to work out their own solutions to the Reformation conundrum. Importantly, the legal processes used, and the rights recognized in those processes, slowed the pace of Reformation. Occurring within a recognized judicial framework, they meant that Reformation, real change, happened at different paces in different localities. Communities dealt with the crisis in their own ways and in their own time, or not at all. As Sir Geoffrey Elton once put it, the victor in the Reformation was the law.

We can only speculate on the lessons taught by the dissolutions of 1536–40, 1545, 1547, and 1559. Certainly, literal disillusionment was one of them, for people learned to devalue sacred properties and objects. The livery men whose cushions were made of altar clothes, the woman whose crystal perfume bottle once held the finger bone of a saint, the Oxford carpenter who made his living making and dismantling sacred objects, the yeoman whose doorstep had been an altar, and all the families whose fortunes were improved by the dissolutions had lost their fear of the sacred. They had lost some of their respect for the church, too, learning to see it as a source of wealth rather than a source of spiritual comfort.

Another outcome, a cause as well as an effect, was the re-mapping of the afterlife. The belief that the dead need the prayers of the living to help them through Purgatory had been in decline since the 1530s. As Robert Whiting observed, intercessory institutions, even in the presumably conservative southwest of England, had already lost much of their vitality by 1547. The attacks on Purgatory launched by Protestants were combining with pragmatic responses to government seizures and gentry hostility to kill them. Consequently, when Mary came to the throne there was no rush to recreate chantries and guilds.[117]

The dissolutions taught people to put their own interests before those of the community. If Justice Porte was willing to dissolve and acquire a monastery he had once sought to endow, or Richard Pate made a fortune out of church lands, they were making a statement that can not have been lost on others. If others are getting theirs, get yours while you can. Some, like Pate, clearly felt bad enough about his profits to give some of them back to his community, but many other people took the former chantry, closed the school attached to it, and tore the lead off the roof, uncaring about the impact on the community, ignoring the commonwealth ideals expressed by the preachers. The Crown had purchased their support of the royal supremacy by creating and guaranteeing a property interest in the former ecclesiastical lands.

Of course, many impropriators of church property did the same thing. They took the tithes and presented the benefices to poorly prepared clergymen, or to no one at all. Too often, livings in the church were treated as sinecures, stripped of their assets and neglected, or, worse, granted to men who provided no cure of souls. The dissolutions compounded this problem by transferring so many livings into lay hands.

It is not surprising that a note of cynicism creeps into Elizabethan writings when church property is mentioned, for it was not just Puritans who were disturbed by the greed that took precedence over godly ideals.

Describing the parlor of a country inn, decorated, "London like," with allegorical paintings, William Bullein's characters Uxor and Civis had no trouble identifying their messages. In one, a man of small learning gets church livings with the help of a covetous patron. In another the "gaper" catches advowsons by reversion, selling his church's well to his patron. In a third we see "covetous men spoiling the church by the names of patrons and givers, which are extortioners and sellers." Was it for this that Thomas Cromwell was a "noble cutter down of the wood of AntiChrist"?

Later, they talk about how King Henry had dissolved the "dens of idolaters," the abbeys, giving their lands to the temporality. Ironically, they note, though many of the recipients of these rich lands love papistry, "they would rather the city of Rome with the Pope's holiness, were utterly burned, yea, and Christ also together, than they would lose their abbey lands . . . for all this, I think they are Protestants."[118]

People and institutions took advantage of the dissolutions as best they could, changing the balance of power and enhancing the authority of the Crown. But the lessons in civic virtue taught by the experience were not edifying. They demonstrated the victory of greed and self-interest over virtue and godliness. Self-interest more effectively converted the propertied classes than evangelization.

5

Redefining Communities

On September 16, 1581 the Reverend Richard Greenham, vicar of Dry Drayton in Cambridgeshire, confronted the ethical dilemma of one of his parishioners. He had received a letter from a godly man asking "whether a Christian might use the help of a papist who had been known to do many cures." Greenham's response was to pose ten questions, questions making papists sound like an alien species. Has this papist dealt faithfully with "Christians?" Is the papist "an open blasphemer and whether he be a papist of conscience or no?" "If he be but a simple silly papist or more obstinate?" Does this papist use his medical practice "for a cloak of sorcery?" And has the patient the strength to let a papist minister to him?[1]

The fact that the pastor of Dry Drayton in the Cambridge Fens was giving advice of this sort indicates how self-identity had changed. For this godly minister and his petitioner there were now "Christians" and "Papists." Papists they lumped with heretics, sorcerers and servants of Satan. Greenham himself had been a child in Mary's reign, but for him the division was clear. And yet, to his horror, papists were to be found all over the nation. And the nation had to adapt to living in a divided world. Every community of every kind had to find new ways of relating that permitted business to be done around the developing religious divides.

William Alabaster, late of Cambridge University, made application to join the Jesuits in 1598 when he was 31. As was customary, he was questioned about his relatives and their religions. His father, he said, was "a Catholic, as I hope." Some of his other kin, especially the Winthrops, Adam and John, were "morose heretics." Yet others were dissemblers, hypocrites who passed as Catholics in Spain, but were not.[2] Like Greenham's parishioner, Alabaster had become adept at parsing religious identities.

This ability to know who to hate was not the result expected when the Reformation began in England. Possessed with the humanists' optimism about what would happen if everyone read the Bible and abandoned superstition, its first apologists thought a brave new world was at hand. As the earl of Derby wrote in 1539,

FIGURE 4   Miniature of Queen Elizabeth, crowned by angels and presiding over Archbishop Parker preaching. Corpus Christi College, Cambridge, MS 582, front end paper.

Englishmen have forsaken Satan, his satellites and all works of darkness and dedicated themselves to Christ's words and faith, and to the works of light. . . . They have now in every church and place, almost every man, the Bible, and New Testament in their mother tongue, instead of the old fabulous and fantastical books. . . . The Ten Commandments of God are observed; Sundays and feasts hallowed and observed, confession, communion at Easter at the least, the four Embers, the Lent vigils and fasts, Friday and Saturday with abstinence of flesh. The states of the realm have, by a law, provided to avoid idle people and vagabonds, to cherish and sustain the impotent, and live so that the works of charity are observed better than ever. Such being the case, how can any wise man call them heretics or schismatics, or slander them as infidels?[23]

Fifty years later English people were happily calling one another heretics, schismatics, infidels, Anabaptists, Puritans, Papists, and other divisive terms. How that came to happen, and how English society learned to live with the social fragmentation such epithets suggest is the theme of this chapter.

In the first instance, distinctions had to be created among people who, immediately before, had been indistinguishable from their neighbors. Their behaviors had to be understood as repulsive, ignorant, and dangerous. At the same time, however, ways had to be found to work together, since these same people who, in the abstract, were to be hated and feared, were one's kin, business associates, and neighbors. If the English Reformation process had not made pragmatic accommodation possible, England would have had a civil war in the sixteenth century. But it did not. Instead, people sharing communities of interest were allowed to evolve social arrangements that made them capable of hating the abstract enemies that surrounded them while quietly doing business with the real people who held those hated views.

This process of pragmatic adaptation went on throughout the land as the Elizabethan Settlement subsided into habit and all but the most ardent believers realized that each was in the role of the Lord High Executioner. To cut the head off one's neighbor, it was necessary to cut one's own off. It benefitted no one to draw the religious lines so rigidly that they interfered with business. Sometimes this lesson was learned the hard way, but once it was learned, it was seldom forgotten.

Learning to Hate

In the beginning, the proponents of the new understanding of scripture were vilified. The Convocation of Canterbury in 1529 took a firm position against heretics who "damnably blinded" the people, condemning as heretical books by Martin Luther, Martin Bucer, Johannes Brenz, Huldrich Zwingli, and other continental reformers along with English works by William Tyndale, Simon Fish, and John Frith. They even forbade reading the "protest" or confession presented by the reformers to the emperor at the Diet of Augsburg, when they called for unity among Christians. These books, agreed the clergy, abounded in "unspeakable and most pestilent heresies and blasphemies, full of innumerable errors."[4] The bishops of Lincoln and Ely were instructed to visit Oxford and Cambridge to ensure that those "founts from which the rivers of science flow" were not contaminated.

A palimpsest fragment of a chronicle noted the result of the Convocation's assertion of Catholic truth. Concerning 1530 it notes, "This year were many honest and good . . . men persecuted [?] for the truth which the gospels own holy doctrine [teaches?] and called heretics both priests preachers and lay men. . . ."[5]

William Tyndale and John Frith died heretics' deaths, but they were joined in their martyrdoms by Sir Thomas More, Bishop John Fisher, and the Carthusians of London. In the mid 1530s it was as dangerous to be too strong a supporter of the Pope as it was to voice the wrong opinion about transubstantiation. It became important to hate the "usurped authority of the Bishop of Rome" as much as Martin Luther; a confusing situation to say the least.

To muddle things even more, the ground of heresy kept shifting. Thomas Cranmer and Thomas Cromwell participated in the destruction of "poor miserable sacramentaries" like John Lambert, burned in 1539 for refusing to admit that Christ was really present in the elements of the Eucharist. Henry VIII, recently excommunicated by the Pope, presided in person over Lambert's trial. Archbishop Cranmer, as senior cleric, began the examination of the accused, upholding, as he himself claimed during his trial in 1555, the "papists' doctrine." After Henry VIII had pronounced sentence Lambert was kept in Thomas Cromwell's home until he was burned at the stake.[6]

Henry VIII's turn toward conservatism in the early 1540s was marked by the passage of the Act of Six Articles and the burning or exile of Protestants who refused to conform. John Hooper fled the country rather than face prosecution, but others were not so lucky or so fleet. With the wind clearly blowing back toward the traditional faith, Bishops Gardiner and Bonner used the opportunity to attack their evangelical enemies, attempting to bring down Cranmer and his supporters. The "Prebendaries' Plot" at Canterbury failed, but many of the clergy who supported the reformers were arrested on suspicion of heresy, as were many of London's booksellers.

In reaction Henry Brinklow wrote his angry *The Complaint of Roderyck Mors*, in which he railed at Parliament for having "shamefully . . . driven men from reading the Bible."[7] 34 & 35 Henry VIII, c. 1 flatly forbade women, artificers, apprentices, journeymen, serving men, husbandmen and laborers from reading it, on the grounds that the Bible bred division and error. In this the Act was correct, for tensions between the proponents of the Gospel and the Mass frequently triggered disobedience and violence. These disturbances played into the conservatives' hands, since they sought to portray the evangelicals as enemies of the state as much as heretics.

However, if Protestant preachers could be charged with sedition, so could Catholics, since the Supreme Head of the Church in England distrusted people who showed any allegiance to the papacy, or to friends of the papacy, such as Reginald Pole, in exile in Rome.

By 1544 Parliament moderated the backlash set off by the Act of Six Articles, making prosecutions more difficult. Thus encouraged, the evangelical party continued to spread its message, and many people broke their Lenten fasts with political intent. But the King, as John Hooper told Heinrich Bullinger in 1546, had destroyed the Pope but not popery. "As far as true religion is concerned," he wrote, "idolatry is no where in greater vigor." "The impious mass, the most shameful celibacy of the clergy, the invocation of saints, auricular confession, superstitious abstinence from meats, and purgatory, were never before held by the people in greater esteem than they are at the present moment."[8] This halfway reformation was too little for Hooper and his ilk, and too much for those who yearned for the restoration of the old ways. Both parties operated in the Court, in the pulpits, in the streets, and in the ale houses. The balance of power swayed from day to day. In 1546, when Dr. Crome attacked transubstantiation in a sermon in the Mercers' Chapel, he was ordered to recant his opinions. But the sermon he preached in response was not a recantation. He reasserted his views of the mass and the papacy, rejoiced that King Henry was dissolving chantries and religious houses, and said he was adamant in the truth he spoke.

Crome's sermon set off another round of prosecutions. Lists were made of those who heard the sermon, people were arrested if heard defending Crome in the street, and a number of his supporters, like Robert Huick, found themselves in the Tower. In the end, Crome chose to recant rather than burn, to the horror of his evangelical supporters.[9]

The conservatives, having won the battle over Crome, attacked the evangelical circles in the Court. Their investigation turned around Anne Askew, a Lincolnshire woman, and Robert Wisdom. Wisdom escaped to the continent, but Askew was subjected to an intense interrogation, part of which was designed to implicate leading women of the Court, including the Duchess of Suffolk, the countesses of Hertford and Sussex, and even the Queen. The interrogators could not convince her to confess voluntarily, and so, she recalled, "they did put me on the rack, because I confessed no ladies nor gentlewomen to be of my opinion, and thereon they kept me a long time. And because I lay still and did not cry, my Lord Chancellor and Master Rich, took pains to rack me with their own hands till I was nigh dead."[10] Although they tried to get her to sign a ready-made recantation, she refused.

With three others she was burned at the stake in July of 1546. "Thus," wrote the Protestant apologist John Bale when he published her prison writings in 1547, "she is a saint canonized in Christ's blood, though she never have other canonization of pope, priest, nor bishop."[11] But Bale's opinion was not shared by all. Certainly

Bishop Bonner, Bishop Gardiner, and their conservative allies were delighted with Askew's fiery end, even if they had failed to catch any courtiers.

The slippery slope of heresy and treason was a tricky place, full of false handholds and falser friends. The building tide of alienation and distrust in the 1540s burst the dikes in Edward VI's reign. The power struggle between conservative and evangelical factions was won by the Protestants in 1547 and their anger, hatred, and horror toward "idolatrous" Catholic worship and the persecutors of the earlier 1540s poured out in an orgy of officially blessed destruction. Images of all sorts were not just removed; they were destroyed with relish. The royal visitor who jumped up and down on Durham's giant Corpus Christi processional monstrance was not simply destroying it, he was rejoicing in the destruction.[12] He would have probably stamped the heads of idolaters with the same zeal, had it been allowed.

Heads were stamped in the West Country in 1548 and 1549. In the Cornish speaking areas of the West the Catholic Church had always been responsive to Cornish culture, while English culture and intentions were suspect. As the religious changes began to bite early in Edward's reign a series of disturbances broke out. In Helston, Archdeacon William Body, sent to dissolve the chantry in St. Michael's church, was met by a mob reported to be 3,000 strong. Sheltering in a house near the church, Body was discovered, dragged out, and stabbed to death. Their leader, John Ressigh, declared that anyone who sided with Body or followed the "new fashion" would be punished in the same way. Naturally, Edward's Council responded with force and twenty-six men were arrested and charged with treason. Ten were found guilty, five of whom were later pardoned. The rest were hanged, drawn and quartered.[13]

Cornish anger over the religious changes was heightened by the imposition of the English language Book of Common Prayer in 1549. When Parliament passed the first Act of Uniformity, requiring the realm to use English in worship, it either forgot or ignored the fact that in Wales and West Cornwall, as well as in Ireland, English was not the native tongue. Latin was the old, familiar language of worship, untainted by English imperialism, so the Cornish speakers of the West Country saw the prayer book as an attack on their traditional culture. The rebels of 1549 wanted a prayer book in their own language, or in Latin, but not in English. This baffled the King's Council, which retorted "How do your children learn the *Pater Noster, Ave* and *Credo?* Cannot your children learn so much in English?"[14] So for many Cornish rebels the defense of Catholicism was linked to cultural identity, just as it came to be in Ireland.[15]

The Prayer Book Rebellion was triggered, contemporary John Hooker tells us, when Walter Raleigh (the elder) met an old woman in the road saying her beads as she walked to church. Stopping her, he demanded if she knew that there was a law against "her and all such as would not obey." Apparently the confrontation turned into a denunciation of sacramentals, for the old lady roused the parishioners of Clyst

St. Mary, telling them that Raleigh threatened "except she would leave her beads and give over holy bread and water" he would "burn them out of their houses and spoil them."

Coming a week after the imposition of the new English prayer book, this so incensed the parishioners that they beat Raleigh nearly to death and fortified the bridge into their village. Later in the Rebellion, Lord Russell attacked Clyst St. Mary. The largest battle of the conflict, it ended when Russell ordered that all his 900 prisoners be butchered.[16] Clearly the old woman and her neighbors had chosen the losing side, paying with their lives and setting an example that would not soon be forgotten. People of that generation would long recall the lesson in obedience taught by Lord Russell's foreign mercenaries.[17] They were intended to remember the force with which the revolt was extinguished, as a matter of policy. The Council had ordered Russell to withhold his pardon to the rebels until he had picked out the "most sturdy and obstinate" to be executed "as an example of terror."[18] For many in Cornwall and Devon "Reformation" would be linked with repression, while for many in the King's government, the West Country was defined as a dangerously Catholic and disobedient place.

As the rebels were repressed, the King's Council took action against clerics who were unwilling to conform to the new Protestant establishment. Bishops, especially Gardiner of Winchester and Bonner of London, were charged with disobedience and removed from office. Bonner, who stopped preaching and enforcing discipline upon the imposition of the Protestant reforms of 1549, was ordered in the King's name to preach against the rebels in Devon, Cornwall and elsewhere, as traitors deserving eternal damnation. He was also to say that anyone using the "old ceremonies" out of devotion was committing an act of disobedience that canceled the value of the devotion. Given this order in August of 1549, he refused to preach the prescribed sermon. He was removed from office shortly thereafter and, on April 12, 1550, Nicholas Ridley was installed as the new Bishop of London.[19]

The persecutions of evangelicals under Henry VIII had prompted Edward VI's first Parliament to repeal the laws against heresy, but the resistance, both passive and active, of adherents of the old church drove the evangelicals to make sharp distinctions as they tried to set their religion apart from the one they hated. In the proposed reform of the ecclesiastical laws, drafted in 1551–2 by a committee of thirty-two divines and lawyers, hard, even cruel, distinctions were made between the scriptural truths endorsed by the evangelicals and the blind, stupid ignorance of those who disagreed with them. Denouncing transubstantiation, or "the so called impanation of the body of Christ," the central event in the Catholic mass, as a heresy, Cranmer's team was very clear in its aim. "We wish," they said, "to get rid of the whole of this Papist dream-inducing drug." A drug pushed by "the insanity" of those who believed the "intolerable error" that the pope was the rock of the church.[20]

Contemplating the list of heretical offenses in this proposed code of ecclesiastical law, F. W. Maitland noted the continuity between the evangelical attitude toward heretics and the Roman Catholic tradition. Under the new Edwardian canons "Not only Arians and Anabaptists, but intractable Romanists and intractable Lutherans would have been burnable." Contumacious heretics were to be turned over to the civil magistrates for punishment, as they always were when heretics were burned.[21] The Edwardian commissions sent out to find heretics are proof that these were not idle threats. They were issued annually, and in 1551 the commissioners, who included many who were drafting the new ecclesiastical laws, were told to hand any obstinate heretics, anabaptists or libertines over to the secular power. Moreover, they were to punish all those opposed to using the Book of Common Prayer.[22] That they were in deadly earnest is proved by the execution of Joan Bocher, burned in 1551 because she refused to recant her denial of the virgin birth of Christ.

This reformed law code was rejected by the House of Lords, but the second version of the Book of Common Prayer, now with its prayers against the "detestable enormities of the Bishop of Rome," became law. This suggests that in the Edwardian years the Protestant leaders were contemplating exactly the kind of extremity that is associated with Bloody Mary. Perhaps it is to the credit of the House of Lords that the reformed ecclesiastical laws were never passed, but in 1554 Parliament happily revived the heresy laws of the Roman church.

Only their hatred of Catholicism united the Edwardian Protestants, for they were divided theologically and politically. John Hooper, who believed fervently in the complete destruction of Catholic remnants, almost refused his bishopric because he had to wear "popish" vestments at his ordination. Archbishop Cranmer, who, as a gradualist believing in slow conversion and who served Henry VIII even during the persecutions under the Act of Six Articles, quarreled with Hooper's taste for destruction. What held such men together was the Crown, the certainty that the national church was the only path to national Reformation. The lesson taught by the vagaries of the Reformation to that point was, to paraphrase a later assertion, "no Protestant king, no Protestant bishop."

It was undoubtedly for this reason that the attempt to make Jane Grey queen was attractive to King Edward and his Protestant councillors. Though the ambition of Northumberland certainly played a role, the attempt to keep the state in the hands of a monarch who would protect Protestantism almost certainly convinced Edward to disinherit Mary.[23]

By the end of Edward's reign complex battle lines had formed among the varieties of English Protestants concerning the structure and liturgy of the national church, but they soon forgot their differences in the face of a Supreme Head of the Church who was a Catholic woman.

Meanwhile, the defenders of Roman Catholicism remained adamant that "Protestants" were another form of an old heresy, deserving the harsh treatment always given to pestiferous sects. For a time after Mary's succession, before Parliament agreed to the restoration of Papal supremacy and Catholic worship, there was a "phony war," as the sides jockeyed for position. By now, England was so riven with religious quarrels that everyone who cherished order sought to walk a fine line between the competing factions while performing their duties as they saw them. But where that fine line was, was not clear. Thoroughly imbued with the royal supremacy, almost all the bishops of Edward's church, including Archbishop Cranmer, were slow to resist the return to Catholicism. In many places the mass returned by popular demand, without resistance, while in others disturbances broke out between competing religious groups. Robert Parkyn, in Yorkshire, reported that in many places priests were commanded by "lords and knights Catholic" to say mass in Latin, consecrating the body and blood of Christ under the form of bread and wine "as hath been used beforetime." Those of heretical opinions, he said, "might not away therewith but spake evil thereof, for as then there was no act, statute, proclamation or commandment set forth for the same, many one dared not be bold to celebrate in Latin, though their hearts were wholly inclined that way."[24]

This anomalous situation did not last long. Mary issued a proclamation a month after her accession declaring that, though she was a Catholic, she was not going to compel anyone else until "further order by common assent may be taken." In short, until Parliament changed the law, she would neither force anyone to be a Catholic, nor enforce the laws against being Catholic. And she ordered her subjects to "live together in quiet sort and Christian charity, leaving those new-found devilish terms of papist or heretics, and such like." To prevent the tumults she feared, she stopped preaching in the churches and forbade the sale of seditious books.[25]

Most of the Protestant leadership was left confused by this turn of events. Worse, many of them were convinced that the early death of King Edward VI was providential. It was a divine punishment caused by their failure to take advantage of the opportunity Edward provided for the conversion of England. Mary was a scourge, sent to chastise them for their laxity. Under these circumstances, fatalism set in. It was an entire year before Catholicism was officially imposed on the nation, with the injunction that "every bishop and all other persons . . . do diligently travail for the repressing of heresies and notable crimes." This sentence rested upon the heresy laws of Richard II, Henry IV and Henry V. Reenacted, they made the Justices of the Peace responsible for detecting heretics, putting the weight of the Crown, now shorn of its supremacy over the church, squarely behind the Pope's episcopal courts in England. As of March 4, 1554, the clock was turned back to "the latter time of Henry VIII" and all the actions of the heretics condemned. Priests who had married were to be removed, vows of chastity were to be enforced, monks and nuns were to return to their cloisters, and those ordained by Protestant bishops lost their ordination.[26]

It was the beginning of a new round of persecution. Heretical Protestants had to be punished as the criminals they were. Beginning on February 4, 1555, the burnings lasted until Mary's death in November of 1558. In that period, more than 300 people were executed, many others died in prison, and perhaps 800 fled to Protestant cities on the continent. The persecutions arose from conflicting goals on the parts of Mary and her new husband, Philip, Chancellor Gardiner, and the new papal legate for the reconciliation of England, Cardinal Reginald Pole. Gardiner, recently restored as Bishop of Winchester, was attempting to force submission to the policy of the church; the King and Queen saw themselves as punishing criminals; and Cardinal Pole saw persecution as protection of the newly restored church from evil influences. They all hated heretics, but disagreed on their goals. To the people of southeast England who were burnt, the policy disagreements meant little, but it was clear, even by late 1555, that persecution was not going to work. The burnings fueled resistance in some, sullen discontent in others. In communities grudging conformity marched with joyous revival. Sometimes neighbor turned on neighbor.[27]

Philip Hughes, studying Foxe's martyrs, concluded that a majority of those punished for heresy were arrested on the reports of justices of assize, constables, and sworn inquests, not clerical officials. A number were reported by neighbors or family members.[28] Given that most detections were local affairs, involving local officials who probably knew the accused, Hughes' numbers suggest the levels of religious dissent in the parishes of southeast England where nearly all the persecutions occurred. They also suggest that very little prosecution of heretics was possible in a state that depended upon lay volunteers to make the state work.

As Christopher Marsh has noted, "it is impossible to argue that the persecution of dissenters had little or no grassroots impetus," repeating with approval Sir Keith Thomas' dictum: "'Indeed if the records of Tudor and Stuart life leave any single impression, it is that of the tyranny of local opinion and the lack of tolerance displayed towards nonconformity or social deviation.'"[29] Story after story makes clear how heresy persecutions occurred within the limits of a known, established community. For example, take the case of William Hunter, age 19.

Foxe tells us that a "neighboring justice" named Brown had heard that young Hunter had heretical opinions, so he sent for Hunter's father and asked him where his son was. The old man claimed he did not know, but Justice Brown threatened him with prison if he did not produce him, despite the elder Hunter's pathetic question "Would you have me seek out my son to be burned?" The Justice certainly would, and young William returned home with his father to face the charge that he denied the corporeal presence of Christ in the Eucharist. He cheerfully agreed that Christ was not in the elements and was sentenced to burn.

On the morning of 27 March, 1555 he was led to the stake between one of the sheriff's men and his brother Robert. In their way they met his father, who, with tears flowing, said "God be with thee, son William." William replied happily that they would meet again with great joy.

The young man read from his prayer book until the pyre was lit, handing the book to his brother before it perished with him.[30]

This little vignette of family and neighbors burning a 19-year-old underscores the local nature of much of the persecution, but it ought to remind us of the obverse, too. Most families and most neighbors did not participate in heretic hunting. In Colchester, where six people were indicted for heresy in 1556, the detections were difficult to obtain and biased. The jurors, pressured to present, refused to name any of their powerful neighbors, sending only lower class people to their deaths. Their awareness of the danger to local hierarchy presented by the persecutions is summed up in the story of the servant who went to the justices with the report that his master was sheltering heretics. For his pains he was put in the stocks to teach him to "speak good of his master."[31]

A good measure of the reluctance of local authorities to participate in the hunt for Protestants is the lack of martyrs in much of the nation. In cities like York and Lincoln there were no prosecutions for heresy in Mary's reign, and in the entire southwest there was only one burning. This may be interpreted as proving that there were no Protestants, but it appears that there was no enthusiasm for hunting them either, which, given the conservatism of the north and the southwest, is surprising.[32]

The experiences of the 1550s shaped the ways in which community came to be defined in Elizabeth's reign. The values of communal solidarity and neighborliness were reshaped in the experience of religious persecution and social division caused by persecutions.

In some, if not most, communities, the local elites showed themselves very reluctant to violate the social bonds in the ways demanded if religious persecution was to work. In others, where social bonds had been violated, they had to be repaired. In all cases, the fiscal impacts of the Reformation combined with the social damage it did to force reconstitution of the social bases of communities.

As the martyr Hugh Latimer wrote in the "Homily Against Contention" in the Edwardian homilies, reprinted in 1562, "What would he [St. Paul] say if he heard these words of contention, which be now almost in every man's mouth? he is a Pharisee, he is a Gospeler, he is of the new sort, he is of the old faith, he is a new-broached brother, he is a good catholic father, he is a papist, he is an heretic! O how the church is divided! O how the cities be cut and mangled!"[33] Christians, he insisted, quoting St. Paul and echoing Erasmus, were to love one another, eschewing revenge, leaving it to the Lord. Ironically, Latimer, (noting that "in zeal Moses brake the two tables," and "caused twenty-four thousand of his own people" to be killed) was well aware that the Bible was not always a peaceful book. And so, lest his homily against contention be overcome with Biblical violence, a note was added to the text: "these examples are not to be followed of everybody, but as men be called to office and set in authority."[34] The necessity of this gloss underlines the tenuous, dangerous line being walked by the magistracy.

It is hard to say when it dawned on people that the confusion of the 1540s and 1550s was creating an almost untenable situation for the local ruling elites who valued order and neighborliness, but it is clear that by 1559 many recognized the problem and were seeking *modi vivendi* that would allow reconstitution.

Perhaps the oddest thing about the Elizabethan Settlement was that so many local magistrates were so willing to ignore religious divisions in the name of social order. In institution after institution we can see that when external pressures for persecution were reduced the leadership turned a blind eye. Sometimes the tensions were so great within institutions that external intervention was necessary to lance the boil, but most communities handled the problem quietly and internally until it either went away or the compromises made became customary.

The generation that came into positions of leadership early in Elizabeth's reign seemed, on the whole, to agree with their Queen. Better to have order and good business than squabble about religion. The youth of the 1520s and 1530s who did not migrate to the radical ends of the religious spectrum seemed to prefer the sort of erastian, Bucerian moderation exemplified by so much of their national leadership like Thomas Cranmer. They were the heirs of Erasmian humanistic ideals as much as of Martin Luther, and they feared the violence just under the surface of their communities.

Elizabeth's reign began as an echo of Mary's. She set out to return the nation to Protestantism by using the same tools available to her sister. On December 27, 1558, five weeks after her accession, Elizabeth issued a proclamation, much like the one issued by Mary a month into her reign, prohibiting unlicenced preaching and regulating ceremonies. It was clearly an attempt to reassure the Protestants and keep the lid on the religious tensions rife in the country. Even though she intended to resume Protestantism and the royal supremacy, Elizabeth would not let Edwardian preachers disturb the peace. "Understanding," she proclaimed,

that there be certain persons having in times past the office of ministry in the Church which now do purpose to use their former office in preaching and ministry, and partly have attempted the same, assembling in the city of London in sundry places in great number of people; whereupon riseth amongst the common sort not only unfruitful dispute in matters of religion, but also contention and occasion to break common quiet

she silenced all those called to preach or teach in the Church, while granting them the right to use the English litany used in her own Chapel, until Parliament changed the law.[35]

In the meantime, advice on transition was offered by trusted advisers and would-be advisers. Armigal Waad, submitting a brief on the "Distresses of the Common-wealth and the Means to Remedy them," drew on his credit as a Clerk of Edward VI's Privy Council to warn of the hatred between the meaner sort and the gentlemen, and of the divisions caused by religion. Religion, he said, was to be handled warily, with great cunning and circumspection, if both Reformation and political unity were to be achieved. "And as I pray God to grant us concord both in the arguments upon the cause, and the state of religion, and among ourselves for the account of Catholics and Protestants."[36]

Richard Goodrich, a leading lawyer and Edwardian administrator, was equally concerned that restoring Protestantism should not disturb civil peace. He stressed that the forms of the law must be followed, while encouraging the Protestant party. Preachers were to be chosen in the interim who were the "discreet sort," who could preach the gospel without inveighing against any sect except Anabaptists and Arians. Dissimulations were recommended by Goodrich to keep the papists and the Pope confused about the Queen's intentions, while the supporters of Queen Mary should be disarmed.[37]

The anonymous "Device for Alteration of Religion" recognized how complex the possible quarrels were. If Elizabeth changed back to Protestantism, the Pope would excommunicate her, the French and Scots would threaten an invasion, the Irish might rebel, the papists would make trouble, and those who would gladly break with Rome would complain that the new Protestant establishment (which he assumed would use the Book of Common Prayer) was a "cloaked papistry," demanding that the realm embrace some other Protestant doctrine. Its author recommended that bishops and clergy who are "good papists" be treated with severity, following the example of Mary's imposition of Catholicism. Better, he opines, that a few people should suffer than that the commonwealth should suffer.[38]

These Protestant politicians feared the breakdown of public order during the transition to Protestantism. Catholic observers had the same sense of the times. The Jesuit Peter Ribadeneira, watching events from London in January, 1559, reported that the "heretics" were elated at the changes Elizabeth had already introduced, while the Catholics were dispirited. Father Ribadeneira, however, urged caution. Precipitous action against England might push the situation too far, forcing things to irremediable extremes: the business was in such danger that all might be lost. There is no point, he told Philip II's confessor, of adding oil to the flames.[39]

Faced with the perilous political situation, Elizabeth and her advisers moved with great caution, a caution which, whether intentional or not, left local institutions with latitude for dealing with religious dissent. Some of this latitude was undoubtedly based on their shared conceptions of how religion and the state related to one another. The group of men that controlled Elizabeth's government in the 1560s were loosely described by Winthrop Hudson as "the Cambridge Connection" because they shared so much common background. William Cecil, Matthew Parker, William May, Nicholas Bacon, Walter Mildmay, Nicholas Throckmorton, Edmund Grindal and a number of other early Elizabethan leaders were Cambridge men who had played important roles in Edwardian Protestantism. They knew one another well, worked together, married one another's sisters, and participated in the same intellectual milieu. Deeply influenced by Sir Thomas Smith and Sir John Cheke, leading intellectual lights of mid-Tudor Cambridge, they were "Athenians," men who believed in the "corrected" system of pronouncing Greek that drew them together against Stephen Gardiner, Bishop of Winchester and Chancellor of the University. Their classical enthusiasms lead them naturally toward humanist ideas of biblical interpretation and Erasmian populism.

When Martin Bucer came from Strasbourg to Cambridge in 1550 he had a profound impact on this group of men. Believing in unity and concord, Bucer thought reconciliation and peace were possible among Christians, be they Lutherans, Calvinists, Catholics, or even Anabaptist. Bucer insisted that the doctrine of adiaphora, which asserted that much ecclesiastical custom was unnecessary for salvation, made it possible for all Christians to live together so long as they recognized the primacy of scripture. Bucer's vision of the Christian commonwealth spelled out in his *De regni Christi* neatly complimented the "commonwealth" thought already prevalent in some English circles and came to influence the early Elizabethan episcopate.[40] Bucer taught them that because the Kingdom of Christ could be found in many kingdoms, with differing practices, a national church was an appropriate thing.

Besides ties of blood, education, theology and marriage, these men shared the Marian persecution. Some, like Edmund Grindal, became exiles and participated in the disagreements between those who wanted to continue using the English prayer book and those who wanted to abandon it for a more reformed liturgy. Some, like Cecil and Princess Elizabeth, stayed home and conformed (presumably with some reservation in conscience). Some, like Latimer and Ridley, were burned for their faith; and yet others, like John Cheke, were persuaded to recant under pressure. Taken together, their Marian experiences drove home the civil dangers of religious fanaticism and attracted them to the Bucerian *via media* that made room for them all. As Nicholas Bacon, speaking on behalf of the Queen at the close of Parliament in 1559, said, the national goal was civil tranquility in the face of dangerous social and religious currents. The MPs were sent home with instructions to avoid all manner of frays and riots through swift justice, to "appease all brabblings and controversies," and to draw the nation together in a single religion. On this point he warned them that

great watch should be had of the withdrawers and hinderers thereof and specially of those that subtly by indirect means seek or procure the contrary. Amongst these I mean to comprehend as well those that be too swift and those that be too slow, those, I say, that go before the law or beyond the law, as those that will not follow. For good governance cannot be where obedience fails and both these alike break the rules of obedience, and these be those which by all likelihood should be beginners, maintainers and upholders of all factions and sects, the very mothers and nurses to all seditions and tumults, which necessarily bring forth destruction and depopulation.[41]

In another 1559 speech, this time in the Star Chamber before those who had "charge and governance" of the counties through the lesser courts, Bacon said: "my Lords [of the Privy Council] would wish you to flee and eschew chiefly and above all the rest . . . all manner of factions and sects, and specially such as concern religion, for these are the most deadly enemies that may be to unity and concord.".[42]

Lord Keeper Bacon, his Queen, his fellow councillors, and all other leaders, local as well as national, were faced with a crisis in 1559, brought on by plague, famine, war, and religious strife.[43] Their response was to seek order, to stress neighborliness and external obedience, and to encourage peaceful conformity, unifying the nation through a national church. Although Protestantism was being reimposed, it was being done with a gentleness that stressed conformity over theology, allowing space for local institutions to build their own jury rigged and roughly tailored ways of keeping the religious peace. Each community and institution began reshaping its local ways of relating that would allow its business to be done within the tense world surrounding it.

The Elizabethan Settlement, then, was a political response to the fracturing, bruising, nastiness of the 1550s. By 1559 people had learned to sort their neighbors into religious camps. Attaching labels, they were focusing their hatreds and fears on the "others" among them. It was this divided society that Elizabeth set out to preserve.

The Book of Common Prayer was a perfect answer for this problem, embodying an emphasis on the imitation of the sacrifice of Christ that moved the congregants to conceive their lives in terms of service. A very effective tool for education, its creation showed that Cranmer appreciated that reform would only truly come when habits and hearts changed. Polemic was not the foundation of a reformed Christian lifestyle.[44] Coupled with the Homilies, which instructed their hearers in the essentials of their faith, the Book of Common Prayer assured that people knew their Bible in context, heard it explained, and understood their duty. But, most importantly, the Elizabethan regime's attitude to conformity preserved the peace long enough. The hatreds were muted until the new religion had time to become habit.

Like water dripping on hard stone, the words of the liturgy slowly bored into the hearts and minds of the congregants. The goal was to create automatic religion, an internalized set of responses that guided the individual in his or her duty. When it worked, it worked through patient repetition. Thus, by the middle of Elizabeth's reign prayer book worship had become natural and right to many because it was the habit of the communities in which they were raised. By the 1580s the pattern of worship enforced by law in 1559 had penetrated to the grass roots.[45]

The most politically valuable thing about the Prayer Book was that it imposed structure, not ideology. To people slowly becoming accustomed to the changes forced by the Reformation, it permitted local interpretation, and, to a remarkable extent, local adaptation of the liturgy. It did not put the congregants who had no religious zeal to a test.[46] Attend, listen, and conform were the orders from on high, but over time attending and listening became habit and habit informed faith.

The Prayer Book as used and enforced, was an excellent tool for the slow creation of a new religious culture without the wrench of civil conflict. The Elizabethan Settlement was a political attempt to put into effect Thomas Wilson's prayer of December, 1560: "And God save the Queen's Majesty, the realm, and the scattered flock of Christ, and grant, Oh merciful God, a universal quietness of mind, perfect argreements in doctrine, and amendment of our lives, that we may be all one sheepfold, and have one pastor Jesus, to whom with the Father and the Holy Ghost, be honor and glory, world without end. Amen."[47]

By the time Richard Greenham was advising people against papists the Elizabethan Settlement had stabilized the nation long enough that people were beginning to see their own Catholic forbears as members of an alien, dangerous sect, or alternatively, as the heroes of a drama of faith. In either case, pre-Reformation religion had ceased to be a part of common experience. It was transmogrified into myth.

In the process, English institutions had to adapt their customs and self-identities in ways that allowed them to survive the religious divisions that threatened their operation.

Adaptations

The cultural patterns that emerged from this struggle to maintain civic order in the name of secular security, if not in the name of God, developed at different rates in different institutions. The 1560s were a rocky time, when people felt their way. The first clear evidence of the cultural adaptations appeared in the 1570s. By the 1590s they had gone so far that the old customs were irretrievable, forgotten by all but the oldest people.

As we look at institutions of various sorts we can see phases of adjustment. First, of course, are the formal responses to the legally imposed changes. But removing an altar or hiring a preacher was only the beginning. There followed changes not legally mandated. Commemorations of benefactors, funeral customs, and other ways of celebrating identity and status demonstrate the slow but steady encroachment of new customs. The language in which people spoke about their daily business changed, too, as did the weights they gave to various civil and religious practices. The speed of the changes was often dictated by the governing structures of institutions. In places like livery companies, where older men dominated, things changed slowly. In places like colleges, the fairly rapid turnover of fellows and the occasional official intrusion hurried the process. Sometimes a local settlement emerged when tensions burst like a religious abscess, forcing local leaders to seek ways to find peace; sometimes the adjustments crept in on little cats feet as customs fell out of use and were replaced with actions and understandings more modern. In those places, the change waited on generational change, as did the larger society.

London livery companies

The London livery companies provide good evidences for the ways in which the new customs replaced the old over the second half of the sixteenth century. They conform to the gradualist model of adaptation.

The records of the Grocers' Company show the livery intelligently sailing past the rocks of Reformation.[48] They scrupulously responded to the religious changes dictated by the Crown, while judiciously maintaining a balance in their responses. In 1556 the livery went to St. Stephen Walbrook, their church, had dirge sung, and returned to their hall to drink. They followed the dirge the next Monday with a mass of requiem sung by note and a sermon preached by John Christopherson, the Bishop of Chichester. All of this was done "according to their old custom."[49]

It was their "old custom," and old customs die hard. Even though they replaced the dirge with evensong in 1559, the internal politics of the Company did not encourage rapid Reformation. Its leaders in 1559 were men who had been adult long before Edward VI's destruction of the mass. They remembered a time when England obeyed the Pope, when there were monks, and when the solemn dirge was sung in all the churches of London for the soul of Henry VIII. Political experience had taught them caution. Fifteen years later, younger men, ascending their professional ladder into the ranks of the Court of Assistants, lacked that direct experience.

These new men had a different sensibility, taking religious umbrage at things that the older men hardly noticed. It was only in 1567 that they decided to dispose of the Company's vestments, copes and "other old church work." Some of the altar clothes were made into cushions for Grocers to sit upon at meetings and dinners.[50]

At the Court of Assistants meeting on October 2, 1573 the burial cloth, used to cover the biers of members of the company, was brought out for discussion. Embroidered with the symbols of Catholic faith, perhaps including the image of the Company's patron saint, St. Anthonin, it was under scrutiny because "some of the company had heard that divers men, were offended at certain things in the same." Apparently they decided that it was not too offensive, for it was a year and half later, in May of 1575, when they decided to replace it with one bearing the Company's arms. In October 1575 a design was approved, with borders decorated with "camells" and other things, which satisfied the complainants. The embroiderers were told to make it with "convenient speed." By the time it was made, there was not a single member of the Court of Assistants who had been in a position of power before 1559. They were younger men of a different religious sensibility, finally ready to surrender the old hearse cloth with its superstitious design and its deep connection to the Company.[51]

The curious case of the hearse cloth is not the only instance in which the Grocers' can be seen evolving a new community culture in the place of the one destroyed by the Reformation. Their pattern of Company feasts and commemorations was evolving at the same time. We can see this in the slow degradation of their observance of St. Anthonin's day, May 18. In the "old days" the saint's day was celebrated with a requiem and dirge for departed members, followed the next day by a mass and dinner. All members of the livery were expected to attend the mass. The Company's election day, in July, was the other great day of communal expression, and it too included a mass. These customs, easily restored after Edward, began to change shape in Elizabeth's reign.

First, the Company entered the obvious halfway house. Instead of mass and prayers for the dead, they substituted analogous Protestant ceremonies. In 1569 the members were instructed to come to their guildhall on St. Anthonin's Day, wearing their best liveries, and process together to St. Stephens Walbrook church to "hear service," returning to the hall for dinner. On their election day in 1571 they went in their liveries to St. Stephens Walbrook "where was evening prayer solemnly said and sung, and from then to the hall for the drinking and nomination of wardens." They returned to church the next morning for a sermon, and to hear morning prayer.[52]

By 1584 these copycat traditions had largely ended. That year saw the last evening prayer service for the livery at election day, but by then even the tradition of the sermon on the next day had ended. The disappearance of these customs may be explained by the disturbed times, which, for the next decade, caused frequent cancellations of election dinners, but certainly the Company no longer saw it necessary to associate corporate worship with communal identity.

In 1592 the minutes of the Court of Assistants shows how the meaning of St. Anthonin's Day had changed shape. It was now noted as the "commemoration day of the beginning of the Company."[53] This commemoration of the foundation stood in the place of the old prayers for the departed brothers of the Company that had always been said on that day. The Company was bound by tradition and legal duties to remember its departed and its benefactors, which had been the function of the requiem. In 1568 the Grocers, still governed by men who were raised believing in Purgatory, were worried about how to keep the memory of their benefactors alive. This undoubtedly had a spiritual dimension – remembering the departed was akin to praying for them – but it also had a fiscal dimension. Encouraging benefactions was important to the Company. Consequently, the Court agreed that the names of the benefactors, living and dead, should be rehearsed at least once a year.[54]

But remembering the benefactors was only a part of the problem. The Grocers oversaw bequests that left them with ex-bedesmen on their hands. Sir William Laxton's will had created a school and almshouse in 1556. Although bedesmen no longer prayed for the souls of the departed, they were still expected to give thanks for them in their prayers. Interestingly, by the mid-1570s the almsmen were expected to conform to a godly standard. The Assistants found the 12 elderly almsmen to be ignorant in religion. They ordered them to learn the Lord's prayer, the creed, and the ten commandments by the next Whitsunday, and live godly and quietly, or they would lose their accommodations.[55] That this occurred at the same time that the hearse cloth was being reformed suggests that by 1576 the Court had come under the influence of a more ardently reformed group.

The Grocers evolved from the habits of their Medieval charter, to a halfway house in which the new forms were used in the place of the old, to a stage, by the 1590s, when they had ceased to view religion as integral to their community. In the middle stage the Company saw fit to employ preachers and enact the piety of the new religion. By the end of the reign they had ceased doing this, too. They had become a group of men who traded in groceries and spices, but whose worship occurred elsewhere.

The Pewterers followed a similar path. The Company records show that they had an active corporate religious life before the Reformation, maintaining an altar in All Hallows (London Wall) church. There the parish priest celebrated their Lady Day dirge at night and a mass on the following morning. The members of the livery were expected to attend, and were served spiced bread, buns, ale, and cheese afterward. Most years they spent thirteen shillings and some pence for the service. The first break in this custom came on Lady Day 1548/9, when they paid the curate 4d for communion, 3s4d for the clerk and singers, and 20d rent to the churchwardens for ornaments, so that their total expenditure on the reformed services fell to only 5s4d, down eight shillings. These "reformed" expenses continued at exactly this level for the rest of Edward VI's reign, so much so that by 1553 the expenses were noted as "for all necessaries as hath been accustomed in times past.[56]

In the reign of "King Philip and Queen Mary his lawful wife," as the Company clerk called them, this pattern changed.[57] In 1554 they only spent 8s2d on their mass and dirge, but by 1555 they were back to the 13s6d they were spending a decade before.[58] It does not appear that the Company ever saw fit to restore their altar in All Hallows. Interestingly, on Lady Day 1559, March 25, the Pewterers had already returned to Protestant services, even though Parliament had not yet settled the form of Elizabethan religion. That day they paid the curate for "taking pains at the communion," the clerk and other singers for performing "at the communion," and

3s 4d for a preacher. They spent 9s 8d for this new service, but even that half reformed service soon ceased to be detailed in the records. The term "Lady Day" disappears in 1560, the entries simply referring to "our feast day." One suspects that the communion and sermon may have continued since the expenses remain the same, and even today the Company holds its election day services in All Hallows.[59]

The Pewterers administered obits for departed members, like most companies.[60] Their largest was that of Lawrence Ashlyn, a former master who died in 1546. It was celebrated every October 3 by the parson and several priests at St. Mary Abchurch. The mass cost 8s 2d each year, including a payment of 6d to the Master of the Company and 4d to each of two wardens for attending, with a further 12d to pay for their drinking afterward. The total cost in the obit's first year, 1547, was 9s 10d. The next year, with the mass stopped, the Company spent 2s 10d in Ashlyn's memory, all but 4d of it being the 2s 6d which Ashlyn left to 30 poor men and women of the parish.[61] Throughout Edward's reign the Company paid the poor of the parish, even though they lost the property supporting the obit to the Crown and had to buy it back. In Mary's reign the masses resumed, though they only cost 8s 2d, a savings of 1s 8d thanks to reduced ecclesiastical costs. The master and wardens were still paid for attending and drinking. In 1559 they stopped the mass and reverted to their Edwardian custom of paying the poor their alms.[62]

The Ashlyn obit entry for 1561/2 indicates the political correctness of the Pewterers. That year the word "obit" in the entry was crossed out and the word "bequest" written in.[63] "Bequest" established the Company's opinion that they were bound to carry out the terms of Ashlyn's will, in so far as it was legal, and so in 1564 they scrupulously observed all the acceptable provisions. They paid the Master 6d, two wardens 8d, and spent 5s 10d on a dinner for them. The total cost of the dinner was exactly the amount spent on the mass in Catholic times, so that they were spending what Ashlyn had commanded to be spent to preserve his memory.[64] These annual dinners in memory of Master Ashlyn continued far into the next century.[65]

The Pewterers had done as the Grocers, although they seem to have been more zealous in their willingness to abandon their old religious life. They continued to honor the intentions of their benefactors by converting what had been requiem masses and gifts to bedesmen into a commemoration feast. This seems to have been a nearly universal pattern, in that the City companies interpreted the gifts of benefactors to be binding, even if they could not continue the masses for their souls. As the Lord Chancellor held in 1841, these bequests to Companies had been made for their benefit subject only to certain charges that had been declared illegal by Edward VI. Consequently, it remained necessary to pay the charitable part of the bequests and it was legal to divert the rest into a dinner.[66]

Other Companies followed the pattern. The Carpenters always collected an offering before their annual dinner. Traditionally, the parish priest received half this offering, and the Protestant minister continued to receive it. Then, in 1567, they diverted the offerings to the poor box. By 1571, however, both the offering and the collection for the poor ceased. Sometimes the Carpenters had a preacher at their dinner in the 1560s, but the last sermon was in 1571.[67] In 1572 they walled up the altar in their hall, quit hiring preachers, and ceased communal religious exercises.[68]

For the Founders Company, the Marian restoration of masses forced communal worship where there is no record of any before. Their wardens' accounts show no payments at all for masses after 1528 until, in 1555, they began having them. Newly Protestant in 1559, they spent 5s for a sermon, and they had a preacher at the master's dinner in 1564. Then they resumed their tradition of ignoring group religious activities. They did not bother to reform their hearse cloth until 1645, when they had the cloth, embroidered with gold and "popish ornaments," burned.[69]

As the City companies were recasting their customs they, like all other organizations which sought benefactions, reinvented the purposes and memorialization of benefactions. Robert Tittler and Ian Archer have demonstrated that the Protestant benefactor, bereft of prayers for his soul, was still remembered as a good man or woman. In hall after hall portraits, in paint or glass, memorialized the great donors and leaders, creating a secular genealogy to replace the connection to the saints. At the same time, a rising tide of historical enthusiasm created a new collective memory for organizations, one that discounted the religious connection and celebrated the communal virtues. These were all moves, taken in the post-Reformation confusion, to "inspire the harmonious interaction of the community's members, to sustain a common purpose, to legitimize the contemporary political order."[70]

In short, as the Reformation progressed, institutions altered the forms of their rituals by focusing on their essential purpose, communal solidarity. As Ward says of the Grocers, "While the Reformation transformed the religious practices of the company, it did not divide members into discrete, opposing camps of conformists and heretics. As a community, the company remained open to individuals with a variety of attitudes toward theology and religious practice."[71]

Universities

But harmonious interactions were not always possible in the highly charged atmosphere surrounding the Reformation. Especially in institutions which were carefully watched for conformity. In the universities, charged with creating the professional clergy needed to make any change in religion work, there were deep tensions, heightened by the youth and enthusiasm of the students and fellows. Consequently, each regime accompanied its changes in religion with visitations to enforce conformity. Heads of colleges, regius professors and fellows were removed, reinstated, expelled, exiled, or reappointed as the winds shifted around the religious compass. These created a great deal of trouble in the small, intimate worlds of the colleges, sometimes breaking into such great boils that external intervention was needed. Such was the case of Merton College, Oxford.

An ancient foundation, it had a reputation for academic distinction in medicine. But in Mary's reign Merton was the home to two of the leading Catholic theologians in the University, William Tresham and Richard Smith.

Tresham was elected a fellow in 1516, becoming Registar of the University by 1523. He rose to become a canon of Christ Church in Henry VIII's re-foundation of 1546, and Vice Chancellor in Mary's reign. He went to congratulate Elizabeth on her accession in 1559, but he refused to conform to the new religious settlement. Although he had done so under Edward, he would not take the oath of supremacy again.

Smith, a younger man, was elected a fellow of Merton in 1528, succeeding Tresham as Registrar in 1532. He became the Principal of St. Alban Hall and the first Regius Professor of Divinity. In the latter post he conformed to Henry VIII's regime, taking the oath of supremacy. By 1547 Smith was denouncing Catholicism, preaching a sermon at Paul's Cross in which he retracted his two "papistical" books, which were burned during the sermon. His retraction was later printed, but he did not seem to have meant it. In 1548 he was deprived of his chair and his prebend in St. Paul's.

Smith's Regius chair was given to the Protestant reformer Peter Martyr Vermigli after the two of them had disputed theological points. Briefly imprisoned for the views he expressed in the debate, Smith fled to Scotland, and then Louvain.[72]

In 1554 Smith came back to Oxford on the triumphant tide of Marian Catholicism. He was restored as Regius Professor and appointed a royal chaplain. Refusing to turn the other cheek or forgive seventy times seven, he used his recovered power to persecute his persecutors. After disputing with Cranmer, Latimer and Ridley at their show trials, Smith was given the honor of preaching at Ridley's and Latimer's joint burning.

Only one member of Merton was removed from the College by the Marian restoration, John Parkhurst, who became an Elizabethan bishop. But the new members elected in Mary's reign turned out to be good Catholics. The Warden of Merton, Thomas Reynolds, though he had conformed to the Henrician and Edwardian changes, prospered under Mary. Made a Vice Chancellor and chaplain to Philip and Mary in 1555, Reynolds had been selected to become the Bishop of Hereford. Unfortunately, Mary died before the temporalities of the see could be conferred, and he was never able to take up the post. Reynolds, too, was deprived of his offices in September 1559, though the College register makes it clear that they were sorry to see their "most illustrious" warden leave them.[73] Reynolds died in prison.

Over the next two years a battle was fought in the College between the conservatives and their enemies, most of whom were probably Protestant. The story has all the earmarks of a petty academic squabble in a small department, but the weapons they used on one another were fashioned from competing theologies.

On October 30, 1559 the fellows of Merton met to nominate a new warden. The visitors desired them to choose some illustrious man by unanimous consent, but it was not to be. Four senior members, George James, John Broke, James Leech, and Henry Atwood voted for James Gervase, master of arts, bachelor of law, and fellow of Merton since 1548. The other three senior members had less consensus amongst them. Roger Gifford refused to nominate anyone; William Hall, a physician who later became a Catholic exile, suggested John Parkhurst, the fellow deprived for his Protestantism, and Robert Searles, a former fellow who was an important benefactor for whom the College had agreed to celebrate requiem masses after his death. Among Searles' gifts to his college were the works of Duns Scotus and Thomas Walden's book against the Wycliffite heretics. These nominations show that Hall was not thinking about the problem of collegiate leadership from a theological perspective. At any rate, the visitors, lacking a consensus, chose Gervase, since he had the majority of the votes.[74]

What happened over the next year is obscure, but it is clear that serious internal disputes broke out in the College. In November 1559 Thomas Binion struck Willam Danbee, a servant of Master Smith, with a dagger, when he was "naked and unarmed." The Warden and masters agreed that the Warden could expel Binion for this, but someone (it turns out to have been William Hall) "falsified" the College Register with an entry claiming that this was a false accusation.[75] The way in which the fellows lined up in this dispute indicates a nasty internal rift in the College, along roughly religious lines. The eight seniors were divided between the Catholic party of Hall, Binion, Pott, Appleby, Gifford, Martial and Jackson, and the Protestant party of Broke, Leech, and Atwood.

The rancor increased throughout 1560. When books were removed from their chains in the library, the Warden and masters ordered a search. They agreed that whoever had them would be expelled "for Mr. Martial and the rest thought sure to have found them in one of the Protestants chambers of the bachelors." However, the books were in the Catholic Pott's rooms, at which point, according to their enemies, Hall "remembered" he had allowed Pott take them off their chains and the charge was dismissed. Of course the Protestants believed Pott should have been expelled.[76]

In December 1560 one fellow, Anthony Atkins, and two scholars, were expelled by Bishop Grindal for refusing to take the oath of supremacy; provoking Hall to write a scandalous libel, which Binion circulated among the Bachelors. It mimicked the form of Bishop Grindal's official titles, beginning "Edmund, by provision of the Devil apostate bishop of London, to all and singular clerks of our diocese and anywhere lying, cursing and hypocrisy are established." According to the libel, Grindal ordered his clergy to corrupt scripture, ruin souls, and overturn good feeling. Grindal's chief minister in this, the preacher John Veron, was described as the

Bishop's demon, a minister of Satan, corrupting the young and misleading the flock of Christ.

This was stout stuff, but another libel, in the form of a personal letter, attacked the members of Oxford who had conformed, abandoning their consciences as soon as they saw which way the majority was running. Atkins, that strong tower, it said, was expelled, but it mocked the rest, concluding that they were living in a sty full of urine, stinking feces and other excrement.[77]

As Christmas 1560 approached the tension increased. Hall, the senior Dean, Gifford and Martial had been called to London to appear before the Ecclesiastical High Commission. In their absence the second Dean, James Leech, took the opportunity to replace the Latin hymns sung in the hall on festivals with metrical English Psalms. Leech had just begun the *Te Deum* in English when Hall, arriving unexpectedly, stormed in like a madman, shouting at them to stop. He struck at the book of Psalms "to have smitten it into the fire," and then wrenched it from Leech's hands, throwing it down the hall. Trembling, Dean Hall shouted at the Bachelors "Are you piping still after his pipe?" "Will you never have done puling? I shall teach you to do as I bid!"

This outburst put an end to singing in the hall until Roger Gifford, falling "from that faction" joined Leech's faction for a time, giving it enough strength to begin the singing of English psalms again. Leech insisted that Hall was trying to provoke him to physical violence against his senior, and that all the papists of Oxford were delighted with Hall's stoutness.[78]

By now Merton was clearly shattered along religious lines. When the three junior fellows were interviewed together they explained the episode of the English Psalms in a fully reformed way: "whereas by the ancient decrees of our college it has been appointed that at every solemn feast we should before and after meat praise God in hymns and psalms, and whereas by injury of time certain superstitious songs were appointed, which afterward by the providence of Godly men and laws of the realm were abolished, and in their place appointed certain psalms of David to be sung," the change was attempted. However, Mr. Hall prevented the abolition of the superstitious hymns.

The deposition of the three junior fellows is pathetic in the angst it expresses. Their seniors were engaged in one of those academic brawls that all citizens of the academy know too well. Keeping their heads down, the juniors just wanted to be told which of the College customs were superstitious and which were not, "for so our consciences shall be eased of great burden."[79]

Things were going from bad to worse. Early in 1561 the sub warden, George James, resigned, owing the College the huge sum of £69 from his time in office. It is difficult to know if his resignation had anything to do with the quarrels in the fellowship, but his bad management was another blow to the institution.

In February 1561 Archbishop Parker, the Visitor, found things so rancorous that he thought it necessary to forbid the College to do business without his permission. He charged them to "cease of all displeasures and quarreling one with another" and apply themselves "to virtue and study," thinking only of advancement of learning, the cherishing of honest students, and good order.[80]

For reasons that are unclear, but which probably had to do with the tension in the fellowship, the regular scrutinies, or meetings of the governing body, were postponed for the whole first half of 1561, while some members of the community scurried around undermining Warden Gervase, claiming he was an "ill husband." William Martial seems to have been a ringleader in the anti-Gervase faction, and he, in turn, was accused by his colleagues of being a papist (which was logical, since he was attacking Gervase's marriage, and marrying was a very Protestant thing to do. Martial was expelled in 1567 for being papist). Martial spent a short time in the Marshalsea Prison because of these charges, but Gervase did leave the wardenship late in 1561.[81] However, despite the tensions, Gervase was given a golden handshake. The fellowship, out of "gratitude and kindness," granted him a lease in reversion upon his resignation.[82]

The resignation of Warden Gervase reopened the sore festering in the fellowship. Archbishop Parker's letter ordering an election was received by the College on January 14, 1562. In it Parker suggested that Alexander Nowell, the Dean of St. Paul's, Robert Huick the Queen's physician and former fellow of Merton, or a Master Masters, another of the Queen's physicians, would be good candidates. Despite these heavy hints, sometime that month someone wrote a letter to Cecil supporting the appointment of William Martial Warden, insisting that the charges he was a Catholic were untrue.[83]

The senior members were ordered to provide three names of possible wardens to the Archbishop. They reported their vote on January 28. Five men had been nominated, including Huick, Nowell, Masters, and two others. Martial received no votes. Huick was named as acceptable by all seven of the seniors, and it is probable that they assumed Huick, Parker's nominee, would be appointed.[84]

Parker, claiming that they had submitted five names rather than the three required, ignored their consensus on Huick and appointed someone not on anyone's list, John Man. It seems probable that Parker, reflecting on the mess at Merton, had decided to appoint Man to break the impasse in the College, since Man had no ties to any of the parties. His letter of appointment exhorted the fellows to live in concord and obedience, and it must have been his desire to use Man to that end.[85] Any Dean today would do as much for an ailing department, but in this case it did not work. Many members of the College, temporarily distracted from hating one another by an opportunity to blame the administration, rebelled.

When Man, escorted by Vice Chancellor Babington and other University officials, arrived at the College at 9 a.m. on April 2, 1562 they found that a majority of the fellows had sworn not to let him in, locking the gate. This majority, as it turned out, was led by the papist faction in the fellows. Dean Hall was at the head of them, and they were incensed at what they took to be an insult to the College's statutes, agreeing together to pay the legal costs of resisting the Archbishop's choice. After a standoff, Broke, of the Protestant faction, ordered the gates opened and Man came in. But he came into a College that was by now completely divided.

Archbishop Parker sent a team of visitors, led by Dr. Thomas Yale, to Merton in May of 1562. By then they had heard the charge and countercharge from the fellows, and created a list of twenty questions about events there. They wanted to know who the "movers of discord" were, who the Catholics were, and what roles particular fellows played in keeping Man out. They were also interested in any other breaches of the College statutes. They interviewed all the fellows, leaving us a record of those happy days.

Of course the members of the Protestant faction denounced the papist faction, accusing them of refusing communion, of hiding Catholic books and objects under the stairs, of libeling the University and Bishop Grindal, of stopping hymns in English, of breaking the social hierarchy by associating with their inferiors, and of generally disrupting College life. The papist party, unable to denounce their colleagues' religion, blackened their morals. John Leech was accused of sodomy and "that he did abuse himself oftentimes in mollicie [effeminacy]." John Broke was accused of adultery with one Ward's wife, and with dining outside the common hall. Henry Atwood was accused of being a usurer.

One of the Protestant party suggested that the election of Huick as Warden, overturned by Parker, had been the result of "shameful packing," for "besides that the true religion of Christ was by that means thought should be oppressed and professors of it shortly shaken out of the college." John Hemming, who made this accusation, refers to the other party as "our papists."[86] Of course there were other accusations made as well, such as fiscal malfeasance and infractions of the statutes.

"Papist" and "heretic," the language of sect and division that so worried Lord Keeper Bacon, were deployed in Merton with devastating effect. The visitors, in keeping with Bacon's belief in sharp law to curb such things, examined the evidence and made their decision. The next afternoon the visitors called the members of the College together for a solemn meeting. After admonishing the fellows for their general sins, they expelled Hall and suspended Gifford from his offices and benefits in the College. The grounds were not that they were papists, but that they had committed offenses against the authority of the Archbishop and the good of the College. The remaining fellows, led by their new Warden, Man, and their new Dean, Broke, wrote Archbishop Parker a groveling letter of submission.[87]

Ironically, Hall, for all the evidence of his conservative opinions, did not leave Oxford. He moved across the street to University College, where he died the next year. Gifford, the messenger from the College to the Archbishop, returned with a letter ordering them to allow him to continue giving the Linacre Lectures in medicine.

He moved to All Souls and eventually rose to be President of the College of Physicians.[88]

If the "papist" survivors thought they had escaped lightly, Warden Man had other ideas. Just a year after the visitation, he charged John Pott and Ambrose Appleby with lying under oath during the investigation. Hall had said in his defense that the majority of the fellows had agreed to spend College money in a lawsuit to fight Warden Man's entry. The rest of the fellows denied this, but Pott and Appleby had signed a an oath swearing that the others had agreed. Consequently, the fellowship voted to expel them for perjury.[89]

Binion voluntarily resigned, but only after he was given the living at Embleton by the College.[90] This suggests that his Catholicism was not too deep.

On New Year's Day 1565, the archenemy of the "papists," John Broke, was excluded from the fellowship for defrauding the College. Three months later he turned up, "iam pridem uxoratus," (*already* long since married) as the register notes, to pay back £10.[91]

The crisis of the early 1560s in Merton divides the Catholic history of the College from its Protestant history. Although there were undoubtedly personal issues and personalities underlying the trouble in the fellowship, the crisis was cast by the participants themselves as a struggle between the adherents of the Pope and the adherents of the Queen's religion. Archbishop Parker, canny academic politician that he was, understood that personalities and ideologies had been conflated, and took a different tack. His visitors were looking for bad citizens of Merton, the men who caused trouble, who broke the statutes of the College. They found them and expelled them. Then Warden Man, after waiting a year, used the same evidence to expel two more. The heart had been cut from the conservative faction in the College and it never revived.

Although the quarrels between the old religion and the new were ended by the intervention of the visitors, it is striking that in these battles, as in many others, the fellowship often bent over backwards to be good to their own, even when they were causing trouble. Roger Gifford's reappointment; the lease granted Warden Gervase when he was forced out, and other incidents suggest a decency and fellow feeling that transcended their religious differences. They were, after all, members of Merton even if they could not get along on all points.

Moreover, it is striking how the visitors and the fellows used the College statutes as their touchstone. They may have accused one another of religious deviance, but when it came to personnel decisions they were taken within the framework of the College bylaws.

Merton was now a safely Protestant place and, since the fellowship naturally turned over every eight years or so, by 1567 the last Marian fellow left the College when John Leech resigned.[92] Although the College suffered from minor rebellions against Warden Man, who was away most of the time serving as a diplomat, religion ceased to be the club with which the fellows beat one another. By the mid 1570s most of the fellows, who were only in their twenties, had no adult memories of Catholicism. They may have been religiously confused, but their religious experiences were far different from those whose formative years were the 1540s. These youngsters did not have the habits of Catholics.

As the College entered the 1570s new patterns emerged, indicating an increasingly different style of corporate behavior. The chapel ceased to be a center of community activity. Its accounts show that less and less money was spent on it, and less and less time was spent in it. Now the parish made only one communion offering, at Easter. Across the 1560s the accounts for the chapel and library (kept on the same roll) showed the liquidation of the remnants of the old service. In Autumn 1562 they decided to sell the copes, vestments and other ornaments, and a fellow was sent to London to consult with merchants. In December 1566 Henry Atwood was asked to pay the College the 41s. he obtained from selling the "papistical equipment" from the chapel.[93]

In 1564 they chained John Foxe's new *Acts and Monuments* in the library.[94] In 1568, they purified their library, making 50s from the sale of the "superstitious" books left to the College in 1558 by Richard Ewer.[95]

In 1563 special allowances associated with the feast Nominis Iesu, August 7, were transferred to the feast of St. Peter ad vincula, August 1, which marked the beginning of Merton's fiscal year. Agreeing "we should have a preacher," the fellows allocated 10s for an annual sermon, converting communal worship and remembrance into a time of exhortation and personal reflection.[96] Having reduced the number of chaplains from four, to three, to two by 1570, the College gave the chaplains a new duty, and an extra stipend, for reading the Bible in Hall.[97]

Perhaps most telling of all was the decision, taken in 1586, to discontinue the chapel accounts. There was too little business to make a separate roll necessary.[98]

Merton's troubled transit of the Reformation was not unique. In Cambridge a very similar drama was played out in Queens' College. There, the Protestant Dr. William May was deprived of the presidency in 1554, making room for Dr. Glynn, who was shortly promoted to a bishopric and resigned. He was followed in November 1557 by Dr. Thomas Pecocke, who inherited a mess. At the time he became President, Queens' was divided into two parties. The one, siding with the President, was self-identified as Catholic, even though it included John May, nephew of ousted Protestant President William May. (John, though ordained a Catholic priest in 1557, was destined to become the Anglican bishop of Carlisle.) The minority, opposing the President, favored reformed theology. At issue was the election of the three bachelors of arts of that year as fellows. In 1559 both parties complained to Sir William Cecil as Chancellor, and Cecil ordered them to stop the election until an investigation could be conducted. As in the Merton case, this story ends with the expulsion of two fellows, though it looked like a victory for the

Catholic party. However, the new fellows all left Queen's shortly after their election, so the atmosphere may have remained turbulent.[99]

Doctor Pecocke left Queen's in May 1559, resigning his presidency to William May, who resumed his duties interrupted in 1554.[100]

New College, Oxford, noted for being one of the most Catholic of the Oxford colleges, had a similar history. Although it had conformed under Henry and Edward, there were tensions among the fellows. In 1550, Henry Cole, an ardent Catholic, was complained against by his colleagues and removed from the wardenship by the visitors, perhaps because of his religion. He was replaced by Ralph Skinner, a married Protestant. In his turn, he resigned at Mary's accession and was replaced by Thomas White, one of the two heads of Oxford colleges permitted to continue by the Elizabethan regime.

Lacking the kind of internal divisions that were cloaked in religion in Merton and Queens', New College was not purged from without, at least at first. In the first four years of Elizabeth's reign four leading Catholic intellectuals simply resigned and moved to the continent. But in 1562 Bishop Horne moved against what was becoming known as a nursery of Catholic intellectuals. Expulsions on religious grounds began in 1562, so that by 1569 thirty-three had lost their fellowships from a society of about seventy. By 1577 Horne's visitation found no evidence of Catholics in New College. The expulsion of Catholics and their replacement with conforming if not ardent Protestants, had turned it into a Protestant foundation, and perhaps had killed much of its intellectual *élan*. The society was now firmly governed by the Warden and thirteen senior members, survivors of the purges. For the most part, they were concerned with managing college estates, appointing to benefices and granting leaves of absence to fellows. Rather than concerning themselves with dangerous ideas, they had turned to the one thing they could agree on, making life comfortable for the members.[101]

In all these cases, the colleges were reconstituted through external intervention. And in all cases, the result of the intervention was a quick settling into the new religion. Forced changes in personnel soon altered their character, so that the Elizabethan fellowships were rapidly conformable to the Queen's religion, no matter what their predecessors' inclinations had been. At the same time, the interventions stressed the purpose of the institutions, reminding them to stick to their appointed tasks.

The change in the university communities between 1559 and 1570 was dramatic. The colleges, which were clearly the tools of the people seeking to impose reformation, had been singled out for careful attention. The masters and wardens and presidents had been granted new powers over the universities, and they were, for the most part, bent on creating Protestant institutions for the coming century. Curriculum and staff had to change as the demand for preachers increased, and the interests of donors mutated. But most of all, it was their godly duty to see to it that their communities reformed, lest there be another Mary Tudor, in the form of Mary Stuart, sent as divine punishment.

Through it all, due process was honored in the universities. Statutes were to be followed, and, if the college statutes conflicted with the current order, they were altered by proper procedures. It is not surprising that the fellows of Merton saw fit to temper the changes occurring around them in Edward's reign with a decree that all the ancient orders of the College were to be observed, as long as they were not contrary to the King's laws and injunctions. They understood that those rules and orders embodied their identity and had to be protected.[102] For the same reason, visitations to the colleges always began with an inspection of their statutes. Each one was different, and, so long as they did not include forbidden activities, that difference was accepted.

In so far as the communal relationships within the universities and colleges were defined by their statutes, they were overhauled by each succeeding regime. The statutes of the universities were altered several times in the 1550s and 1560s. But the changes were always cautious, leaving the societies worshiping as prescribed, but otherwise operating as usual. The conservatism of these changes is encapsulated by the Oxford statute decreeing, in 1564, that "wherever in these statutes the words 'The Book of Sentences' shall occur, they shall be taken to signify nothing other than the books of sacred scripture."[103] By this one editorial amendment Peter Lombard's *Sentences*, the standard interpretation of the Bible in the late Medieval universities, was overthrown, replaced by the Bible itself. The statutes themselves were good, they just needed small corrections!

In July of 1577 Warden Bickley of Merton College described the horrors of an outbreak of plague that was killing townspeople, masters, students, important bureaucrats and nobles alike. Its cause was debated, he said, and some thought it was the result of fetid air from the prisons, where the disease had appeared first. Another explanation, which Bickley seemed to like, was that it was sprung "ex artificosis diabolicis et plane papisticis flatibus e Lovaniensi."[104] Whether diabolical tricks and papist flatulence floating over from Louvain was sufficient cause is unclear, but it made sense to a collegiate world that, by 1577, had come to equate the Devil and papists.

Inns of court

Nicholas Sander, a Catholic refugee from New College, Oxford, claimed that the Inns of Court were predominantly Catholic in the 1560s, though, as he ruefully observed, most lawyers "submitted to Caesar and went with the times, giving the second place to God."[105] Looking back from the distance of a century John Milton confirmed this when he complained that the conservatism of judges and lawyers explained the slow establishment of Elizabethan Protestantism.[106] These legal servants of mammon, were not, unlike members of the universities, subject to government pressure for conformity before 1569. The lawyers of the Inns, for all their litigiousness, seem to have navigated the shoals of reformation rather well, developing an internal policy of live and let live, so long as no one made a point of thrusting his religious persuasion on fellow members.[107] This allowed the Inns to become accustomed to the changes of the Reformation slowly, almost naturally.

The records of the Inns for the Henrician period make it clear that they were maintaining a corporate religious life. Members were expected to pay their share of the charges for chapel wax to maintain altar lights, the St. John's or Midsummer lights were lit, masses were said for the dead, and obits were accepted from the wills of deceased members. These entries continue in a regular succession until 1549/50 when they come to an end, as they did everywhere.

There are signs, however, that there were religious tensions within the legal community. Though lawyers might be generally classed as conservatives, not all of them were, and the young men attending the Inns for legal training were, like teenagers everywhere, attracted to the more radical messages.

In the summer of 1546 the members of Lincoln's Inn discovered that someone had taken down the St. John's light in the Hall and hung a horse's head in its place, "in despite of that Saint, as it could not by common presumption be otherwise intended, to the very perilous example of other." Within the week a man named Eldrington had confessed to the act, and implicated two others – though they refused to admit their guilt. The offense was considered so serious that they two who remained silent were committed to the Fleet prison by the Lord Chief Baron on the order of the Lord Chancellor himself. Eldrington was put out of commons, and the two prisoners were expelled from the Inn for a short time. The last we hear of Eldrington and one of his confederates is a note in the Council's records that they "made a frey" in the commons, hurling butter at someone's head.[108]

As the Edwardian Reformation proceeded, the Inns conformed to the new liturgical requirements, but they quickly reverted in Mary's regime. The expenditure on wax in the Lincoln's Inn tells the tale clearly, with its purchase suddenly dropping to near zero in 1550, then jumping back up in 1555.[109] The Inn's Treasurer, Serjeant William Rastell, laid out significant sums of the Inn's money to reequip the chapel with images, tabernacles, and vestments. Significantly, his accounts show a penny was paid to remove the reader's desk from the chapel, marking the end of Edwardian liturgical practice.[110]

As Treasurer Rastell spent what was necessary; as an individual he went further. In May of 1554 he gave the chapel of Lincoln's Inn a large "picture in a table" of the deposition of Christ from the Cross, along with two yellow and green sarcenet altar coverings, and paid 4s to gild the knobs of the canopy covering "the sacrament." In exchange for this, the Benchers agreed that in every mass said at that altar the priest would pray for William, his wife and all of their kinfolk, as well as naming them in their bede roll.[111]

In Queen Mary's time, Lincoln's Inn was dominated by an elderly bench. Its senior member, William Roper, had been born in 1496, admitted to the Inn in 1518, and called to the bar in 1525. His father-in-law was Sir Thomas More, whose biography he wrote. Roper was a governor of the Inn first in 1549, and from 1553/4 he served continuously until 1569. Roper's Catholic sympathies are beyond question.

Roper's closest colleagues, in age, were Edward Griffin (or Griffith) and Clement Higham. Griffin had been admitted in 1521. He had been a governor of the Inn since 1540 and would, like Roper, continue until 1569. Higham, admitted in 1518, was a governor by 1548, remaining one until 1559. Thomas Hemming and William Tankard were also Marian governors, admitted in 1521 and 1522 respectively. William Forester had been admitted to the Inn sometime before 1525. He had been sitting as a governor since 1552 and would continue until 1567. Henry Haydon was admitted in 1526. In this group of grey beards Henry Payne was a mere child, since he had been admitted as recently as 1531, remaining active in the Inn until his death in 1568.[112]

In short, most of the Marian governors of Lincoln's Inn were born before or shortly after Henry VIII came to the throne. It is not surprising that men of their age and conservatism were willing to expel James Dalton. Born about 1535, he was educated in the newly founded Christ Church, entering the Inn under special license only in 1555. In May of 1558 the governors expelled young Dalton because of his religious opinions.[113] It seems to have been the only case of official intolerance in the Inns during Mary's reign.

The governors of Lincoln's Inn were a long-lived group, but, like the Marian bishops, they began dying around the time of Elizabeth's accession, allowing new blood into the governing body. The leadership skipped a generation, passing to men admitted in the late 1530s and early 1540s. Teenagers in the opening years of the Reformation, this group proved itself very cautious in the face of the religious changes. Or perhaps they appear cautious because they had to share the government of the Inn with men like William Roper, Edward Griffin and William Forester, all of who continued to be elected governors into the late 1560s. In Elizabeth's first decade there seems to have been an balance of power between the elderly Catholics and the younger men. William Roper continued to be a power in the community, securing admission for his relatives and lending the Inn money, and there is no evidence of direct action against him, or any of the other known Catholics. The Inn conformed, but it did not show itself to be overly concerned about the religious propensities of its members.

If things had been allowed to take their natural course, Lincoln's Inn would have slowly turned Protestant. Its elderly Catholic leaders were, in due course, dying, leaving the field to men whose religion, if not Protestant, could not be the kind of Catholicism represented by the old men. But the course of history beat the course of nature to the post. The danger of a rebellion in support of Mary Queen of Scots, born out by the Northern Rebellion of 1569, frightened the Privy Council into its first hunt for Catholics, who were now assumed to be seditious. In May 1569 the Privy Council wrote to the Inns, naming suspected papists within them and demanding that they be excluded from commons until they conformed. Worse, the papists were barred from practicing in court.[114]

Questioned about their absences from church, the lawyers responded with careful vagueness, attempting to walk a fine line between their consciences and their careers. Robert Atkinson of the Inner Temple, whose speech in defense of freedom of conscience in the Parliament of 1563 was really a plea for toleration for his family's religion, insisted that he went to church when he was in the country, but when he was in London he was too busy to attend.

Pressed as to whether he had heard mass or matins in Latin, or confessed his sins "after the popish manner," Atkinson indignantly said he had not offended in that way since he was hauled before the Ecclesiastical Commissioners eight or nine years before. As to whether he had taken Protestant communion at least three times a year since Elizabeth came to the throne, Atkinson said he had taken it twice, once when forced to and the year before at Easter.[115] In 1572 Atkinson was formally expelled from the Inner Temple, along with four others, for failing to reconcile themselves with the established church.[116]

In theory Atkinson could no longer practice law, having been formally prohibited from appearing in court, but that was not the case. In 1566 he had become Recorder of Oxford and he kept the post for the rest of his long life. This is especially telling because Oxford, under the influence of Sir Francis Knollys, its high steward from 1564 to 1592, became a deeply puritan town. Atkinson continued to hold the city's chief legal position, and his relative, Sir Francis Stonor, served as its sheriff. Both men had known Catholic sympathies, going home each night to openly Catholic wives.

Over in the Middle Temple, Edmund Plowden was in difficultly for the same reason. In early November 1569 the commissioners of the peace were ordered to subscribe to the "book and statute" for the uniformity of common prayer as a test of loyalty. Plowden, who had been reported by his bishop as a Catholic in 1564, unsuspectingly attended a meeting of the bench, discovering to his surprise that he was expected to subscribe on the spot. Brilliant lawyer that he was, he refused to sign until he had read the fine print, concluding, after due consideration, that he could not agree "generally to all things in the act and book." This legal answer, with its concern about the "generality" of a law, had not, he claimed, kept him from attending church more than any other lawyer he knew, but he could not take the oath. Subscription required that he believe in the things set out in the prayer book, and, since he did not, it would be impious to say that he did. He hoped they would not take his refusal as resistance to the Queen, to whom he swore love and obedience, but he simply could not betray his conscience. As was required in cases of refusal, his fellow justices made Plowden give his bond to appear before the Privy Council if summoned.[117]

Oddly, he was not expelled from the Middle Temple, even though he was removed from the commission for the peace in Berkshire. Nor was his legal practice interrupted. In 1577 a list of the benchers of the Inns, detailing the religion of each one, named Plowden as a papist, very learned, of very good living. He was so respected as a lawyer that he counted the Queen among his clients.[118]

In Lincoln's Inn William Roper was fighting the same battle. One of the oldest and most eminent men of the society, Roper exercised great influence. But in 1569, having been one of the four governors of the Inn since 1553, he left office. His departure was probably caused by the Privy Council's attack on known Catholics in the Inns, but William Roper, having been bound for his good behavior in 1560, was never bothered. He kept his legal offices under the Crown and moved quietly into the shadows – though at 73 or 74 years of age he may have been old enough that the authorities saw no point in forcing him to conform, even though all Readers, Benchers and Utter Barristers were supposed to take the oath of supremacy.[119]

The stories of Atkinson, Plowden and Roper show us that underlying the official intolerance there was great latitude left to lawyers who refused to subscribe. Even though the Privy Council had ordered the expulsion and disbarment of men who did not subscribe, neither Plowden nor Roper lost their memberships or their legal practices. Atkinson was expelled from his Inn but Oxford knew a good lawyer and kept him on. In the legal community there was a tolerance that seemed to grow from the common bonds among lawyers and a certain disregard for the letter of the law. As in the colleges, these communities tried not to be too hard on their own.

Even those members of the Inns who were clearly Catholics found their colleagues took a leisurely attitude toward disciplining them. Thomas Roper did not escape as his father had. He was one of those named by the Privy Council as a known Catholic in 1569. Lincoln's Inn did not rush to judgment. Frequent threats of expulsion were made to convince Thomas to conform, but he did not lose his chambers in the Inn until 1579, a full decade after he had been first threatened.[120]

Thomas Roper's case is not unusual, since many suspected Catholics were handled with the same courtesy. In 1575 the council minutes show that three men, including Anthony Roper, were given more time, "to the intent they may use conference for their better satisfaction of their conscience, are spared from the expulsion of the Fellowship of this House until the end of Hillary term next, so that they in the mean time receive the Communion in Lincoln's Inn." Eight more were identified as "to be talked with all at the Bench for not receiving the Communion."[121]

The tolerance shown by the governing bodies in the Inns of Court began to wain in the late 1570s. There was increasing governmental pressure, complete with the attempt to identify all the benchers' religious orientations, and the leadership of the communities was moving forward another generation. In Lincoln's Inn the generation of William Roper had passed, in about 1564, to a group of men admitted in late 1530s and early 1540s. By the late 1570s those men were being displaced by men admitted in the late 1550s and early 1560s, all of whom had been called to the bench in Elizabeth's reign. They had taken the oath of supremacy, and it is clear that the Inns, though still containing Catholics, were increasingly Protestant.[122]

We can see this in actions of the Council of Lincoln's Inn. In May 1578 James Dalton, expelled from the Inn for his Protestantism in 1558, when William Roper's generation was in control and Mary was on the throne, was formally readmitted. The rhetoric in the Black Book of the Inn betrays the revulsion of the Council for what had happened in the bad old days. Dalton's expulsion, it says, "odiously prosecuted and odiously registered in the time of Popery, must be utterly blotted out and put to perpetual oblivion, and yet that he shall be so adjudged of the Fellowship of this House as through he had been never expulsed."[123]

In 1581 the same Council officially repudiated their predecessors' promise to pray for the souls of William Rastell and his family. Made in Mary's reign in exchange for rich altar furnishings, it was obviously unenforceable under the Elizabethan Settlement. Nonetheless, they officially disassociate the Inn from it. Written beside the Marian entry in the Black Book is this Latin note: "This order, because of its stupid, abominable superstition, was abolished by the Council held on 16 November, in the twenty-third year of the reign of Elizabeth."[124] This was more than a rejection of purgatory. It was a loud rejection of the values of a previous generation.

The 1570s were a time of occasional sermons in the Inns. They had not bothered with them in the 1560s, but pulpits were placed in their churches around 1570, and payments for sermons start appearing. It may be that these occasional sermons, always associated in Lincoln's Inn with the feasts of the Purification and the Ascension, were arranged because their old chaplains did not preach. But by the late 1570s it was becoming common to have permanent preachers. In Gray's Inn William Chark was hired in 1576, serving until 1581, when Thomas Crook took over for the next seventeen years. The Temple Church hired Laurence Chaderton in February 1578 for £20 a year.[125] In Lincoln's Inn the search for a permanent divinity reader began in early 1581. Desiring to have one "like the others," they tried to hire Lawrence Chaderton, who had left the Temple, but took William Chark from Gray's Inn instead.[126]

Interestingly, these preachers were all on the more puritanical end of the theological spectrum, little tempted to tolerate papists. Whether this suited the more tolerant leaders of the legal community is unclear, but something made the Ancients of the Inner and Middle Temple choose Richard Hooker over Walter Travers to be master of the Temple Church in 1585, stopping Travers' salary.[127] Travers, an enthusiastic Presbyterian, had been appointed to preach in Richard Alvey's place during his last illness. Travers was successful, drawing enthusiastic audiences of citizens and, as Izaac Walton tells us, "younger gentlemen of that Society." By rights, he could have expected to succeed to the mastership, but Hooker, only 30, was brought in from Oxford instead.[128]

Hooker opened his preaching career at the Temple with a morning sermon on March 20, 1585, in which he asserted that papists who lived and died in the Roman church might nonetheless be saved, since their ignorance could be excused. Further, he reminded his listeners that Roman Catholics, unlike pagans, acknowledge the work of human salvation was wrought by Christ alone, differing from Protestants only in the manner of applying that understanding. This meant that even the Catholic church was under Christ's new covenant of salvation.[129]

Travers was outraged. That afternoon he preached a refutation and a preaching battle began that raged for days in the pulpit, spilling into print and the Privy Council, and involving continental reformers. The Puritan party, so devoted to stamping out all remnants of Catholic worship and belief, were horrified that such opinions could be expressed in such an important pulpit.[130]

On the other hand, Hooker's opinions, shaped by his circle at Corpus Christi, Oxford, was undoubtedly more comfortable to the members of the Temple, since they included men like Edmund Plowden.

Hooker, stimulated by this debate to begin his meditation on religion and the state that became the *Laws of Ecclesiastical Polity*, was a good fit for a group of men who were tolerant, if not indifferent, to nonconformity. As Geoffrey de Parmiter noted, "In the tolerant atmosphere of the Inns . . . a man was unlikely to be unduly harassed on account of his religion provided that he was not detected in any kind of proselytism or participation in forbidden rites, and such penalties as the Inns from time to time imposed on their non-conforming members were mild by the standards known to Catholics elsewhere."[131] In the end, Milton was right, though perhaps for the wrong reason. The Inns of Court were not so much conservative as latitudinarian. This latitude on the part of the nation's legal community meant, however, that it was not a group inclined to enthusiastically impose reformation. By about 1580 they had become Protestant by default.

Lawyers, taught to split hairs, were, like the rest of their culture, mastering the art of discrimination. Most obviously, they had left the world in which all Christians were assumed to be brothers and entered a world where some Christians were worse than pagans and akin to devils; where the Christian Antichrist in Rome was more feared than the Muslim Antichrist in Istanbul.[132] Less obviously, but just as certainly, they were learning to discriminate between ideology and social function.

Religious guilds

Logically, one assumes that all religious guilds in England passed away in 1547, sometimes reviving briefly under Mary, to die again in 1559. Most did, although the number of Marian revivals seems to be relatively small. However, not all religious guilds could be suppressed, since they had independent legal identity that protected their property, even if they could no longer pray for the dead.

In Norwich the Guild of St. George had been chartered by Henry V, making it a permanent body. An important civic institution, its members, which included all the aldermen of the city, kept it going, adapting to the changes as the times demanded.

Each year on April 23, St. George's Day, the guild members paraded through the streets portraying St. George, Princess Margaret, and the Dragon slain by St. George to rescue the Princess. It was a one of the high points of the civic year, as the procession marched to the Cathedral for mass and prayers for the departed, leaving the Dragon outside on the Dragon Stone.

The Guild was important enough to Norwich that when the Edwardian injunctions forbidding all religious processions were promulgated and the chantries were closed, its members reorganized. Renaming themselves the Company and Citizens of St. George, the reinvented their celebration. No longer processing with St. George and the Dragon, they attended evensong on April 22 and divine service on April 23, followed by a banquet. On April 24 they met again for a sermon and the election of officers.

With Queen Mary came the opportunity to revive the Guild. Accordingly, the members of the Company once more named themselves the Guild of St. George and declared that they would celebrate the feast as they had done 20 years before. Oddly, they moved their celebration to a different day, no longer keeping the feast of St. George. Now it was a fixed rather than moveable feast day, and it was no longer directly associated with the saint.

In 1559 the Elizabethan Settlement forced another reworking of the Guild's title, and it became the Company and Fellowship of St. George. Once again the Company went to evensong and heard a sermon on election day. Still processing through the streets, they no longer portrayed St. George or Princess Margaret, but the Dragon still marched.

This halfway house of the 1560s ended in 1574 when the Company moved its feast to June, joining it with the celebrations surrounding the election of the city's mayor. Tellingly, the Company's clerk no longer called it the feast of St. George. It was now described as the "feast of the mayor, shreves, and company."

The Dragon, known affectionately as "Snap," continued to prowl the streets of Norwich for centuries after, but by the late sixteenth century the feast of St. George had become a celebration of civic unity, ceasing to honor either the saint or the departed members of the Guild. The fun of the procession was kept, but its original meaning was lost. It had survived because, in its new guise, it continued to perform its civic duty. As Muriel McClendon has remarked, this desacralized St. George "represented practically everything except the continuity of tradition."[133]

Within communities this ability to adapt was especially important. In a family, ideological tensions could be overridden by affection and the absence of direct external interference. Institutions that functioned in the public arena were more visible, more publicly regulated, and more susceptible to internal conflict if communal solidarity was not maintained. The Reformation had removed many of the tools of communal identity and solidarity from the institutional tool kits, forcing them to be reinvented. Those reinventions often looked much like the old tools – commemoration of benefactors might seem like prayers for the dead – but they rested on a new ideology and depended on a reinvented corporate history.

Most of the destruction of institutional solidarity occurred in the 1540s and 1550s. The repair work lasted into the 1570s, and its effects were visible in the 1580s. The destruction was more than top-down Reformation, though the dissolutions and persecutions certainly had their effects. The "purification" of parish churches, the end of prayers for the dead, and the sudden appearance of large amounts of ecclesiastical real estate on the market, with all that implied about local employment, opportunity and government, marked the people of the 1540s and 1550s in significant ways. These imposed changes, however, were outward and visible signs of inward and less visible transformations. Some people welcomed the change, ecstatically dancing on the fallen images of Dagon; others were horrified, and some, perhaps the majority, were more confused than religiously offended. But as the dust settled all groups were still living together. In the long run, they had to repair the destruction, which meant mediating the disagreements between individuals within communities about the proper role and function of those communities. It was in this mediation that the semi-autonomous nature of institutions and local governments softened some of the impacts. It was done in the name of order and security, but the officials who did it were, as a group, reorienting their institutions away from the troubling religious issues toward shared institutional concerns. The lawyers and the members of the livery companies are good examples of the way in which their status allowed them to work out the issues over time.

This working out happened at different paces in different places. Within ecclesiastical institutions and the universities, the shock was short and sharp, though mitigated by a respect for law. In other sorts of communities the change took much longer and was more gentle, reaching maturity in the 1570s as the generation of the 1520s and 1530s handed control to those raised in a time when the old ways were already collapsing. In community after community the 1570s and 1580s saw the arrival of this new generation, bringing with them new ideas of social relations.

The reality of Tudor government was that the monarch could only do what the local magistrates agreed to do, which gave the local magistrates a great deal of breadth in interpretation and imposition. Parishes, companies, town, colleges, and cathedrals had varying degrees of Reformation according to the nature of the compromises made by their leadership. But in each of them, the compromises were quickly hardening into custom by the 1580s. By then a new set of definitions, religious and therefore political, were at work.

Most visibly, these new definitions placed neighbors and kin on one of two sides of a thin line. Some took communion and some recused themselves, refusing communion. The term "recusant" first appeared in official documents in 1568, becoming common only in the mid-1570s, as this new body of people took on an identity that gave common identity to everyone else. Finally the English had a mirror in which to see their common, national, religious culture.

Of course much of the impetus for these new definitions came from without, as Catholics became a believable enemy in the wake of the Northern Rebellion, the presence of Mary of Scotland in England, Elizabeth's excommunication, papal support for the Irish rebellion, and the St. Bartholomew massacre.

The result of this compound was the birth of a new political culture. Rooted in local variety but sharing national characteristics, it adapted established customs and forms. It recognized religious difference as a matter of conscience but insisted that order be the first priority. The nature of that order was becoming the question of the day. In a fractured world how could social peace be maintained?

6

Reinventing Public Virtue

In October 1565 the congregants at Paul's Cross were told that they were more iniquitous than ever because they enjoyed the freedom of the Gospel. "In time of [Catholic] ignorance," the preacher boasted, "there was no such abundance, such going to law, such drinking, and pride, such usury, etc." Why? In the time of superstition Satan "had so lulled them asleep in blindness that he was sure they were his own, and now, seeing he can work no more by ignorance and withstand the truth of the gospel, he hath turned himself into an angel of light, and crept so subtly into our bosom that he persuadeth us that no sin can do us any harm." The minister rebuked the Londoners, yearning for the good times of persecution, when people cared about religion. Now, free preaching of the gospel had made their hearts cold to its message.[1]

This sermon probably left its auditors confused, but it stated a potent irony. Free preaching of the central Protestant message of salvation by faith convinced many that they need not worry about their sins, lulling them, the clergy feared, toward the antinomian heresy. If they felt sure in conscience, they could do what they wanted, knowing their election was certain. If they were not graced with faith, they could do nothing about salvation anyway, and they could do as they pleased. And no one could estimate their salvation by their works. The public face of virtue had been veiled.

In the midst of the rapid institutional and intellectual changes of the mid century, people's conceptions of public virtue were confused. As traditional certainties shattered, they had to invent the rules as they went along, conducting the business of their lives as their understanding of their place in society evolved. They changed out of pragmatic necessity, and they explained the change using the new language of Protestantism. The result was a modified social morality that placed the individual in a new relationship with those around him or her. Closely allied to the old expectations, it gave the individual more choice, depending upon conscience and self interest as regulators.

Social morality could change because English government in the Reformation era was essentially local government. The parishes, the towns, the incorporated boroughs, the universities, the colleges, the guilds, the companies, and even the counties were governed by local leaders working without pay and under haphazard supervision. Their relationship to the Crown was strong, but it was reciprocal, as members of Parliament understood. Consequently, government was the exercise of local self-interest mediated through the structures of law and custom, and self interest was defined by the values and concepts of virtue possessed by local governors.[2] If order was to be kept, if security was to be maintained, these men did it as a matter of local politics, as informed by local experiences. Hence the history of the institutions is also the history of the Reformation's effects. The people running them applied their experience and their understanding to the problems of the moment, revising and creating as the need arose.

In each institution, in each community, the Reformation produced private treaties of toleration among the members. These unwritten agreements generally avoided ideological conflict by concentrating on the pragmatic purposes of the community. A Puritan could do business with a Catholic as along as the business was not about their conflicting religious values. Economic interest could override a good deal of distrust in other areas. It was equally true that local leaders had learned a high degree of relativism from their experiences in the Reformation. If the Crown and the theologians kept changing what was true, all truths became relative and scarcely worth fighting about. They could demonstrate what Bob Scribner labeled "the tolerance of practical rationality."[3] There was a lot of practical rationality going around in Elizabethan England.

Out of these *ad hoc* reformulations grew a new Protestant culture. The national energies had been absorbed by the Reformation in the middle of the century, and the Reformation had severely damaged many traditional cultural practices. Rebuilt willy-nilly, a new set of practices began to emerge in the 1570s, leaving to the younger Elizabethans a process of exploration and redefinition that can most easily be seen in the artistic brilliance of the period, but can also be found at the counting boards and taverns. Accompanying it, however, was a new paternalism encouraged by people frightened of the troubles unleashed by religious tensions and heightened, widened and deepened by the wars and economic crises of the later sixteenth century.

The result, by the early seventeenth century, was a social morality alien to that of their grandparents. It was a social morality that is recognizable to modern people, marking the divide between late medieval and early modern England. Historians have often noted this change, and debates have raged over the chicken-and-egg problem of capitalism and religion, mercantilism and state formation, and the rest, but fundamentally the change that produced early modern culture arose from the daily concerns of people who used their contemporary understanding to define and solve pressing personal and public concerns. Those contemporary understandings were rooted in changing social experience and changing religious values, the one rubbing against the other so that both wore down together. We can see this change everywhere in the Elizabethan age, which subsumes all those people who came to adulthood before the first decade of the seventeenth century. Experiencing rapid population growth, inflation, rising crime rates, religious warfare, international ideological conflict, rapidly expanding international trade, and the rise of a new industrial base, they understood these issues using the values of a logocentric religion hammered home by increasingly ubiquitous preachers, moderated and adapted through the evolving values of their overlapping communities.

The Elizabethans were building on the ruins of late Medieval culture in England. Their parents and grandparents had experienced its destruction, responding as best they could to the chaos of the Reformation, soaring inflation and all the other problems of the mid-century. By the second decade of Elizabeth's reign English people were becoming comfortable with the adaptations they made to survive the Reformation era, handing their children new "old" habits on which to base their cultural responses. As Edward Bicknoll lamented in 1579, "We have quite forgotten *Mariana tempora*."[4] Bicknoll meant that religion had become slack and God might send another chastisement, but his complaint was true. By 1579 the memories of the mid-century convulsions were fading into folklore and propaganda, used as a bogy-man to frighten the nation in moments of tension like the Anjou marriage negotiations.

We can see English culture settling into new modes everywhere we look by the 1580s. Popular festivities have become nationalized, with the Queen's providential accession day, November 17, replacing the celebration of St. Hugh of Lincoln's feast, and other traditions, like the Corpus Christi Day pagents being abrogated.[5] Economic behaviors have adapted to the use of credit and bills of exchange, consolidating London's dominance of the nation's economy.[6] Economic rationales were being recognized as separate from moral imperatives in business decisions. Parliaments stopped talking of "commonwealth" business, increasingly using reason of state as its rationale for legislation, just as leading intellectuals were embracing the lessons of Tacitian humanism, stressing a civic virtue learned from the Romans.[7] Individual piety, marked by emotional self examination, is becoming popular, encouraging a literature of self-exploration. In education Ramist dualism is undermining Aristotelean induction, and the English language is acquiring new appreciation and some of its greatest authors. In religion personal choice, even conversion, became a formal possibility, even as the English nation adopted a new "other," the satanic papist, and learned to distrust a significant number of its citizens for their refusal to worship as prescribed by the Crown. Even congregational self-government seemed a possibility by the 1580s. The list could go on and on, but all these things were growing from the rubble of the Reformation. They were the product of men and women attempting to find their way through life in a culture whose habits, damaged and distorted, had to be reformulated.

The purpose of this chapter is to explore some of the ways in which the adaptations made in the mid-sixteenth century influenced the public virtue of individuals, changing conceptions of duty and reciprocity. These new consensuses of virtue produced and justified a new economy and the new, paternalistic style of government, blessed by an emerging Anglican theology.

Practical Politics

Right and wrong, and even the paradigm of virtue itself, was poorly defined because of the Reformation confusion. The essential message of Protestantism, salvation by faith alone, was not fully understood by most people, though, if wills are any indication, by the 1580s many people knew the formulas. On the street solafidian theology, often combined with doctrines of election and predestination, had the effect of undermining communal certainties and throwing the individual back onto his or her own devises. For many it was a liberation of a sort, since it was less and less easy to know if the intention of an act was Godly. The compromises of mid-century made this confusion almost natural, since the only forum in which one could be convicted with certainty was that of one's own conscience. And skepticism was a common result.

The prolific Bishop Thomas Morton, writing in 1606 against the "heinous and heathenish" equivocations of Catholics, acknowledged, in a back handed way, the existence of this private sphere of conscience, separate from the public sphere of action, when he insisted it could not exist for Jesuits. Arguing that each person has a stable, constant conscience against which the truth and falsehood of any statement could be tested, he claimed that conscience speaks to the soul as certainly as if it had a voice. Quoting Augustine he insisted "the mind cannot think other than what it thinks." This, he said, made it impossible for a Catholic priest to deny his priesthood before a royal officer. To reach this conclusion he recognized the existence of a private self, known only to the individual conscience, which is beyond the control of law. A self which knew when it was lying. It was wrong, thought Morton, to deny that one was a priest, since one could not deny it in conscience. Besides, there was no other way to discover the papist snake in the nation's bosom.[8]

William Alabaster, one of the golden lads of Elizabethan Cambridge, chaplain to the Earl of Essex at Cadiz, and a convert to Catholicism, tried to encapsulate this Protestant approach to religion of the individual heart and head in his conversion narrative, written in 1602. One of the things that had troubled him during his contact with Catholics in Cadiz was that they took sin seriously, believing in penance and restitution. His Protestant colleagues took a different view of sin. They held that the heart was the seat of judgment about sin, not the law. "And if our heart reprehend us not for our life," he wrote, "we [shall] have hope in God, and not otherwise." Knowing, as a Protestant, that he was excused from the law, Alabaster "thought I might challenge to myself as well as the best, (to wit), to be able to judge of all matters alone, and so I framed myself to be that spiritual man that St Paul talketh of *qui omnia iudicat ipse vero a nemine iudicatur.*" After he became a Catholic, he recognized that enjoying liberty and sensuality hardened men's hearts, leading them away from God by blinding them to their sins.[9]

John Bossy described this changing relationship between the individual and the law in a seminal article exploring the shift away from the Seven Deadly Sins, which taught social obligation as the basis for a Christian life, to the Ten Commandments. The Decalogue could be read as a law code which put greatest emphasis on offenses against its "first table," concerned with God's honor. Thus blasphemy and swearing would be given greater theological weight than offenses against one's neighbor. The second table contained things that need only be regulated for social harmony, like theft or adultery, since the intentions behind them could not be known. The first table concerned God directly, shaping God's attitude toward the community.[10]

This was a convenient doctrine for those who lived pragmatically, since their consciences, not so tender as some, allowed them broad toleration in many arenas. If people lived as a good neighbors, paid debts, and refrained from blasphemy, their internal religious convictions were not the business of the neighborhood. God would punish or reward them according to His intentions, not according to human judgment. Only those actions outwardly visible could be certainly criminal. Murder, theft, and adultery had a clear physical reality to them that could be judged and punished. But as for belief, only outward conformity could ever be expected. Only God and the individual could know the secrets of the heart.[11]

This evolving standard of conscience and stress on the Ten Commandments was born in the iconoclasm of the Reformation, which sprang directly from the commandment "You shall have no other Gods before me," and the attack on "works" religion. As works were rejected and faith stressed, the behavior of one's fellows and one's self declined in importance. Communities experiencing these attacks, however, did not simply abandon the value they placed on neighborliness or their need to get along. Instead they turned to the secular law and self interest to enforce standards traditionally maintained by religion.

Elizabethan judges, pondering the nature of the royal supremacy and the sorts of crimes it could produce, separated offenses against God from offenses against the supremacy and from criminal offenses. Importantly, Chief Justice Whitelock put the trial of felonies first, the regulation of civil offenses second, and what he called the "onus providentia" third. This last category was watched by the law because it fostered unity in the church, peace and tranquility in the community, and security in the family. In all these concerns the law was not interested in sin, it was interested in order.[12]

By the same token, the church courts, now a department of state, were charged with maintaining good order. No longer needed to herd people toward salvation, they were still charged with maintaining the Christian virtues of social harmony. The churchwardens who presented their neighbors for misbehaving, the parsons who tried to reconcile fractious parishioners, and the archdeacons who heard the charges, depended on the norm of neighborliness as the bedrock. "Love thy neighbor as thyself" was a crucial teaching to these people unless they belonged to the little flocks of the separating elect. The church was the community, a *corpus permixtum* that contained every one in the parish, not just the elect. As John Darrell would put it, the English church was a "mixt company compounded of christians true and false: the greatest part being the worst."[13]

Since the greatest part were the worst Christians, it is not surprising that many of the social and political responses to the Reformation message were less than enthusiastic, tending toward maintenance of harmony rather than the imposition of God's will. Or that, in practice, this meant allowing the individual a good deal of latitude in personal belief. The famous *via media* of Anglicanism rests directly on this.

Where it came from is an interesting question. In the context of the second half of the sixteenth century, the English appear astonishingly tolerant in their response to religious conflict. Civil wars in Scotland, in the Low Countries, in France, and in Ireland were fueled and justified, if not actually caused, by religion. The English exception seems to arise from the nature of English government and the attitudes of English leaders. As Dairmaid MacCulloch has pointed out, the incremental Reformation directed by Thomas Cranmer rested on the principal of concord which, though ultimately intolerant of Catholics and Anabaptists, assumed the slow but sure conversion of the nation to Protestantism. Cranmer built this on his Augustinian concept of predestination, which allowed him to see in even the most ardent Catholic a person not yet awakened by grace. The Archbishop joined this to his conviction that the church needed a Godly prince to guide the faithful through law. This law defended the middle ground against the sects on either side, making it possible to proceed with the national conversion by persuasion, teaching the people through reformed liturgies and sermons rather than slaughter.[14] Obviously, Cranmer's irenicism was not shared with all his reforming colleagues – the isertion of the "black rubric" into the Book of Common Prayer of 1552 is proof of this – but his spirit infused the liturgies Cranmer created.

Queen Mary's Catholic Church had a different philosophy, even though Cardinal Pole was inclined to be more irenic than his queen. The Roman and Spanish Inquisitions were active when Mary's restoration began, and Philip II's Spanish clerics were experienced with both. It would have been surprising if the Roman church had accepted Cranmer's model of concord and slow conversion, since it so clearly believed in the iron fist within the episcopal glove. But Elizabeth, by returning the nation to the *status quo ante*, endorsed the maintenance of harmony within a broadly tolerant church.

The Queen's political ideal of order and harmony did not match the desires of some of her subjects. In William Bullein's wonderful dialogue a world traveler, who had seen Cuba and Ethiopia, described the best reformed city, Nodol [London], in the best reformed nation, Taerg Nattirb [Great Britain]. In this Utopia the biblical slogan "Maintain Brotherly Love, Fear God, Honor the King" is over every gate. But brotherly love is narrowly defined. In this model Protestant city disobedient children and adulterers are hanged; swearers' tongues are cut out; and known papists are burned. Informers are well regarded for reporting on their neighbors, and even cats and dogs are kept off the streets in sermon time.[15] An evangelical regime might have tried to enact this model, but not Elizabeth's. Peace and conformity, gentle persuasion, and good order were her ideal state.

Given this emphasis on harmony and slow conversion, the rising acceptance of conscience as the only sure guide, and a legal system which saw order as its primary concern, it is not surprising that the mid-Elizabethan period produced a culture that was often self-contradictory about religion. The Elizabethan Settlement positively encouraged people to use their practical rationality to evade the nasty parts of religious division. We can see this distinctly in the reality of recusancy.

In 1607 John Ridgeway applied for admission to the Jesuit college of St. Ignatius. As was customary, he was interviewed about his religious history and his family in England. John, just past 20 at the time, gave this account of his family:

My father is [was] a learned lawyer, a schismatic, my mother is a Catholic, and both are of high families. I have an elder brother, Thomas, a Catholic, and two others, as far as I know, heretics, namely, Peter and William; six sisters heretics, I think. I have several relations; one called Stonor, other Lental and others Atkinson. I claim Mr. Southcott, a Catholic, as my guardian; I have also an uncle and maternal aunt, the latter a lover of Christ, the former of the error of the schismatics.[16]

Ridgeway's account of his family connections is a perfect demonstration of the way in which Elizabethan Catholics lived in the heart of the community, related to, and doing business with, the "heretics" and "schismatics" around them, just as the heretics and schismatics were related to and did business with the papists in their midst.

John Ridgeway's schismatic father was Thomas Ridgeway, of Torre Abbey, Devon and the Middle Temple. Thomas sat for Dartmouth in the Parliament of 1584, carrying on the tradition of John's grandfather, another John Ridgeway of the Middle Temple, who sat for Dartmouth and Exeter in various Henrician and Marian Parliaments.

His Catholic step-uncle and guardian, Thomas Southcote of Bovey Tracey, Devon, sat in three Parliaments in the 1550s, representing Dartmouth once. The Southcotes of Devon were related to the Chief Justice of the Queen's Bench, John Southcote, who conformed in religion despite the Catholicism of his wife and family. (His recusant family later invented a family story of how he, trying recusants, resigned rather than sentence a priest to death, spending his last years in penance.) Southcote's daughter married Sir Francis Stonor, the conforming head of an Oxfordshire family, in 1579. Stonor's mother sheltered Edmund Campion in their family home.

John Ridgeway was tied to Oxfordshire through the Atkinson family, too. Robert Atkinson, who was Recorder of Oxford from 1566 until his death in 1607, sat in the Parliament of 1563, where he made a notable speech against the treason bill, calling for toleration in matters of conscience. His demand for religious toleration is not surprising when we realize he would be expelled from the Inner Temple for papistry in 1570. He later conformed, but his wife never did.[17]

So John Ridgeway's family was riddled with religious contradiction. He was surrounded by schismatic and Catholic kin. Most of his older male relatives held positions of honor and power in their communities, as did his brother, Thomas, who sat in Parliament for Devon in 1604, was an Irish MP, and would become the first earl of Londonderry. They disagreed over religion, but they were still family.

Catholics and other dissenters in England did not withdraw into fastnesses and retreat to mountain tops to survive. They lived on the high street and in the manor house, doing business with their neighbors. Religiously they were separate, they were suspected in times of national crisis, and they could not sit in Parliament or graduate from a university, but they remained in the community, occasionally persecuted and fined, but made distinctive only by their refusal to take an Anglican communion.

In the middle of Elizabeth's reign English Catholics were just learning that they were Recusants, and they were everywhere. Families were fractured along religious lines, just as all other social institutions were fractured. This happened especially in the families of the political and economic elites – the parliamentary classes – since they were more likely to be placed in a position that required them to declare their loyalty to the Elizabethan Settlement. Moreover, these religious fractures were not just between distant cousins. They often split the marriage bed, divided filial loyalties, and threatened fraternal relations. Not even the leaders of Elizabeth's regime were immune from these conflicts, which were often inter-generational battles wrapped in religious mantles. The earl of Leicester's son became a Catholic, as did Lord Buckhurst's son, a daughter of Sir Francis Walsingham, and one of Burghley's grandsons. Several bishops had Roman Catholic relatives, too. Like all Elizabethans, these people were living in a world of unofficial religious plurality. Their wives and sons, fathers and daughters, mothers and god parents refused to accept the officially established religion, yet life went on.

Contemporaries recognized that the official rhetoric of intolerance, though truly meant, did not describe reality. Archbishop Whitgift, under attack in 1584 for encouraging Catholics when he prosecuted Protestant nonconformists, observed wryly to Lord Burghley, "O! My lord, would to God, some of them which use this argument had no papists in their families, and not otherwise also countenance them, whereby indeed they receive encouragement." James I had the same reaction when people complained about the lax prosecution of recusants, observing that the law would be better enforced if the recusants were not kin or friends of the judges. In case after case, connection and kinship intervened to create a more bearable climate for Catholics than the one officially espoused by church and state. As Antony Milton has observed, this did not mean that magistrates were not Protestants. Their flexibility toward their Catholic neighbors and kin "simply manifested the interplay of different codes of conduct which were not necessarily confessionally driven. Local community values bonded neighbors together, while members of the gentry could feel bound by a code of honor and conduct in which issues of confessional allegiance had no place."[18]

In the Jesuit John Ridgeway's family group, Sir Francis Stonor presents a textbook case of how religious tensions within a family influenced the behavior of a man who was the Escheator of Oxford, Sheriff of Oxford twice, justice of the peace, Member of Parliament, and an important client of Robert Cecil. Almost all his kin were recusants.

His mother, Cecily, had allowed Campion and Parsons to print the *Decem rationes* at Stonor Park. Consequently, she was made a prisoner in her son's home. There, she and her confederates were to see only "Francis, and such other godly and learned persons as he shall think meet . . . to reduce [them] to conformity."

In a typically Elizabethan way, Sir Francis Stonor became the farmer of his mother's lands, which had been seized to pay her recusancy fines. This lease kept the land under family control and generated the income to pay for Lady Stonor's expenses. So her son was her warden, and her financial manager, because of her recusancy. A situation not unlike what would have been done in the natural order of things, since her widow's third was made up of portions of manors that Francis had inherited as eldest son. From 1585 until 1594–5 he was leasing his mother's property for £30 a year, against her debt to the Crown of £340. In 1594 he became Sheriff of Oxford and collector of recusancy fines. Interestingly, his annual lease in following years was reduced to only £18 4s 10d.[19]

Sir Francis' brother fled to the continent and his wife, sister, and daughters were all imprisoned for recusancy, but he was trusted enough to be the sheriff of Oxford twice and a justice of the peace.[20] Clearly his strategy, if not his personal religious conviction, was to protect his kin and his family property by conforming and taking responsibility for their religious error. Head of the family, he could absorb the impact so long as he was trusted by the Crown. Perhaps he was a crypto-Catholic himself, but his conformity allowed him to be a maker and enforcer of the laws.

The Stonors' extended kin network was of a kind familiar to most families of the parliamentary classes. If we add other kinds of connections, such as guilds, companies, colleges, inns of court, judicial benches, patronage, and plain friendship, the picture becomes even more complex, making religion only one of many influential categories. It is necessary to ponder what that diversity might mean for an Elizabethan member of the ruling elite. Did he put these complexities away when he attended the House, served as churchwarden, or sat on the JP's bench? Or did he debate, vote and judge with them in mind?

For most these questions are very hard to answer. Only lawsuits allow us some access to the activities of magistrates, and there is insufficient evidence to show how the House of Commons served as an arena for family experiences of the Reformation. But in a few cases the evidence is less murky. Take, for instance, Francis Alford.

Francis Alford's attempts at moderation in Parliament blighted his career, giving him the reputation of being a papist, though he probably was not, and making it nearly impossible for him to get lucrative patronage despite his powerful kin, like Lord Buckhurst, who tried hard but could not help him. The trouble was, Alford had a family full of Catholics to look after, and he was a civil lawyer, an occupation sympathetic to episcopal administration. The resulting refusal to rush to condemnation of all Catholics and his dislike of Puritans made him suspect.

Francis was the son of Robert Alford, a London citizen and draper, who died in 1546, after writing a pious Catholic will leaving his soul to the Virgin Mary.[21] Robert Alford's children did not share his piety. His eldest son and heir, Roger, who made a career in the household of William Cecil, clearly shared his master's Protestant leanings, and was in some danger in Mary's time.[22] The second son, Francis, always claimed to be a Protestant.

Francis married a recusant *avant la lettre*. In 1562 he espoused Agnes, the widow of Henry VIII's physician, Augustine de Augustinis, a Venetian resident in England since 1529. By this marriage he acquired considerable property, and considerable trouble.

In April of 1582 Agnes Alford was caught hearing mass in their home in Salisbury Court. Secretary Walsingham did not prosecute her, however, simply taking Francis' promise to make her go to church.[23] But her arrest confirmed in the minds of many what had been suspected for a decade.

Alford was branded a Catholic because he had opposed the unreasonable penalties in the bill against Mary Queen of Scots in 1572. By his own reckoning his defense of justice in that Parliament ruined his chances of advancement. In the 1572 debates Alford took a moderate position that haunted him forever after. In the midst of the hysterical reaction to the plots of Norfolk and Mary, when most MP's were calling for blood, Alford called for due process.

First, in May of 1572, he spoke in support of Arthur Hall's right to defend Queen Mary and the Duke of Norfolk in a speech in the Commons. When Hall's speech was nearly drowned out by "shuffling of feet and hawking" Alford called on the members to let every man speak his conscience.[24] His attempt to protect the freedom of debate in the Commons was not appreciated by the House.[25]

In June of 1572 the Commons were debating a petition to the Queen to use the sword of justice against Mary if anyone revolted in her name, and urging that anyone who assassinated Mary be exempted from punishment.[26]

In response Francis Alford "made some scruple of conscience." Beginning with an *apologia* asking that his intentions not be mistaken, he argued that if a rebellion began in England, to which Mary Stuart was not privy, it would be "the greatest injustice in the world" to "lay the pains of treason upon her," "for so she should receive punishment for the offense of another."[27] Further, he argued against licensing anyone to kill an anointed ruler outside the law, especially since Mary was an heir to the throne.[28]

Despite his plea for prudence, the House disliked Alford's speech. Thomas Norton, the rabidly anti-Catholic member for London, spoke after Alford. Even at this distance we can hear the sneering tone he adopted. "The matter," he said, "is greatly mistaken by the gentleman that thus spake." Wicked rulers must be put to death, as the Old Testament demands, and the Queen of Scots was a wicked, treasonous woman, "no queen of ours, she is none of our anointed."[29]

This episode blighted Alford's career, perhaps because his kin associations provided all the extra proof needed that he was a Catholic, but Alford insisted he was a devoted member of the Church of England. As he told Christopher Hatton,

many are the injuries that I have sustained in my time, yet never more have grieved me more than to be charged with the infamy of that sect, which ever I have abhorred from my youth, and whereof I have ever professed the contrary, not without danger of my life even when the flame was hottest ... Neither is there any living that ever heard me defend popish opinion contrary to the public opinion received now in England; or ever heard me silent in the face of a papist, if he defended any of the popes trumperies ... I think my voluntary profession of my faith in open Parliament without compulsion ought to satisfy every honest person.[30]

Although he protests too much, he did strongly support the established church against the attacks of more radical Protestants. In 1571 he spoke against the assault on the Court of Faculties, as a good civil lawyer ought.[31] In a debate over the need for a learned ministry in 1585 Alford expressed his distaste for the democratic enthusiasms of Presbyterian preachers in language that paraphrases his Queen:

We speak much of duty, but we do none. In other countries the sheep are so well taught and are so dutiful they will follow their shepherd through a market town, but our sheep will teach their shepherd, he can not drive them before him, but if one fall a leaping a ditch or hedge, all the rest will follow though they break their necks for it. I like not of these verbal sermons. I dare boldly affirm it, one homily doth more edify than C of these verbal sermons.[32]

In 1587 he defended the clergy against Puritan MPs who denounced them as idle and superstitious.[33]

A friend of the ecclesiastical hierarchy, Alford willingly stood on his record when asking for ecclesiastical patronage. Rehearsing the attempts of laymen to seize church property, he traded on his influence as an MP, reminding the Bishop of Bath and Wells "you ought to have great care to arm yourselves in parliaments," offering his services. Lord Buckhurst, in a letter to the Bishop of St. Asaph, urged him to help his kinsman Francis Alford, "to whom the church hath greatly been beholding, as to one who hath opposed himself against the calumniations of the same in all the parliaments in her majesties time, a thing well known to all the clergy and an action whereby himself hath reaped many displeasures of the adversaries, to his great hindrance."[34]

Alford's dislike of the godly comes through in a letter written at the close of Parliament, probably in the 1580s. He rejoiced in the blunting of the "fanatical humor of the precisian and the puritan most impure."[35]

Francis Alford had to endure the suspicion that he was a Catholic all of his career. But, whether or not Francis himself was inclined to Rome, he was certainly a moderate in religion, a friend of episcopacy, due process and freedom of conscience, and an enemy of the puritanical for the very good reason that the Elizabethan Settlement gave the Catholics in his family some protection. Any anti-Catholic legislation threatened his kin.

In Alford's letter book in the Inner Temple we find hints of how things like bills for coming to church, increasing fines against recusants, and lack of due process for religious dissenters affected his life. In a letter "to have papists delivered out of prison," he petitions that a couple, identified only by initials, imprisoned and deprived of their property for popery, be released to "go home to their house where their children and family remain without guide, putting in sureties for their good and loyal behavior and forthcoming at all times."[36] It appears from the rest of the letter that he is doing this because they are in some way a charge to him, suggesting a family connection.

One lesson to be drawn from the life of Francis Alford is that the religious complexities of his family influenced his behavior as a lawmaker. Certainly any changes in the treatment of recusants hurt those closest to him, and threatened his purse. He had good reason to demand moderation and due process for Catholics. Another lesson is that, although he was suspected of Catholicism and his family was certainly guilty of it, Alford continued to be returned to Parliament. He was not shunned, and, though his prospects may have been damaged, he was not prevented from practicing his profession. The same could be said for Sir Francis Stonor, Robert Atkinson and many, many other members of Parliament.

Perhaps part of the explanation for the refusal of Parliament to enact some of the more radical kinds of reformation proposed to it had to do with the personal *via media* followed by members and peers whose families and friends stood to suffer from any move to the right or to the left. The History of Parliament Trust found that only 74 percent of Elizabethan MPs were assuredly Protestant. Of the rest, about 8 percent in a given Parliament were "Catholics," "Catholics conformed," or known to have close affiliations with Catholics. But every member of Elizabeth's parliaments had Catholic connections, living or dead, forcing them to recognize that no matter how they defined themselves theologically, any strict distinction excluded loved ones and friends, tenants, fellow members of guilds and town governments, other justices of the peace, and even their servants. The Elizabethan polity could only work if these ideological tensions were not allowed to overwhelm the common interests of the various communities to which members of the political elite belonged.

Of course, the shoe on the other foot was Puritan. About 9 percent of the membership of an average Elizabethan Parliament was classified as preferring further Reformation. Naturally, the number of Catholics decreased and the number of Puritans increased over the years, but, clearly, these were men used to living with divergent religious opinions, and ready to ignore them in favor of other consider-ations. Thus Henry Hastings, the Puritan Earl of Huntingdon, was a patron of Robert Brokesby, MP, despite his recusancy.[37] The virtue this class cared most about was loyalty, as Lord Burghley tried to make clear in his apologia *The Execution of Justice in England*.

Ironically, the ability to make common cause for non-religious purposes cynically made religion a convenient way of getting the attention of the authorities. Established as an issue of public order, it lost its theological meaning, becoming a weapon in battles far removed from salvation. The Llŷn recusancy case from Caernarvon demonstrates the ways in which a dispute about honor could be turned into a case about religion.

In 1578 Bishop Robinson of Bangor was ordered to search the house of Thomas Owen of Plas-du, an important and powerful man whose family had connections with Morus Clynnog, rector of the English College at Rome. Ostensibly, Owen, and three other justices of the peace, all of whom were arrested, were in contact with Hugh Owen, Thomas Owen's brother, who was a "runagate" Catholic priest.[38]

At the time of the search, Thomas Owen was at his sister's home in Shropshire — either hiding or visiting, depending on whose story you believe. But when he heard of it, he returned to the county, where he was arrested and imprisoned for six months.[39] Richard Vaughan, the sheriff, tried to get Owen indicted for treason under both the anti-papal Act Against Treason of 1563 and, weirdly, the Act condemning Lollards of Richard II. In order to do this, he attempted misleading the grand jury and forging an indictment, but the justices detected the fraud and threw it out. In righteous indignation, Thomas Owen appealed to the Star Chamber, beginning a long, complicated suit against Richard Vaughan, his brother-in-law Hugh ap William ap Madocke and Richard Owen ap Res Vaughan.

It appears that the trouble had begun in a fight between Thomas Owen and Hugh ap William ap Madocke over a pew in their parish church. In the ensuing feud, ap Madocke and the Vaughans invented the charges against Owen. They claimed he had called England's religion superstition, that he supported Catholics abroad, that he had convinced more than sixty people to stay away from church, and that he denied the royal supremacy. Under oath they could produce no evidence for any of this. They were using a charge of popery to trouble Owen.

The fact that the justices refused to send Vaughan's forged indictment forward speaks volumes about the nature of the county and their understanding of law. Thomas Owen was linked by birth and association with known Catholics, but there was little proof of his treasonous activities, and a great deal of evidence pointing to the use of treason as a charge used to harass and damage him as a part of feud.[40] The justices understood this sort of feuding, and they applied the law, freeing Owen. In this case, they were not blinded by the mere charge.

In practice the communities of England looked less like the New Jerusalem than like confessionally confused commonwealths in which people of varied opinions about ecclesiology and soteriology mixed indiscriminately and used religion when it was convenient. Ignoring confessional divisions on most occasions, people did not see all Catholics as bad, or attempt to disassociate from them. As Anthony Milton observed, the Crown and the laity worked on the practical assumption that most Catholics were loyal and dependable subjects. "Bad papists" certainly existed, but they were alien and exotic, not at all like your "good papist" neighbors, kin, and ancestors.[41]

In the manor of Havering we can see this sort of attitude in practice. The churches at Romford and Hornchurch had, by the late sixteenth century, taken on a distinctly reformed cast. Their church aisles had been replaced with pews, over which the Parishioners argued enthusiastically, and they only rang their bells for national holidays like Elizabeth's accession day. Many among them were Puritans, and three-quarters of the people took communion annually. And yet, though there was a small group of committed Catholics in the community, very few people were reported to the archdeacon as recusants.

Marjorie McIntosh suggests that this tolerance might have been the result of occasional conformity on the Catholics' part, but speculates that the Catholics had the tacit sympathy of the churchwardens and vicars.

She gives an example of the complicated way in which this sympathy played out, telling the story of Thomas Reading, presented in 1596 for failing to attend services. Reading had been living in Havering since 1568, when he had purchased land from the locally important Legatt family. When summoned to appear in court, Reading did not come. Instead, Thomas Hayes, a churchwarden of Hornchurch, appeared on his behalf. Hayes explained that everyone knew Reading was a recusant, since he had been sent to live among them by the Archbishop of Canterbury. Apparently Parker had placed Reading in the custody of his cousin, John Legatt, and he had been living quietly among them for years. This assurance of his place and connection seem to have been sufficient defense. As McIntosh observes, "toleration of quietly Catholic gentry houses" like Thomas Reading's was a common phenomenon in the nation.[42]

That the Elizabethan elites successfully separated pragmatic interests from religious prejudices well enough to run the nation is clear. It is the historians, whose fascination with "recusants" and "puritans" have kept us from seeing what any thinking Elizabethan politician knew: *mediocria firma* was the only way to prevent the collapse of civil society.

At the same time, Elizabethan leaders believed gentle persuasion was more effective than force. Although the fines for recusancy increased across the reign, and although churchwardens were required to file returns of recusants beginning in 1582, most officials were willing to let financial pressure and time bring people into conformity. Today's crypto-Catholic, it was assumed, would produce Anglican children. Tolerating half-hearted resistance was a way of undermining resistance altogether.

Christopher Marsh's study of the Family of Love demonstrates this. The followers of the Dutch prophet HN, the Familists were mystics who outwardly conformed and lived as good neighbors. Although some of the clergy saw them as a threat, many others did not. Andrew Perne, the vice-chancellor of Cambridge and Vicar of Balsham, is infamous for his willingness to adapt to theological alterations. It was a trait shared with most of the establishment, and it had practical implications in his dealings with the Family. His parish had more Familists than any other, but he treated them with gentleness and respect, pursuing a policy of "moderate persuasion." Perne's attitude was widely shared by Elizabethan clerics and the Queen, and, Marsh argues, the ultimate disappearance of the Family of Love occurred because the establishment refused to persecute them.[43]

The refusal of most magistrates and ecclesiastical authorities to systematically and viciously persecute recusants allowed religious minorities to survive and fit in, without pushing them to revolt. This tolerance and neighborliness was the result of their experience of the complexity of everyday life, a willingness to recognize that doing the business of the family and the community required latitude in the enforcement of the state religion at a time when its definition was imprecise beyond its demand for Christian neighborliness.

That there is a pattern of tolerance is confirmed by outbursts of genuine intolerance. Richard Topcliffe, famous for his vicious pursuit and interrogation of

Catholics, was odious to the public. Although he certainly carried out his investigations under orders, his enthusiasm for the job was so appalling that he spent the final years of his life under a cloud. His nephew Edmund changed his name so he would not share in his uncle's reputation.[44]

One did not have to be of the elect to be a good citizen of Elizabeth's England. The answer to the Aristotelean Oxford examination question "Whether a good citizen is a good man," was a resounding "no," if a good citizen had to mean a godly man.[45] As a member of Parliament observed in 1601, "Aristotle saith, a man may be *bonus civis*, but not *bonus vir*; And though I abhor the sin, yet I deny not but a sinner may be a good member."[46]

Conversions

One of the problems besetting historians of the Reformation is the refusal of the people they study to clarify their religion. Sometimes it seems that they had no idea what they believed in. But that is not really surprising. Until 1571 there was no official definition of English Protestantism. The enactment of the Thirty-Nine Articles by Parliament gave the Church of England articles of belief against which identity could be measured, though it was perfectly possible to subscribe to all thirty-nine and still believe the church needed further purification.

By the same token, Catholics, until Elizabeth's 1570 excommunication, had no clear directions about how much conformity was permissible. Although a trickle of Catholic refugees flowed to the Continent in the 1560s, people like Edmund Campion stayed on until the end of the decade, tolerated but unsure of their position. After that, their identity was defined by an external standard – "recusant" is not something they called themselves. Moreover, Catholics had the added confusion of the Council of Trent. After it ended in 1563 continental Catholicism, aggressively formalized and hostile to folk religion, was increasingly different from English popular Catholicism. As we saw in Augustine Baker's memoir, there was a vast confusion over religious identity in the mid-Tudor period. Conforming but lacking in religious zeal, his parents provided no religious education for their thirteen children. "What their children's belief or practice should be, in matter of religion," said Baker, "they heeded not."[47]

Even important members of Elizabeth's government had imprecise ideas about what they were supposed to believe. In 1567 Elizabeth named the earl of Sussex ambassador to negotiate a marriage between herself and Charles of Austria. Before he went, Sussex asked for some help on a vexing point: "as to the question of religion he wished to be quite clear about it before he left, because, although he was a native born Englishman and knew as well as others what was passing in the country, he was at a loss to state what was the religion that really was observed here."[48]

All of this raises the confusing problem of identity and conversion. How did one distinguish the act of conversion ("I did subscribe to A, now I consciously abandon A and subscribe to B") if A and B lacked definition? Is there an easy distinction between believing that one is reforming the church and believing one is converting to a theologically exclusive form of Christianity? Were people certain they had changed religious identities?

In the early years of the Reformation, there was no formal conversion for there were no denominations. The goal of reformers was not denominational success, it was renewal of the one church. It was a widely shared goal, and, though there were many versions of what a renewed and reformed Christian society looked like, it was assumed that the true church was singular, embodying the one truth. Thus in the early 1530s Robert Huick could declare himself convinced by Luther's arguments without declaring himself to be a Lutheran.

John Hooper, writing to Heinrich Bullinger in the 1540s, described his arrival at Protestantism as a dawning spiritual conviction. He did not say "I was a Catholic, I am now a Protestant." Mentioning Zwingli and Bullinger as the two authors who had weaned him from the "evil ways of my forefathers," he speaks of his rebirth into a new life. "Nothing now remains for me," he says,

to the remainder of my life and my last hour, but to worship God with a pure heart, and know my defects while living in this body, since indeed the tenure of life is deceitful, and every man is altogether as nothing; and to serve my godly brethren in Christ, and the ungodly for Christ: for I do not think that a Christian is born for himself, or that he ought to live to himself; but that, whatever he has or is, he ought altogether to ascribe, not to himself, but to refer it to God as the author, and regard everything that he possesses as common to all, according as the necessities and wants of his brethren may require.[49]

He was "born again," not moving from one established doctrinal tradition to another. Living God's will was his objective, not arguing about ecclesiology. There was a simple dichotomy between the "true church," and the "false church," and a desire to correct the false one. This began to change once the "true Church" in England took official form in 1549, changing loose theological consensus into arguments about details.

The "true Church" in England became fractious and factious. Hooper fell out with Archbishop Cranmer about how clergy ought to dress, and, though in the end he was ordained Bishop of Gloucester in full costume, their argument set the tone for the fights among the English religious exiles in Frankfurt, and the disputes over vestments in the 1560s. At the same time, reformed theologians and politicians quarreled over the prayer book, requiring a revised edition in 1552.

By the time Elizabeth came to the throne the debates over the varieties of soteriology among Protestants, with the divide running between Lutherans and

Calvinists, were less important than battles over the form of the liturgy and the structure of church government. It was assumed that in a rightly reformed community proper ideology accompanied proper liturgy and structure, awakening faith in the participants.

Thomas Earle, the vicar of St. Mildred's Bread Street, noted in his commonplace book that the end of the Latin mass in June 1559 was "to all mens comfort except a few of Calvin's church" and "peevish obstinate" papists. By 1564, however, he was one of those that would evolve into a Puritan. His complaints did not center on doctrinal teachings – he seemed content to read the homilies and to perform the prayer book service. His frustration focused on clothes and organization. Although not a Calvinist, Earle was offended that the English church had no elders, could not elect its pastors, and could not discipline the church deacons and servants.[50] People like him wanted a church that had clear definition and discipline. It should not retain anything that smacked of popery, and it should direct behavior.

The English bishops agreed, and the convocation of 1563 produced plans for the necessary reforms of discipline, as well as a set of articles designed to make clear the theological position of the English church on subjects like predestination and the Eucharist. Elizabeth, however, anxious to avoid definition, and certainly angry that the bishops were acting without her direct authorization, prevented Parliamentary action on the bills until 1571. By then, thanks to the Northern Rebellion and the excommunication of the Queen, she was more willing to see them passed. Nonetheless, it remained clear that conformity and obedience made you a good Christian in the eyes of the state. There were no theological tests imposed on the general public by the Elizabethan regime. Catholics occasionally were asked the "bloody question" of whether they recognized the supremacy of the pope, university graduates were expected to accept the Thirty-Nine Articles, and lawyers, MPs and Crown servants might be offered the Oath of Supremacy, but there was no general test. To be Anglican was to be obedient to the Queen and, after about 1570, to take communion every year or so. You could believe as you wished within those constraints.

This means that formal "conversion" was a new choice for the youth of the later Elizabethan period. Invented by clerics, it was something which, though it had political consequences, was about intellectual commitment to a system of argument found to be more persuasive than other systems.

On the July 13, 1597 Adam Winthrop, father of John Winthrop of Massachusetts, noted in his diary that his nephew, William Alabaster *"fatebatur se esse papistam."*[51] "Fancies himself to be a papist" neatly catches the nature of William Alabaster's conversion. Alabaster himself said his conversion was intellectual, caused by reading a book by William Raynolde.[52] An eminent academic noted for this Latin poetry, Alabaster wrote a little pamphlet entitled "The Seven Motives," in an attempt to convert the earl of Essex, his patron, to Catholicism. It was suppressed with rigor, since no copies survive, but the two refutations written at the time give us a good picture of his intellectual religion. His words are those of a professor arguing logic, not those of one whose heart has been infused with newly felt grace:

Such is the practice of the later [Protestant] religion, they teach that nothing is to be credited, but what is warranted in holy books, and give not infallible rules of interpretation, but such as at last must be over ruled by private opinion: for conference of places, propriety of phrase, acceptions [reception] of words, can make no other conclusion than every ones conceit will afford. So that of an infallible proposition, and arbitrary assumption, must needs ensue a dangerous conclusion, though not ever in the matter which is concluded, yet always in the manner concluding.[53]

Alabaster's arguments were effective in at least one conversion.

John Grosse, who had known Alabaster at Cambridge, visited him in prison at Wisbeach. After much argument with Alabaster and two other priests, they gave him a pamphlet "with seven or eight valid reasons for the Roman Church, which having read and closely examined, my fervour and obstinate spirit began to relax." After returning to his inn, Grosse recounted, "I began to recall the arguments and to weigh them on both sides, and having equally balanced them all, I suddenly rose to my feet, and said to myself, 'certainly this is the true religion'."[54]

William Alabaster spent several months in prison for publishing his "Reasons," before fleeing to the Continent. But he was a Papist from intellectual conviction, and that same intellectual enthusiasm got him in trouble with the Inquisition. Dabbling in cabalism, he was detected and arrested. Escaping back to England after a period of house arrest in Rome, he converted back to Anglicanism.

Uncle Adam Winthrop's diary: "Memorandum that on Thursday the 19th of April 1610 Mr. Furdon of Assington told me that Sir William Waldegrave the elder did tell him lately that my nephew William Alabaster was revolted from the popes Religion to our Religion."[55]

Alabaster had blotted his academic copy book, but his ordination was still good, and his family gave him a benefice on the manor where his mother lived.

William Alabaster's old college roommate, who felt compelled to refute Alabaster's motives, took a similarly jaundiced view of the conversion. John Racster summed up William, the academic star, "But we that know him, know the true cause [of his conversion] to be unthankfulness banqueting with lust and ambition: for having always a great deal more then he deserved, and yet desiring still, much more then he had, growing discontent with fulness, he fell at odds with faithfulness."[56]

Unthankfulness banqueting with lust might be the cause of conversion; it was an easy charge to make, but it might more certainly describe conversions from Catholic to Anglican. John Donne's case is a good example, since it so clearly put him on the path to greater rewards. But he described his movement toward Protestantism as a "survey," an intellectual exploration that left him highly aware of the denominational choices in western Christendom. It also left him with irenic skepticism of a sort that demanded he find something that satisfied his own soul.

His third satire is a pointed interrogation of religion, with its insistence that there is a truth but it is not taught by theological factions. "Fool and wretch," he asks,

> Wilt thou let thy soul be tied
> To mans laws, by which she shall not be tried
> At the last day? Oh, will it then boot thee
> To say a Philip, or a Gregory,
> A Harry, or a Martin taught thee this?
> Is not this excuse for mere contraries,
> Equally strong? cannot both sides say so?[57]

Rather than taking instruction from Pope Gregory, or Henry VIII, or Martin Luther the soul must climb the huge hill, cragged and steep, on which Truth stands.

The existence of these denominational truths around the Hill of Truth could not be ignored by people late in Elizabeth's reign. They had choices to make as they struggled, each on his or her own, to reach Truth. Many, however, never started out. They stayed at home and conformed, even though they knew that choices, and even heart wrenching conversions, were possible.

These practical people, who represented most of the population, were like Thomas Egerton, John Donne's erstwhile patron. Born in 1540, Egerton was a Catholic until the beginning of the 1570s. A lawyer educated in Oxford and Lincoln's Inn, he was 30 and beginning a promising career when the Privy Council noticed him. In May of 1569 the Benchers of Lincoln's Inn were informed by the Council that Egerton and a number of others "have misused them selves in contempt of the laws of this realm and contrary to the laws ecclesiastical, partly in not resorting to the church or other place of common prayers, partly in not receiving the blessed communion at times convenient, but contrariwise, using other rites and services prohibited by law." Nor, apparently, had he taken the oath of supremacy.[58]

The Benchers were leisurely in their response, but a year later, in June 1570, Egerton was presented with an ultimatum: either he prove his conformity by bringing a certificate from the Bishop of London, or he would not be called to the bar. Confronted with the loss of his profession, Egerton yielded.[59] He was duly admitted to practice before the bar and began a stellar career. By 1581 he was a governor of Lincoln's Inn and Solicitor-General. In 1592 he became Attorney-General and in 1594 he was made Master of the Rolls. He remained Master of the Rolls while serving as Elizabeth's last Lord Keeper, and King James chose him to be his first Lord Chancellor, an office Egerton held until he died. In his legal capacities he was happy to prosecute recusants, though in 1588 he made a distinction between real traitors and those misled by ignorance and blind zeal. Though he was an implacable prosecutor of Catholics, he reserved much of his wrath for Presbyterians, whose ideas he saw as a threat to the monarchy. Whether Egerton's forced conversion, sweetened by the prospects of a career, was genuine is hard to know. The acerbic Lady Russell once summed him up as a deep dissembler and arrant hypocrite, though he was certainly loyal to the Protestant regime.[60]

But perhaps Egerton felt about his religion as Robert Cecil, Earl of Salisbury, did. After a career as one of the most powerful men in late Elizabethan England, a career spent defending the Elizabethan Settlement against threats from papists and dissenting Protestants, he addressed the question of a politician's religion in his will, made in March 1612. "Because," he wrote,

I would be glad to leave behind me some such testimony of my particular opinion in points of faith and doctrine as might confute all those who judging others by themselves are apt to censure all men to be of little or no religion which by their callings are employed in matters of state and government under great kings and princes as if there were no Christian policy free from irreligion or impiety. I have resolved to express my self and opinion . . .

There follows a clear statement of his personal theology, a theology that helped him walk between the religious extremes. He believed in his heart, he affirmed, the Apostles' Creed, the "*Summum credendum* I have always observed as the best rule of necessary faith and points of salvation." As for the sacraments, he made it clear that he believed in only baptism and Eucharist, and he took the time to spell out his Eucharistic doctrine. He had never, he said, found any evidence of the flesh and blood of Christ in the elements "because god himself hath taught me that flesh and blood availeth nothing with him but the spirit and life." On the other hand, he could not agree with those who took a memorialist position. He knew that he received spiritual nourishment from the elements, which were the body and blood "to all purposes of special nourishment of life and graces," if they were received with faith and penitence. Expressing his desire to receive communion on his death bed, he left fruits of his life as a testimony to his faith.[61]

Cecil spent no time on ecclesiology. He did not express his devotion to the state church. He simply stated his personal theology as a reflection of his soul and conscience. He knew where he stood amongst the competing theologies.

By the 1590s, reform had become conversion, and conversion had become a trope, marking the stabilization of religious demarcations. Conversion of this kind was only possible when people had definition, so that a wishy-washy young poet could shock his uncle by a conversion that could be reversed.

This was a world in which everyone knew that there were alternative religions, and accepted that families might contain diversity. The question of "How should we live now?" had ceased to be about either retaining or reforming a traditional religion.

It was now about choosing from among established varieties and obeying conflicting authorities. It was also a world in which new reasons for cooperation had to be established.

The Imperative to Behave

In his Fourth Institute of the Laws of England the indefatigable jurist Sir Edward Coke summarized the complex twists and turns of Tyrringham's Case. Tried in 1584, it was a wildly complex dispute about what rights belong to an office, in this case the right to firewood. In a classically pedantic mode, Coke noted that in presenting the case arable land should have been mentioned before firewood, since the law liked arable land best. He proved this by citing 4 Henry 7 c. 19, the grandparent of all the pious laws against enclosure and depopulation. But then he took off the robe of the legal pedant and put on the mantle of political economy. He thought preachy laws about the higher good of farming were silly because they did not recognize that self-interest was the key to securing cooperation.

"I have observed," he wrote, "that the most excellent policy, and assured means to increase and advance agriculture, is to provide that corn shall be of a reasonable and competent value; for make what statutes you please, if the plowman has not a competent profit for his excessive labour and great charge, he will not employ his labour and charge without a reasonable gain to support himself and his poor family."[62]

Born in 1552, Coke had entered the Middle Temple just as the Catholic Roper family was being squeezed out. Becoming Elizabeth's Attorney General in 1593, his later career as a judge was stellar, and his legal commentaries became the standard guide to the law for centuries. Coke's disillusionment with old-fashioned moralizing shows how far the Elizabethan view of public virtue had evolved from that of the earlier sixteenth century. Obedience now began with the individual's conception of self-interest defined by conscience.

One of the remarkable features of Elizabethan life is the increasing intolerance of behaviors associated with the festive culture of Medieval society. The title of Ronald Hutton's famous book *The Rise and Fall of Merry England* catches the nature of the change dubbed "the Reformation of Manners." Traditionally historians have placed the blame for this development on the puritanical, but the causes go deeper and are a part of the great sorting of virtue that occurred in the in aftermath of the Reformation. The appearance and guarded acceptance of religious plurality was connected to the rise of the individual conscience as the primary forum in which God worked. This conscience made the individual personally responsible to God, and could, if ignored, draw God's wrath down upon the community. By the 1570s attention was shifting away from communal prayer and practice that won God's favor, toward individual obedience – toward John Bossy's culture based on the Ten Commandments. In turn, this lessened the antagonism toward sins that occurred in communal relations, such as usury, and increased the antipathy toward sins of individual choice that had fewer major social consequences, such as swearing. Ironically, this made the magisterial class increasingly paternalistic as it tried to do its God-given duty of ensuring that each individual behaved in ways pleasing to God.

Of course rationalization does not occur in a vacuum. The explanatory structures of the Elizabethans were being rebuilt not only because of the damage done by the attack on salvation through works. They had to be rebuilt because the economic and social structures of the nation were eroded by the many headed monsters of economic and demographic change. Their options involving money, social status, and virtue were changing.

For those who came to adulthood in the 1520s and 1530s the language of economic analysis was the language of communal duty. Their thought about the economy and society is so distinct that they have been labeled "Commonwealth Men" by historians. Their ideal society was one in which everyone lived as good Christians serving the common good.

This way of looking at the economy and social relations was essentially static. It assumed that things were ordered as they should be, and that disorder was a result of human sin. Mid Tudor proclamations and statutes constantly complained about the hard hearted, stiff necked, greedy people who caused economic and social dislocation, which was a form of divine retribution. The preamble of the Act Against Usury of 1552 catches this belief that social ills are a product of sin:

But forasmuch as usury is by the word of God utterly prohibited, as vice most odious and detestable, as in divers places of the holy Scripture it is evident to be seen, which thing no godly teachings and persuasions can sink into the hearts of divers greedy uncharitable and covetous persons of this realm, nor yet, by any terrible threatenings of God's wrath and vengeance that justly hangs over this realm for the great and open usury therein daily used and practiced, they will forsake such filthy gain and lucre, unless some temporal punishment be provided. . . .[63]

Those who thought this way believed they were returning to the perfection of the ancient Christians. If the church was properly reformed, if the gospel was properly preached, people's hearts would change, and they would stop those sinful actions that destroyed social harmony. The people who believed this were the same who believed that the imposition of the properly reformed prayer book would lead people to see their errors in religion. Commonwealth men were optimistic about human potential, if people were properly instructed and controlled.

The people they were herding toward awareness of their sins were suffering from high inflation and declining real wages. An unprecedented population explosion was driving up the real price of essential goods, too.

Meanwhile, the dissolutions' reallocation of property and the changing economy were producing wealthy people whose power did not match their social positions. The example of the dissolutions, and the rationalizations for taking God's property that they produced, must have had an impact on the way people estimated their economic and social behavior in relation to their community. To see the Crown and lay people greedily snapping up church property, even if justified by higher ideals, must have bred an opportunistic state of mind and a flexible conscience. To acquire a dissolved chantry and close the village school was not an act of piety. Some people tried to expiate their greed with new schools and other gifts, but the example remained negative.

On any level, religious, philosophic, economic, or social Tudor society, by early in Elizabeth's reign, was being run over by the juggernaut of forced change. In the face of it, Elizabethans gathered their political, religious, and economic tools together and attempted to stave off disaster. From religion they appropriated their changing understanding of spiritual anthropology and scriptural authority; from their understanding of economies they took a monetarists conception of inflation, and from politics they took their vast experience with local government and self-regulating institutions. Applying all of these, they reached a new understanding of people's places and duties, of public virtue.

It took some time for these understandings to emerge, however, as the first generation of Elizabethans felt their way away from the commonwealth assumptions, toward new ones that better fit their new perceptions and experiences. Things crystallized in the 1590s, by which time economic behaviors which were aberrant in the 1540s had become natural and virtuous. By then, as Keith Wrightson has observed, the values and relationships of the earlier economic morality had "eroded in their constraining force." The commonwealth had been redefined, Protestantized and secularized at once. The old values were not exactly abandoned, but they had been reshaped to give them force in an altered world.[64]

The history of usury in the post-Reformation era is a good example of how changing religious interpretations came into conjunction with changing economic realities to produce a cultural sea change.

Usury was forbidden by the law of God. From multiple places in the Old Testament, and from Jesus' command to "lend freely expecting nothing in return," the Christian learned that he or she was not to lend money at interest. Aristotle and Thomas Aquinas agreed that money, barren and unable to reproduce itself, could not be charged for the loan of money. Money was like a sandwich. If I borrow your sandwich and do not eat it, it does me no good. If I eat your sandwich I cannot return it. Therefore, to demand interest on money is to ask for something that I cannot pay back. It did not reproduce, and I spent it. Unlike a rented house, I cannot return it for further use. Classical Christian morality, as enshrined in canon law and echoed by the Commonwealth men, held that usury was a form of theft, hated by God. It was assumed that it was practiced only by people who had surrendered their hearts to Satan. Moreover, it did untold social damage. As John Jewel, the first Elizabethan Bishop of Salisbury and the author of the *Apology for the Church of England*, mildly explained, usury occurred "if I lend £100, and for it covenant to receive £150 or any other sum greater than was the sum which I did lend." This was, he said,

such a kind of bargaining as no good man or godly man ever used: such a kind of bargaining as all men that ever feared God's judgement have always abhorred and condemned. It is filthy gains, and a work of darkness. It is a monster in nature, the overthrow of mighty kingdoms, the destruction of flourishing states, the decay of wealthy cities, the plagues of the world, and the misery of the people. It is theft, it is the murdering of our brethren, it is the curse of God and the curse of the people. This is usury.[65]

By the time Jewel wrote those words in the 1560s European conceptions of usury were confused. Since the beginning of the century academics and civil lawyers had been disputing about the conditions, if any, under which money could be lent at interest. The Fugger banking family of Augsburg was supporting Johannes Eck to argue, against Martin Luther, that commercial interest at a moderate rate of 5 percent was not offensive to God. By the middle of the century many Calvinists and Jesuits were beginning to agree, taking the position that the intention of the lender was the key issue, not the effect on the borrower.

Martin Bucer, the Edwardian Regius Professor of Divinity in Cambridge, began his career there with a lecture in which he explained that Christ's charge to lend without expecting return did not apply to loans made with good intentions. Interest charged to support orphans, widows, or students was good, unlike "iniquitous" or "biting" interest that hurt the borrower and damned the lender.

This infuriated John Young of Trinity College, who challenged Bucer to a disputation. Bucer's side was subsequently published. In it he affirmed that no business was possible without lending, and that gain on a loan was proper, so long as it was measured by the rule of conscience. In order to make this argument he drew on recent philological research into Biblical Hebrew, translating the word used for usury to mean "biting." If, Bucer claimed, the loan did not "bite" – it harmed no one – it was licit. Translating Psalms 15, a proof text for the anti-usury forces, he found that where the word "usura" had been used, the phrase "usuram mordentem" should be used. It was a neat humanist finesse of the issue, cutting the Gordian knot of the biblical prohibition by using the latest in etymological research.[66]

Young and most of his colleagues, Catholic or Protestant, did not agree with Bucer on this point. Indigenous English academic and theological opinion continued in a conservative vein, as testified by the Edwardian law against usury and the proposed reform of the ecclesiastical laws made in 1552.

But voices of economic rationality were being raised, nonetheless. Most of them were heard at the counting boards of merchants engaged in foreign trade. They were used to foreign ways, and to dealing in money "on exchange." Richard Clough, one of Sir Thomas Gresham's factors in Antwerp, was urging his employer to remind William Cecil that Parliament should allow lending at interest. He wanted "order to be taken for some reasonable interest between man and man, which I take should be more commendable before God than as the matter is now used."[67] Clough took the position that God's law against usury was best observed if the extortions of pawnbrokers and other lenders were curbed by allowing some interest. He was against total prohibition for the practical reason that prohibition created greater scope for abuse than did regulation.

In 1571 Parliament joined battle on whether or not loans at 10 percent should be permitted. In a complex debate that drew on the full tradition of civil law, humanist linguistics, canon law, and scripture it was concluded that usury was against God's law and was not to be permitted. However, the legal pragmatists among the members insisted that it was useless to prohibit all usury with a blanket condemnation. The result was a distinction between petty usury, at 10 percent or less, and grand usury at more than 10 percent. Both were punishable, but petty usurers would only receive a light slap on the wrist, losing the interest they had taken.[68]

In the end the members of Parliament were unwilling to go as far as their continental brethren. They clung to the Commonwealth position that usury, forbidden by God and manifestly a danger to society, should not be tolerated. The debate, however, shows us that there were theological cracks appearing in the wall of English condemnation.

William Cecil, working out the problem of usury across many folios of spidery notes, recorded the opinions of his learned friends on the subject. Two of them, Sir Nicholas Throckmorton and Dr. Robert Huick, took a position with which Cecil could not agree. They were willing to leave usury to the individual conscience. Throckmorton insisted that "nothing external is evil *nisi quatenus interna actio animi accedit*," so that only evil intention made usury sin. Huick took the position that the circumstances of the borrower determined the propriety of a loan, making it, once again, a matter to be determined by the individual lender.[69]

Usury remained technically illegal for the next 53 years, but in fact the 1571 Act Against Usury, thanks to its creation of petty usury, had set a ceiling for loans that was carefully observed. Ten percent became the standard rate for lending. At the same time, the arguments advanced by Throckmorton, Huick, and Bucer were accepted by more and more people. In the context of the rapid expansion of the English economy it is not surprising that personal experience suggested that the standard of intent and condition should be adopted as the ways of measuring sin.

And since they could only be determined by the lender, many people concluded that usury should only be regulated if it did manifest damage to society.

By late in Elizabeth's reign there were manuscripts in circulation making this argument, to the discomfort of the more conservative churchmen. In one, reputedly written by Walter Howse, we can see that usury was, in his mind, lending in excess of the legal rate with evil intentions. His usury only occurred when the lender was greedy and unwilling to forgive a loan to a person who fell on hard times. The good lender takes no interest unless it is compatible with the common good, and, although he is always careful to assure repayment with a bond or contract, he stands ready to forgive. The proper lender enters into a contract with "this proviso written on the book of the conscience," that he will be bound by God's conditions. Luckily for the capitalists, God was not displeased with loans that profited both borrower and lender.

Critics of this faith in conscience held that a usurer must know he is a sinner because everyone wishes to avoid the reputation of being a usurer. Howse, however, asserted the opposite. Conscience, he says, derives from knowledge, *scientia*. A lack of knowledge can cause errors in conscience, as when a recusant refuses to attend church because he or she cannot do so in good conscience. If a recusant's conscience can be wrong, it is a blind and ignorant conscience, because recusants minds are not fully enlightened by the truth out of holy scripture. And so it is with usury. Those who condemn it do not understand the Bible. God approves of lending at interest so long as the lender's conscience is informed of God's conditions.[70]

By the second decade of seventeenth century, when the late Elizabethans were in power, this move to make usury a matter of intention had come so far that Parliament explicitly cut God out of the consideration of usury, using the law on usury simply as a means to control interest rates in the interest of the national economy. In their analyses, the issues were economic, and the question was whether to use the power of statute to lower the rate from 10 percent to 8 percent, matching the rates charged in Holland. One of the Bacon brothers, either Francis or Nathaniel, launched a move for lower rates in 1606 by arguing that high interest rates are a disincentive to investment in capital intensive ventures, such as draining fens, planting oaks, and sending merchant fleets to sea.[71]

These new arguments about usury appeared during the difficult financial times at the turn of the century when bankruptcy was rampant and creditors were demanding relief. The understanding they had of credit and its role in the economy was light years away from that of the monetarists of the mid-sixteenth century. It had reached a point where most people accepted loans as a normal part of business and understood the relationship between the cost of money and the possible profit from a venture.

The enthusiasm of secular authorities to control sins like usury declined through Elizabeth's years, evidence of the declining authority of the Church and changing ideas of the individual's relationship to God. Calvinist predestination made sinful acts like usury irrelevant theologically—still sin, but only symptoms of a lack of grace. In law Christian moral obligation, a defining force behind medieval legal conceptions of debt and trespass, was being replaced by a more particularistic approach evidenced by the rise of *assumpsit* and action on the case in the sixteenth century. These, argues DeLloyd Guth, mark the replacement of divine mandate as the source of human law by concepts of social utility.[72] In short, when works salvation and purgatory were banished from English pulpits a new ground had to be found to justify social regulation.

The end of the Medieval concept of the economy as a balanced part of the commonwealth is marked in Parliament by the decision of a committee of the House of Commons to rewrite the usury law of 1571. In 1624 they reported out the bill lowering the interest rate to 8 percent with this comment: "the committee thought good to strike out that conclusion in the preamble that all usury was against the law of God, leaving it to be determined by Divines." The Commons, despite fears of capital flight to Italy and Spain, where rates were higher, passed the bill. In the Lords the Archbishop of Canterbury objected that allowing usury was a scandal to religion. And so an amendment was added: "That no words in this law contained shalbe construed or expounded to allow the practice of usury in point of religion or conscience."[73]

Economic behavior, and with it the right of self-aggrandizement, had been officially internalized. Parliament, no longer believing that economic problems were caused by sin, abandoned sin to the individual conscience, and left it to the clergy to form consciences. Law, theology, and economic experience had combined, quite unintentionally, to create a world in which the measure of one's moral quality equated to one's self-contentment. For deeply religious people this state of mind created the intense introspection found in the meditations of Grace Mildmay or in Nehemiah Wallington's huge spiritual diary. For more people this conception of morality did not send them to their closets to check their consciences; it sent them into the world with lighter consciences.

We can see the same pattern in the way people thought about enclosure, the practice, so hated and denounced by mid-Tudor moralists, of turning arable land into sheep pasture. It was assumed to dispossess farmers, create vagrants, drive up the price of food, and damage the commonwealth. But by the 1580s this assumption was being questioned. Enclosure, after all, was a form of economic improvement, and improvement was emerging as a desirable end.

In 1593 Parliament repealed the anti-enclosure statutes, which, as Justice Coke had noted, had been accreting since the time of Henry VII. The disastrous harvests of the mid-1590s followed, and people reached for the traditional explanations of dearth, blaming the greedy, so the statutes protecting tillage were revived in 1597. However, the new idea that self-interest was a better regulator than prohibitions of sinful behavior was taking hold. As Henry Jackman, a London merchant sitting for Wiltshire, noted in his diary, "Men are not to be compelled by penalties but allured by profit to any good exercise."

Pressure built for the repeal of the anti-enclosure laws across the first two decades of the seventeenth century. Sir Walter Raleigh explained the logic of the repeal when he pointed out that although there was dearth in some places, others had surplus, and that it was easier to buy the surplus than try to subsidize uneconomical farms. The Netherlands, always the economic model for these men, grew almost no corn; it simply imported it. Raleigh drew the moral: "And therefore I think the best course is to set it a liberty, and leave every man free, which is the desire of a true English man."

By the 1620s the practice of agriculture had changed so much that the 1563 legislation protecting tillage was, like the law against usury, abandoned by Parliament. Like usury, it had ceased to be a problem, unless the enclosers deprived others of their lawful rights. This new state of mind abandoned the traditional hierarchy of uses of property. The law no longer preferred cultivation over other uses. Thus the fens could be drained, displacing thousands of people, with the excuse that improving the lands would increase revenue. Improvement was the watchword of the day.

These legal changes chart the alterations in the underlying cultural assumptions experienced by the Elizabethans. The post-Reformation generation inherited a shattered set of values, a world patched together by the ad hoc responses of their parents to psychological and fiscal blows of the Reformation and rapid economic and demographic change. The younger Elizabethans developed from this a significantly different moral economy from that of their progenitors.

Shattering the old ethical world created great opportunity. As Keith Wrightson observes, the shifts in definition and the changes in priority "bred ambiguities and tensions which were resolved in several ways. For the most part they were resolved by expediency in the day-to-day conduct of economic affairs." In a world with alternative acceptable opinions, people, logically, chose those interpretations that best suited their self-interests, adjusting to the changing norms of a competitive economic environment with the help of a theology that gave conscience primacy.[74]

But in the midst of the liberalizing economy, there came a fear of the choices people make when free. The fear of disorder that had prompted the mid-sixteenth-century magistracy to patch and mend their commonwealth to prevent civil war led their children to an obsession with their personal sins. That same Parliament of 1624 which finally liberalized the laws on usury and enclosure succeeded in enacting another agenda, the prohibition of swearing and cursing. Where once usurers and greedy engrossers of arable land had been the wrack of the commonweal, the profane oaths of the drunken and lascivious person now stood. The improver could get on with making the nation more profitable without fear of God's wrath, but woe betide the nation that tolerated people who put on fancy ruffs, drank deep and exclaimed "God damn me!", breaking the peace of the Sabbath.

Like so many of the social agendas of the Elizabethans, we can find the origins of this one among the Edwardian reformers who desired to create a godly community which governed itself by scriptural principles. In late 1551 the select committee drafting new ecclesiastical laws took a stern view of personal behaviors which had always before been minor offenses handled by church courts, if at all. Notably, their draft contained a prohibition of blasphemy in the strongest terms, treating blasphemers as equivalent to heretics. In it, those who swore were muzzled with a shilling fine to the poor box and the shame of standing bare headed while the homily was read, confessing they had abused the sacred name of God.[75]

There was an attempt to revive this discipline in Parliament in 1559, and in the Convocation of 1563 extensive discussions took place about discipline. The last attempt to revive it was made in 1571, when Thomas Norton, John Foxe, and other evangelical colleagues sought to reintroduce the 1552 code, only to be tripped by members who were intent on attacking the prayer book.[76]

Two homilies against swearing were in included in the 1562 book of homilies and read to Elizabethans ever after. These concentrated on unnecessary oaths and on perjury, taking as their texts Malachi 3:5 and Zechariah 5:3–5. In Malachi it is announced that God will be a "swift witness and a sharp judge upon sorcerers, adulterers, and perjured persons." Zechariah says that God's curse will fall on falsehood, false swearing, and perjury, destroying the house of the false man. Although the passage from Zechariah might imply some communal doom, the homily did not interpret it in that fashion. It only promised individual doom for those who swore false oaths.[77]

Because Parliament never ratified the reformed ecclesiastical law, the stricter discipline desired by the clergy was never enforced. Blasphemy, along with drunkenness, was left to the church courts, and to local authorities. In the little commonwealths of Elizabethan parishes and towns, devout Protestant leaders, led by their consciences and their reading of scripture, attempted to create their own discipline by controlling local offenses against the majesty of God.

Of course the root cause of regulation was the perception that order was threatened. But was order threatened by the evil act itself, or by the anger the act engendered in God? Clearly, order was a product of divine blessing, and actions which offended God, making the community impure, had negative social consequences.

This state of mind is well documented among the people who moved to New England to create their godly commonwealth in Massachusetts, and it is epitomized by the people described in David Underdown's *Fire From Heaven*, but it first appeared in political action in the 1570s. It was a product, in these early instances, of committed Protestant magistrates whose social attitudes were formed in the chaotic 1550s. They had absorbed the evangelical commitment to the creation of godly communities, along with a healthy conception of their divinely ordained duty. Their theology justified their political actions, and their political actions were responses to the rapid changes occurring around them.

The Reformation of Manners was nothing new, in terms of the ways in which English communities responded to increases in poverty, demographic redistribution, and economic change. It was a local response. It did not occur everywhere, it often lasted for a short time when it did occur, and its enforcement was often haphazard. But it was fashionable among Elizabethans, and many of its tenets became statute law in the early seventeenth century.

One of the things that makes the Elizabethan enthusiasm for moral reform different from its predecessors is that the Reformation had welded the spiritual arm to the secular arm. The ecclesiastical law of the Roman church had always, with biblical precedent, attempted to control blasphemy, fornication, and a wide range of social crimes. Because it did, the state did not. The Reformation, however, broke down the barrier between the two systems, as churchwardens and local magistrate shared common duties.

This is especially apparent in the towns where the acquisition of monastic and chantry property gave aldermen control of the local ecclesiastical machinery. They nominated to advowsons, appointed chaplains, hired preachers, set up lectures (or refused to fund lecturers), and took responsibility for the moral climate in ways unheard of when the abbots ruled.

In Bristol, for instance, about 10 percent of the population took part in government, but most of the power fell to the much smaller elite that controlled the corporation. They imposed and administered regulations, levied and collected taxes. With the Reformation this group took on religious duties, too. As David Sacks has observed, "To a degree perhaps not reached again until the creation of the welfare state, they oversaw the lives of the citizenry from cradle to grave."[78]

One of the results of this fact of local life was that the conception of a magistrate's place in the world changed. By the late sixteenth century the image of the mayor as the king's vicar and first among equals had been altered. As the preacher of Bristol, Thomas Thompson, redefined the magistracy, it became a Christian *exemplum* of civic virtue, living God's law by grace, endowed with practical understanding of worldly affairs, it was expected to use that understanding wisely and well.

Thompson propounded the principal duty of the magistrates, keeping order. Citing the Book of Judges, Thompson reminded them that before there was a king in Israel, there was anarchy. The mayor and aldermen were to act as the kings in their little Jerusalem, scattering the wicked and judging the poor. Their failure to accept these responsibilities would bring ruin to their city and the commonweal. The very prayers prayed over the magistrates stressed their duties to God, rather than their duties to their fellows citizens.[79]

And what were the magistrates to worry about? In 1579 Edward Bicknoll confronted an essential paradox. The world, he, he opined, was "lying sick of age," for never was there a time so wicked, foul, filthy, nasty, and loathsome: "yet we say, we be clean and wholesome," enjoying the freedom of the Gospel. How could this paradox of sinful England living in the light of the gospel be explained? He expatiated:

This complaint as it may truly be made in divers respects, so specially in this, that God's most glorious name is not hallowed nor honoured, but vainly used, terribly abused, & blasphemed most outrageously. Some faults against the second table, because they concern the common wealth, are somewhat dully executed, nay I dare boldly say that laws for hawks eggs, for coveys of partridges, and yes of pheasants, are with much diligence observed and looked unto: (and good cause that so they should). But this that concerneth Gods honour, and the glory of his majesty, this whereof God hath given a special charge, whereunto God hath annexed his terrible threatening, this commandment of the first Table, concerning the reverence of God's own name, is (fie for shame) too much neglected.

He begs his dedicatees, the educators Alexander Nowell, John Mullens and John Walker, to promote His Glory.

Namely, and most specially . . . that some strength of law earnestly be . . . established for punishment of vain swearing, and for the utter cutting off of forswearing or perjury. The discommodities of the outrageous excess in apparel breedeth much more woe then many deems for: drunkenness is a deathful disease, & it dismaketh a man, so that he ceaseth to be that he was: But this vice concerneth not man so much as God: No tongue can utter, no pen can express, no mortality can conceive the sinful wickedness, the dishonor unto God, the mischief and misery unto mankind, that groweth thereby. . . ."[80]

Bicknoll in this preface laid out the basic issues that would come to dominate thoughts about the legislative control of sin. The protection of the Commonwealth was a secular issue, which made protecting the nation from God's wrath similar to protecting it from a Spanish invasion. It became increasingly important that magistrates protect God's honor lest He rain pestilence, famine, war, and recession on England.

Edward Hutchins lectured the justices, magistrates, and jurors at the Chester assize in 1586 on the clear connection between their duty and God's expectations. The people must be brought to order by the joint operation of pulpit and bench: "the minister by the Word, the magistrate by the sword; the one by love, the other by fear; the one by softness, the other by sharpness; the one by persuading, the other by punishing, if that persuasion may not prevail."[81]

Hutchins was admitting that, once freed from "superstition," the people had not become pure; they had descended into license, anarchy, and "freedom," becoming a threat to well ordered society. The secular causes for this feeling are not far to seek. The rapid population increase was flooding the nation with young people, and the many of the urban areas were experiencing unprecedented growth. The high spirits of a young population combined with the disruption of traditional patterns of social control threatened the peace. For late Elizabethans the results of economic and demographic dislocation called forth a political response explained in religious terms.

The local leaders applied their religiously informed conception of the problem through law, making it the duty of the state to ensure that God's honor was kept intact. What was unusual about their response was that these crimes against God's honor were secularized and made into statute law for the nation.[82]

By late in Elizabeth's reign the national sensitivity to the sins of blasphemy, to the once petty crime of swearing oaths, and to the problem of drunkenness had increased along with the general concern about personal conduct. In the church courts a new offense was created: "common drunkenness." It had been punished by the Church before but the civilians expanded prosecutions, believing they had the right to regulate offenses not preempted by Parliament. The drunkard in the 1562 homily was construed as harming his or her own soul with gluttonous behavior. By late in the reign the drunkard was construed as a threat to the community and prosecutions for swearing began to increase. The episcopal act books contain many *ex officio* cases against people like the man from London who in 1599 was described as "a blasphemer of the name of God a common brawler and a sower of discord among his neighbors."[83]

Traditionally, such offenses were punished by the church with public shaming. In 1591 an Essex man was forced to do penance for being drunk "in service time." He had to sit in the church porch with three empty pots and a white wand before him until the second lesson, when he was to come into the church and read a statement of his crime written by the minister.[84]

But the church courts were not effective enough to solve the problem of disorder so local authorities began to take action on their own. In 1606 Mayor Coldwell of Norhampton proposed to the aldermen that the ale houses should be off-limits to the inhabitants, on pain of a fine of 3s 4d and imprisonment. Moreover, no swearer, curser, drunkard, or idle person was to be eligible for public relief. The aldermen approved his proposal, so "all profaneness, dicing and carding, drinking fled clean out of the freedom of the town." This zeal for the town's good paid off, reported Richard Rawlidge, because "whereas the plague had continued in the said town above two years together, upon this reformation of the Magistrates the Lord stayed the judgment of the pestilence. . . ." The ban was so beneficial that the town petitioned for and received the right to extend it two miles beyond its boundaries.[85]

The limits of blaspheming were extended like the Northampton ban. If swearing and drunkenness offended God and brought the plague, then all offensive swearing had to be stopped. Which ever came first, the ale or the oath, it was the magistrates' duty to prevent it. George Downame developed a list of the sorts of oaths that had to be forbidden, amounting to a ban on all emphatic ejaculations.

Childish oaths, such as "bodkin, lakin, by cock, by my fey," were forbidden, because they are used in place of God's glorious name. God was mocked by them. Swearing by creatures, as "by the sun," is forbidden. Swearing papistical oaths, as by the angels, the saints, the rood, the mass, or by relics, is forbidden. As are blasphemous oaths on parts of Christ's body which, if they proceed from superstitious ignorance, are idolatry.

Queen Elizabeth herself was guilty of offending the Almighty with oaths, swearing by the mass, and often by God, by Christ and by many parts of Christ's body, and by saints, faith, troth, and other things. In 1585 William Fuller dared to tell the Queen that her swearing was an evil example to her subjects, encouraging idolatry.[86]

Apparently Elizabeth did not use the last class of forbidden expressions of emphasis, heathen oaths. Scholars, says Downame, affecting Latin elegance, use in their orations and exercises expressions such as "aedipol, mehercule, per Iovem immortalem," robbing God of his glory by bestowing it on idols.[87]

But the point to Downame, Fuller, and dozens of others was that "we must not only reform ourselves, but also those who are under our government." Magistrates and householders had to eradicate the leprosy of swearing and drunkenness "because where any one enormous sin reigns in any member of a society, which is not suppressed and reformed, or at least corrected and sharply punished, that sin will bring God's vengeance and fearful judgements, not only upon the offender, but also upon the whole body of that society."[88]

The old Queen may not have stopped swearing (one can hear her declaring "by God's teeth I will not!") but the reformed concept of magisterial duty had been internalized by the time she died. The first legislation that linked swearing and drinking to the national good appeared in Parliament in the sessions of 1597–8 and 1601. More and more of it appeared over the length of King James' reign, as legislators strove harder and harder to bring the law of the nation into line with the commandments of God.

The *raison d'être* of all the attacks on drinking and swearing is visible in the 1601 bill against "blasphemous swearing." The preamble of the bill noted that it had pleased God to bless England with the Queen's government for 43 years. In this "blessed time" God had taught people to know not only the grossest sins, "but to make a conscience of the smallest sins, whereby God is dishonored." Having learned from the scriptures that no greater offence could be committed against God than blaspheming his name "by ordinary and customable outrageous oaths," the authors had found "this offence of ordinary swearing to be grown very common, in all places and persons, to the dishonor of his holy name, the contempt of his law forbidding such blaspheming, and to the just provocation of his wrath and indignation to be poured upon us, and the whole land." God had promised "that his plague shall never depart from the house of the swearer."

In order to turn away divine wrath the bill ordered that two or more JPs, in consultation with a minister, could punish habitual blasphemers with fines and prison terms.[89]

Committed and rewritten, this bill lost some of its piety. "Blasphemous swearing" became "usual and common swearing" in the title and the preamble simply stated that taking God's name in vain was a high sin against God's majesty, provoking His wrath against persons and places by whom and where it took place. Gone were the references to God's blessings, to the "schoolhouse" of religion, to consciousness of sin.[90]

The debate over this bill, which eventually passed the Commons only to be killed by prorogation, revolved around the problems of who should have jurisdiction over the punishment of swearing, the clerical courts or secular courts Some, such as Edward Glascock, took the traditional position that swearing was an ecclesiastical matter, of concern to the soul rather than the body and so fitter to be "spoken in a pulpit than in a Parliament," preferring it to be left to conscience. Nonetheless, Glascock did recognize that swearing threatened the nation: "If the God of Abraham, the God of Jacob and the God of Isaac hath sworn (that) his plague shall not depart from the House of the Swearers why should not we seek to repress this vice which brings a plague, which breeds mortality, that breeds destruction, desolation, and the utter ruin of the Commonwealth?"

But what would convince people to refrain from swearing? Not a ten shilling fine. And swearing did not belong to the secular jurisdiction. Glascock went on to attack the corruption of Justices of the Peace, arguing that the effect of laws against drunkenness, swearing and church attendance, would be to enrich the justices not to stop the sin.[91]

Glascock, born in 1577 and possessed of an MA from Cambridge, was a lawyer, with a lawyer's awareness of the difficulties of enforcing vague laws. Moreover, Glascock was hostile to Puritans. But he shared in the common assumption about why God punished Protestant nations. He had the analytical approach of the English Protestant.

In the shires the Reformation of Manners, which included attacks on Sabbath breaking and sexual incontinence, both of which arose from drinking, continued wherever the local gentlemen saw it to be their duty. In North Cadbury the parish received a windfall in the early 1590s when Francis Hastings left them £20, on the condition that they never again profane the Sabbath with a church ale. These fundraisers, he observed, abused God's creatures in drunkenness and riot, corrupting the youth with games of wanton lasciviousness. The parishes of South Cadbury and Maperton received lesser bribes to do the same.[92]

The problem was, as Francis Hastings understood, that the parishioners had to be willing to cooperate. His executors were instructed to extract a promise from the people of the lucky parishes to observe his ban on church ales. It was their free choice in this case. But because they might choose the wrong way, those who wanted to control drinking needed the weapon of law.

The Reformation of Manners was not well received in many places, and in most the evils predicted were less frightening than the social dislocation that an attempt to stop swearing, drinking, and Sabbath recreation would cause. The hatred of the sin was great, but the individual sinner was, if not loved, at least tolerated. As in the case of known Catholics, community standards of tolerance often determined the limits of enforcement.[93]

In Colchester in Essex Richard Smith has identified patterns in the shifts of the religious wind by looking at the prosecution of certain offenses. His work clearly indicates that early in Elizabeth's reign staunch Calvinists took control of the town and began hunting fornicators and other sinners with enthusiasm. But by the 1570s many of the townspeople had been alienated by the uncharitable actions of their godly magistrates. When John Lone, a prominent mariner, was arrested and imprisoned for adultery with the wife of his business partner, a popular backlash began. Lone and his paramour were imprisoned for a week and then carted through even the poorer areas of the town. This high-handed treatment of a prominent businessman and a gentlewoman struck at the hierarchy that held the town together. It was the last straw for many, and a libeling campaign began that ended with the expulsion of some godly aldermen from the borough government. Ironically, the result in Colchester was the establishment of a Protestant social program that recognized the importance of maintaining the social hierarchy. The town created fornication juries to hear cases like Lone's, preventing more embarrassing episodes by this mechanism. And the godly party never again got control. By the 1590s this middling approach to change so frustrated the radical reformers that Separatism began to appear in the town.[94]

Out of these examples we can see a new civil virtue evolving. It demanded a citizenry voluntarily obedient to God and zealous in protecting God's honor. At the same time, it demanded a magistracy willing to make people protect God's honor in defense of the nation, while honoring local concerns. The end result was a stronger and more invasive magistracy with greater concern about personal behaviors, and less concern about economic behaviors. Importantly, this left the parameters of civic virtue to the local communities most of the time, so that it was enacted and lived locally.

The negotiation of these community standards was always highly dependent on personalities and conditions, so that in some places "culture wars" erupted, but the one thing they had in common was localness. The Reformation crises had been weathered in different ways by different communities, and Elizabeth's government allowed parishes, towns and other institutions the latitude to reach their own solutions. By the beginning of James' reign, however, the power of the state was being used to give some parties an edge over others. This would destroy the pragmatic flexibility of the Elizabethan Settlement, just as the local responses it spawned were hardening into custom.

Still a profoundly religious society, the English were not yet ready to leave God out of the law, but God had removed himself through double predestination. Sinful acts, symptoms of reprobation, were still punished, but punished because they were dangerous to society, not because individual souls were at stake. The law was no longer needed to herd people toward individual salvation, but the magistrates still had the duty to protect the commonwealth from reprobates.

7

Learning Private Virtue

"The conscience of a Christian," said Bishop George Downame, "is exempted from human power, and cannot be bound, but where God doth bind it." His 1608 Paul's Cross sermon upheld a vision of a Christian conscience exempt from the laws of men, both ecclesiastical and civil. "Neither," he claimed, "is simple obedience due unto them, neither can they make an particular, which in respect of moral law, is indifferent . . . to be simply necessary."[1] Formerly Professor of Logic at Cambridge, Downame was making yet another attempt to explain the conundrum first propounded by Martin Luther in his treatise "On the Freedom of a Christian." Luther posited that a Christian is totally free, servant of none; and yet is totally bound, a servant of all. Freed of the civil and moral law by Christ's blood, he, in loving freedom, voluntarily serves the neighbor he loves as himself.

It was a beautiful image of the freedom that comes with faith, but it was a very difficult message to turn into rules for living. Downame concluded his sermon by demonstrating that Christians must freely obey their divinely appointed monarch, but not everyone reached the same conclusion. Many took their freedom more literally, and felt bound only by God's law in scripture, so that bishops like Downame had to keep explaining how conscience limited one's actions by freeing them. It was a basic contradiction inherent in the Protestant theology they had learned as children.

The Edwardian regime was the first in English history to attempt the religious education of its young. The Prayer Book of 1549 contained a catechism, and the Primer of 1553, reprinted by Elizabeth in 1560, contained explicit directions for the education of children. Together, the catechism and primer were to teach children their duty to God, country, community and parents, living "every one in his office, according to their vocation and calling."[2] Before confirmation every child was to be examined on his or her knowledge of the catechism.

Invented on the continent in first flush of the Reformation, these tools were used across Europe to ensure that the next generation grew up believing the right things. In England in the 1560s, the first, simple, catechism began to be embroidered and stretched by the new ecclesiastical leaders to counter the threat of continued Catholicism. The royal Injunctions of 1559 ordered catechizing done every other Sunday before evening prayer, on Sundays when there was no sermon, and on holy days; by 1563 there were demands that the catechism be taught more frequently, and that adults be examined, too.[3]

The Elizabethan church produced several educational tools. John Jewel wrote his *Apology*, justifying the Anglican Church in 1560. Articles of faith were proposed in 1563 that became, after political misadventures, the Thirty-Nine Articles defining Anglican belief. The Book of Common Prayer was translated into Latin, for schools, and Welsh, for Wales. A new, extended, catechism, written by Dean Alexander Nowell of St. Paul's in 1562, explained the beliefs and expectations of the church to the young. Nowell's *Catechismus Puerorum* was an ambitious expansion of the prayer book catechism, designed to introduce Calvinist doctrine to England's youth. Although never officially approved by the Crown, it was quickly translated into English and achieved semi-official status.[4]

This textbook made it clear that obedience to God and the prosperity of the state were intimately linked, emphasizing duty to God, the monarch, the clergy, school masters, masters, parents, elders, and social superiors. Youngsters were to obey anyone to whom authority was given by God, since all authority comes from God. These authorities are all constituted by God for the single purpose of disciplining peoples' minds, which are naturally puffed with pride. Magistrates, therefore, had a heavy duty to God. They had to be 'fatherly correctors' of the people.[5]

But there was a worm in the apple of obedience. The students were taught that ultimate authority came from God and was registered in conscience. In which case, conscience, as directed by Bible reading and prayer, had a greater authority than magistracy. This created a dichotomy in Elizabethan culture that could not be easily resolved.

Sir Thomas Wilson unwittingly set out the problem in his popular logic textbook, first published in 1563. His syllogisms were brutally propagandistic, meant to teach young Protestants how to think correct thoughts. But in them we sense the tension between obedience and conscience plaguing Elizabethans.

As an example of a perfect universal affirmative argument, "Barbara," he provides this:

Bar – All honest things are to be embraced.
Ba – All Christian laws made by Christian magistrates are to be embraced.
Ra – Therefore all Christian laws made by a Christian magistrate are to be embraced.

Next, he provides syllogisms that demonstrate the no one who contradicts a magistrate is a good Christian. But then he provides a syllogism under the form of "Caesare":

> Cae – No just man before God has an unquiet and doubtful conscience.
> Sa – All they that trust to be justified by their works have unquiet consciences.
> Re – Therefore none trusting to his works, is just before God.[6]

To follow one's conscience contravened the demand that one obey the Christian magistrate without questioning. It was an almost irreconcilable contradiction, made worse by the rejection of rational faith. In deed-oriented piety, virtue could be defined by outward signs. Protestant election made those signs impossible to interpret, their quality depending on invisible grace. The result was a search for emotional assurance "in conscience" that one was leading the virtuous life of the elect.

By the time the first generation exposed to these contradictory values came into influence in the 1570s, it was wrestling with the problem of identifying, promoting, and maintaining Protestant virtue and morality.[7] Out of their wrestling emerged new "habits of thought" which had profound implications. The first post-Reformation generation created and used these habits to make sense and decisions, and in that making they produced an English Protestant culture. Like their grandparents' culture, it remained profoundly connected to God, but its ways of thinking, its very epistemologies, made sense of experiences in ways alien to its forebearers. Often contradictory within themselves, they were fighting to preserve the religious values that had produced the Reformation. In the process, the individual soul replaced the church as the point of contact between God and humanity, knowledge of this world became distinct from knowledge of God, and history became the record of human activity, not Divine activity, even while particular events were often given cosmological import. At the same time, sacral monarchy came to be both more important and more human, the monarch's soul functioning as the national soul, making the ruler both less and more accountable. These impulses were often contradictory, signs of a society in the process of rapid cultural adaptation.[8]

It fell to the generation born in the 1540s and 1550s to lay the foundations of Elizabethan culture.

A child of the 1540s, Richard Greenham came up to Pembroke Hall, Cambridge in the first class of Elizabethan students. He arrived about the time Edmund Grindal, freshly returned from exile, was elected Master of Pembroke. Before his exile Grindal had been President of Pembroke for many years, and his return to his old college gave him a chance to create the Protestant clergy that he, as Bishop of London, knew were desperately needed. Greenham was one of the young men shaped by Grindal's agenda. He was trained to evangelize the darker recesses of the realm.

In Greenham's case this meant Dry Drayton in Cambridgeshire, where he attempted to create a Christian community on the new model. He went to Dry Drayton to teach the gospel and unify the community. Preaching six times a week, catechizing every Thursday, and counseling those troubled in conscience when they needed it, he was a model pastor. Because he was, people collected his advice. From his "Commonplaces," we get a picture of the problems faced by this first generation of Elizabethan clergy as they struggled to create a new world of habitual Protestantism.

The "Commonplaces" start in 1581, by which time Greenham had been active for a decade. They show a parish in evolution, unsure of itself and how it was expected to behave in the new dispensation.

For instance, traditionally, Christians were expected to abstain from flesh during Lent. Early Protestants had made it a mark of their faith that they openly ate meat during Lent, rejecting its as a superstitious "work." However, Queen Elizabeth annually ordered Lenten abstinence. Greenham's parishioners were confused. He resolved their confusion by explaining that eating or not eating flesh was not the issue. The state of one's conscience was the issue, since Satan could take advantage of those who abstained as easily as those who did not. Abstemious or not, they had to keep a clean conscience[9]

Asked if a person might "go to a place where some ungodly thing is so that our purpose be to breed a greater detestation of that wickedness in our hearts," he said no. Going to plays was not good, even if one's purpose was to "cry out against idolatry." The weakness of our flesh makes it probable that we would fall into the sin if we were in its presence.[10]

But what if one must be in places where there were plentiful occasions for sin, such as the court? Greenham said "although thou have occasion to sin, yet the cause of sin is still in thy self." Therefore, even if they did not have the strength to profess their religion publicly, they must still strengthen themselves by secretly frequenting the exercises of the Godly.[11]

As a preacher he was frustrated by his congregation's hardness of heart, but he reminded his students that preaching the law of God was directing men to Christ. "For," he said, "by the law I drive men out of themselves and send them to Christ if they will, but if they refuse to go worthily to Hell, and so to those whom he could not be the messenger of salvation for their unbelief, unto them he was an instrument of condemnation prepared for them."[12] In short, he could awaken the need for Christ that demonstrated election in those God wished to save.

But Greenham, though accepting the doctrine of predestination, still had to worry about the consciences of his parishioners. What did one say to those tempted with unbelief? You told them to pray to God for help, and then go about daily business knowing that their prayers and the Word worked as seeds in their hearts. Above all, they should never try to defeat to Satan by strength of will. That is the opening

Satan seeks. The troubled mind must rest in Christ, comforted by the certainty that its discomfort was proof of election.[13]

As Greenham knew, rites of passage often produced generational tensions between those with older ideas about religious proprieties and those with more reformed ideas. This was especially true in the rituals of death. Prayers for the dead were deeply ingrained in English culture, as was the idea of a trental or "month-mind" and "year mind," when services were held in honor of the departed. Provisions for obits, month-minds and prayers for all Christian souls remained common in wills into the 1570s, to the irritation of the Protestant clergy. Bishop Pilkington of Durham listed the offending customs, including singing, ringing, trentals, years' and month-minds, doles in the name of the dead, watching the corpse, and funeral banners.[14]

Richard Greenham confronted this problem gently, saying that whatever was not flatly commanded or plainly forbidden in the word, might sometimes be allowed "for the maintaining of love and some times be left undone for the avoiding of superstition." His general rule was that all things should be done decently, without profane disregard for the body or superstition. Even the praying could be left out of a funeral, but scripture reading was necessary. Clearly, he was not suggesting toleration of the things Pilkington condemned, but he was not simply imposing his ideas on his parishioners, either. Like St. Paul, he understood the necessity of milk for babes in these moments of stress.[15]

Points of ritual were also teaching opportunities. Once, when a person, who had not himself been catechized, brought his child for baptism, Greenham asked him if he was sorry he had not been taught? And was he sorry for his offenses known and unknown? And would he promise to be catechized so his child could be brought up in godliness? What was the man to do? Say no, and have his child refused baptism?[16]

Greenham was performing the pastoral art of teaching and leading, gently goading while recognizing the nature of the human animal. He taught the aspiring ministers who walked out from Cambridge to observe him to combine the carrot and the stick in order to awaken in their parishioners a sense of election, and to purge them of their bad habits. Slowly, he was sure, they would amend. As Eric Carlson has observed, Greenham, with his experimental pastoral theology, managed to keep his parish working harmoniously for twenty years.[17] It was twenty years of slow evolution, during which time a generation died and the children he catechized grew up as Protestants.

Greenham was modeling the new Christian commonwealth and ministry for his students and his people, slowly massaging Protestant ideas into the culture. Meanwhile, Protestant intellectuals were constructing Protestant ways of knowing and living the virtuous life.

Back when Robert Joseph had his novices at Evesham reading Terrence's *The Eunuch* and Sir Thomas More's *Utopia* was still a novelty, it was assumed that humanist learning could be combined with Christian faith to renew and reform the

Church. It had not occurred to Erasmus and More that they were launching something that might bring down the Church instead of remodeling it. Their aim was to restore primitive religion, recover the proper meaning of the Bible, and reform the Christian community. They were at odds with some of their scholastic colleagues about the value of a traditional arts education, with its emphasis on dialectic and Aristotle, because they insisted on individual virtue as the foundation of good order.

These Erasmian concerns were widely shared in English intellectual circles, so it was not a particularly Protestant move when Thomas Cromwell sent visitors to Oxford in 1535 to purge the University of antiquated philosophy, attempting to replace it with modern learning in divinity, philosophy, moral law, natural law, Latin, and Greek. Richard Layton informed Cromwell that the philosopher Duns Scotus was being expunged: "We have set Dunce in Bocardo [the Oxford jail], and banished him Oxford forever." His books, "now made a common servant to every man," were nailed up in the privies for toilet paper, or sold for scrap.[18]

As Duns Scotus was dismissed, the intellectual fashion turned toward Greece. Leading academics equated proper classical education with proper Christian ideals, turning toward Greek language and neoplatonic theologies as antidotes to Duns Scotus and Aristotle an theology. They were not necessarily Protestant, but their rejection of the philosophical roots of the high Medieval Church changed their understanding of their relationship to it. Thus the battle at Cambridge in the early 1540s over how to pronounce Greek pitted evangelicals against conservatives, new learning against old. Sir Thomas Smith and John Cheke, the proponents of the new pronunciation, were committed evangelicals. Their enemy, Chancellor Stephen Gardiner, was the leader of conservative reaction at Court as well as in the University. Cheke's translations of Chrysostom into English, dedicated to Henry VIII, suggest how the union of some strains of humanism and Christianity contributed to the establishment of the royal supremacy. It reached its epitome when John Jewel, defending the Church of England, leant heavily on the Greek Fathers to combat the Latin Fathers cited by Rome. The Greeks, with their bent toward caesaropapism, were friendlier to the royal supremacy and the state church.

As a part of the supremacy, the study of canon law was suspended, never to be resumed, and the universities began a long decline. With canon law and theology in total confusion, scholars voted with their feet, not bothering to study theology or seek ordination.[19]

The intellectual confusion and institutional uncertainties provoked by the mid-century troubles began to dissipate in the 1570s, as a new generation of scholars, asking questions born of the confusion, emerged, exploring the meanings and application of their Protestantism, using the latest academic tools. In Merton College this generation's arrival was heralded by men like Thomas Bodley and Henry Saville, with their commitment to the new learning. Their neighbor over the wall in

Corpus Christi, Richard Hooker, was feeling his way toward an ecclesiology for the state church. In Cambridge, a new method began to make sense of the Calvinism popular among Cambridge theologians like Lawrence Chaderton and William Perkins.

Contemporary intellectuals were all interested in the same questions. It was a generation searching for the way out of the intellectual confusion bequeathed them by their parents. Poets and playwrights discovered that words, projecting images on to the mind, were tools of self-understanding. Just as the Word led one to God, so words, imaginatively used, led one to truth. "The historian," wrote Sir Philip Sidney in the early 1580s,

laden with old mouse-eaten records, authorizing himself for the most part upon other histories, whose greatest authorities are built upon the notable foundation hearsay . . . better acquainted with a 1000 years ago, than with the present age, and yet better knowing how this world goes, than how his own wit runs, curious for antiquities, and inquisitive of novelties, a wonder to young folks, and a tyrant in table talk; denies in a great chafe, that any man for teaching of virtue, and virtue's actions, is comparable to him.

Sidney did not think much of historians, and he thought even less of philosophers as teachers of virtue. They were too bound to evidence, too logical, to move the heart. Without poetry, the history of Troy would hardly be interesting. For this ideal courtier-knight, the *beau ideal* of his age, human understanding was cloudy at best. Metaphor was better, for she was a real teacher, not a pompous, didactic, Latinate windbag like history and philosophy.[20]

Conceived in the first year of Queen Mary's reign, Sidney shared with many in his generation the preference for fine poetry, stirring metaphors and emblems over the aridity of logic. Like Petrarch, they knew it was better to will the good than to know the truth, exulting rhetoric over dialectic as a tool to improve humankind.

There was wide agreement that virtue could be determined only from within, and that the evocation of emotion helped stimulate and locate it. As Peter Kaufman has observed, this search for emotional experience is what tied the theatrical world to the world of "practical divinity." The plain man's path to heaven led from black despair, to awareness of one's dependence on God, to an awareness of election.[21] Inducing this despair that brought joy was the aim of preachers of all sorts, because tasting its bitterness led to the joyful certainty of election.

A new casuistry of conscience was built on this perception.

The intellectual necessity for doing this arose from the Calvinist understanding of the practical effects of grace and election. Christians were bound in conscience to obey the law of God in all things, and so they needed practical exercises in applied casuistry. But it was also necessitated by the desperate need for order and certainty in a world that rejected the Catholic system of virtue based on pious works.

Protestant intellectuals took it as their mission to teach a newly Protestant culture how to understand its place in God's creation.

In the process, curricula were remodeled as dons began teaching with different emphases. Thomas Cartwright's advice to a student entitled "For Direction in the Study of Divinity" summed up the situation. In it he wrote "I think the new writers are to be read before the old, for that we understand by them what suits there are depending between us and our adversaries of all sorts, we may both the better know what evidence is laid up in the monuments of the old writers either for us or them, and make our note accordingly."[22] Cartwright's "new writers" were Calvin, Beza, Bucer, and Luther. He was calling for a Protestant curriculum designed to produce minds capable of disputing the intellectual inheritance of their civilization.

Gabriel Harvey, who became Professor of Rhetoric at Cambridge in 1574, summed up the mid-Elizabethan academic state of mind in a teasing letter to a friend at court. The scholars of this age, he reported, are interested in politics and policy, not contemplative theology.Worrying about God in the abstract, he wrote, "was expired when Duns and Thomas of Aquino with the whole rabblement of schoolmen were abandoned [by] our schools and expelled the University."Now tastes ran to contemporary continental authors, especially books written by Castiglione and Guazzo, to histories such as Guicciardini's *History of Italy*, and emblem books. Authors writing on political philosophy were especially popular. Everyone was reading Machiavelli, and Jean Bodin's *Republic*. As for logic, "Aristotles Organon is nighhand as little read as Duns' Quodlibet." But Aristotle's economics and politics, he insisted, "everyone hath by rote."[23]

One of the reasons that people no longer read Aristotle's logic was that scholars of Harvey's generation had been infected with humanist dislike of the arid practice of Aristotelean syllogisms. Many had been taught to ask the question asked by Lutheran Franz Burchard, "Which do you think has served the church better? The one [St. Jerome] who by his eloquence illuminated the Holy Scriptures and diligently expounded many dogmas, or Scotus who, while he elucidated no dogma, brought into the church the most trifling disputations?"[24] They learned that education should prepare one to live well and blessedly, not to engage in trifling disputations. Theology, said Petrus Ramus, was to be studied in order to learn the doctrine of living well, for "the end of teaching is not to know the subject for itself, but to know its use and purpose."[25]

In this Ramus joined Martin Bucer and Philip Melanchthon, Erasmus, Juan Luis Vives, and many other leading intellectuals from across Europe in the first half of the century. All of them were critical of scholastic Aristoteleanism because it lacked practical application. Christian leaders, whether princes or priests, needed, they believed, the tools of rhetoric more than the niceties of logic in order to inspire their people to live the Christian life.

Ramist theory was among the most important methods for applying rhetoric and logic to the Christian life. It was born in the context of University of Paris, where young Petrus Ramus [Pierre LaRamée], frustrated at what he saw as the uselessness of the traditional curriculum, had defended his thesis that Aristotle was wrong about everything. Developing a way of teaching logic that made learning easier, Ramus described his new pedagogy in two books in 1543. One, on the structure of dialectics, showed his method. The other, innocently entitled *Remarks on Aristotle*, savaged Aristotelean method.

This sweeping attack hit the university curriculum hard, since Aristotle was the heart of it. Ramus' books were, Walter Ong contends, "a public announcement to the whole teen-age and younger community of undergraduates, a community which habitually lived in a state of unruliness..." that the curriculum was wrong. Naturally, the faculty turned on Ramus, equating his heresy against Aristotle with the other heresies loose at the time, denouncing his pedagogical proposals as a Lutheran plot.[26] Ramus' job was saved by Francis I, who made him Professor of Rhetoric, but, despite an official order to spare him, his was killed in the massacre of the French Protestants in 1572.

By then, those young people who had found his ideas exciting were introducing his method into the curriculum. In Cambridge Sir Philip Sidney and Gabriel Harvey set about making him a staple of learning, providing a new, Protestant, way of knowing. Men like Lawrence Chaderton, William Perkins, and William Ames, leading minds of the Puritan movement, took the logical tools of Ramus and developed an applied theology. Identifiable by its use of "cases of conscience," this theology sought to teach the believer how to make rational choices in line with God's will. Their method depended upon the identification of true axioms deduced from scripture, which could be used to resolve singular problems. From the axioms, schematics of salvation could be elaborated in a system known as "technometria," showing the relationship of all things to God's intent.

Ramist dialectics were not epistemology, *per se*, but they fit the world view of men who believed in The Word that became flesh and dwelt among men. If the only religion of Protestants was the Bible, as Henry Chillingworth famously insisted in 1638, many Protestants sat uneasily in the councils of the inductionist.[27] The only reality was God, and all human reasoning was unreal, a meditation on the shadow on the cave wall. True understanding could only come through election – only when God allowed people to see clearly would they understand his true desires and intentions. Therefore it was necessary to portray the symbols of election in everyday life.

The popularity of Ramist analysis lay in its pedagogical power. Applied to theology, it could make the arcana clear. Applied to moral predicaments, proper courses of action could be identified. That is why it was so useful in dealing with "cases of conscience." It could help people know how to live.

And it could be understood by all, as the translated handbooks of Ramist method suggested. The first, by Rollo McIlwain, introduced it as "a perfect method," compounding the best of Aristotle's logic with Cicero's rhetoric and Quintiallian's grammar. It was so perfect, he claimed, all arts could be understood using it.[28] A 1584 edition proclaimed its breadth: *The Arts of Logic and Rhetoric . . . for method in the government of the family, prescribed in the word of God: and for the whole in the resolution or opening of certain parts of Scripture.*[29]

William Perkins, born in 1558, applied Ramism to become the voice of English Calvinist casuistry. He took the new theology and created a method of applying it to everyday life, teaching people how to use their consciences as a guide. His *Three Books of Cases of Conscience* asked and answered the question "what is virtue" by setting cases and explicating them.

The virtuous life was easily defined by Perkins. It was "To walk in our particular callings, doing the duties thereof to the glory of God, to the good of the commonwealth, and the edification of the church; avoiding therein fraud, covetousness, and ambition, which cause men oftentimes to set their consciences on the tenters and make them stretch like cheveril."[30] But if their narrow consciences were not to be stretched like a kid skin on tenterhooks, they needed guidance.

Using Ramist dialects, which allowed things to be defined through the identification of their opposites, Perkins wrestled with hard questions. Often, the problem began and ended with the reassurance of election, but in between was the world of virtuous, godly action. How were people expected to behave? Knowing this was complicated by the fact that the test of virtuous behavior rested in the individual's conscience. "Conscience," he wrote, "is a part of the understanding in all reasonable creatures determining of their particular actions, either with them or against them." It is the faculty in the soul whereby we use reason, "serving to rule and order the whole man: and therefore is placed in the soul as to be as the wagoner in the wagon." It rules the will. The conscience has two parts, the theoretical, that considers truth and falsehood, and the "practical understanding," that considers the good or bad of every particular action.[31]

It was "practical understanding" that the "cases of conscience" literature was designed to aid. Before acting, a person was expected to clarify choices by asking four questions. First, is the action against Christian religion – Does it break the moral law of the second table of the decalogue? Second, is the action prejudicial to the honor of God – Does it break the first table of the decalogue? Third, is the action contrary to the justice due men – Does it break Christ's commands? Fourth, does the action pertain to the calling of the actor – Is due order maintained?[32]

In practice, this test allowed people to determine whether it was appropriate to attend a play, to use a Catholic physician, or play football on the Sabbath. But it could also be used to guide political actions. Properly applied, a Christian conscience directed a person to a life of moderation: "A man that hath any conscience, may see how to carry himself, in all these civil affairs, in an even, upright, and equal course,

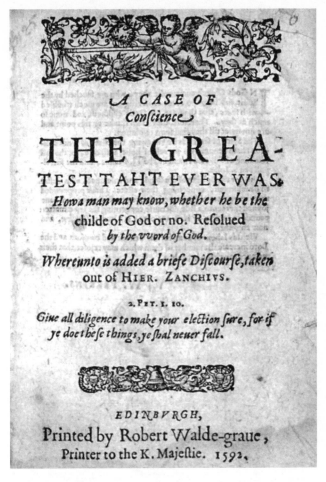

FIGURE 5   Title page from *A Case of Conscience. The Greatest Taht (sic) Ever was....*, by William Perkins. © British Library.

and warrantable not only by the law of the land, but even by the law and word of God."[33]

Of course this application of conscience exalted the individual over the community, with difficult practical consequences. As Geoffrey Fenton observed in his *A Forme of Christian Pollicie*, "civil policy ought to be conformable to celestial government," and governors and judges chosen accordingly, so that "we in our common life expressing an immovable zeal to obedience [to God], may concur with them, and agree altogether in one law and doctrine, one will and judgement." The result is a

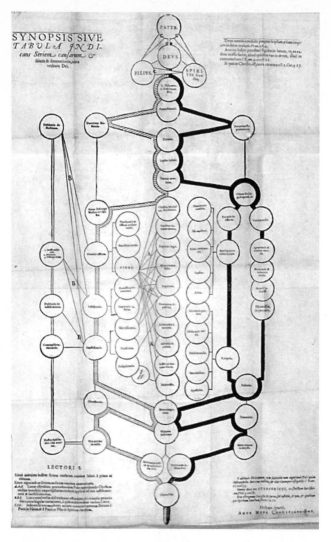

FIGURE 6   Chart of election from William Perkins, *Armilla aurea, id est, Theologiae* ... © British Library.

commonweal knit together by love and harmony in the worship of the true God. Of course, if the magistracy did not excellence in divine and human learning, making decisions consonant with God's will, there would be problems.[34] Some took this very seriously, demanding that government and clergy be guided by divine law rather than covetousness, expedience, and worldly interests.

In Perkins' often copied system, the individual conscience was to be constantly monitored, so that Christian virtue was interiorized, directing behavior and giving assurance of salvation. Theologies of this kind formalized the cultural change occurring in England. We can see this in a new genre, the meditative diary, used to check and refine the conscience.

Samuel Ward, writing in the 1590s, kept a running tally of his intentions and infractions as a way of training his conscience and reassuring himself of his election. By and large, it was a dismal record. On a single Sunday he discovered in himself seventeen infractions, including an after dinner nap. But Ward's misery about his "blockishness" in serving God was exactly why he kept his diary. He wished to induce wretchedness. The casuistry of Calvinism demanded that one plumb the depths of one's sinful nature in order to soar on the joyful reassurance of God's grace, produced by the knowledge of one's unworthiness. On May 28, 1595, it pleased God to give Ward one of the insights that fed his assurance: he glimpsed His mercifulness toward a sinner like himself.[35]

As Ward knew, prayer was the primary way to refocus and define behavior. In the logic of Protestantism, the proof of election lay in worldly sorrowing, so the act of prayer was a reminder of regeneration. The more people felt their sins, the more they were able to comprehend their election. The preachers believed that though election could not be affected by behavior, behavior could certainly bring acceptance of election. Thus the irony of double predestination was that it demanded great effort on the part of the clergy.

They encouraged a pietistic experience of faith that did not depend on external markers so much as internal pain. Insisting that prayer should "rip up all the inward and secret corners of consciences," the pietists believed that the process of ripping apart was necessary for rebirth in Christ.[36] Dwelling on sins and shortcomings made one aware of one's need of God, and that, in turn, moved you to understanding of His grace. Therefore, it was claimed prayers read from the Prayer Book lacked the desired emotional impact. One had to meditate with fervent anguish on one's faults in order to achieve the catharsis sought for.

This seeking for prayerful catharsis created a new vocabulary of word and gesture that became familiar to late Elizabethans. If their grandparents had expressed their piety in the works Protestants despised, the end of the century expressed piety through interior struggle. The new spirituality required them to labor mightily day and night in contemplation of their unworthiness and God's grace in electing them to salvation.

As Peter Kaufman has shown, this commitment to interior religion, with its ravished hearts and yearning souls, can be found littering the literature of the Elizabethan England, as well as its sermons. Christopher Marlowe, sometimes taken for an atheist because of his skepticism, gives Dr. Faustus the wretchedness necessary to produce awareness of God's choices. Faustus is damned and cannot call on God, even though he wants to.

O I'll leap up to my God: who pulls me down?
See, see where Christ's blood streams in the firmament,
One drop would save my soul, half a drop, ah my Christ,
Ah rend not my heart for naming my Christ,
Yet will I call on him, oh spare me Lucifer![37]

Unable to make the last minute return to the God of the elect, Faustus is dragged down to eternal torment, representing to the audience, in a neat Ramist dichotomy, the "other," the unelected reprobate.[38] In this moment of misery Faustus is alone with the question of his eternal fate. It is a theatrical moment that can easily be found on William Perkins chart showing how the reprobates proceed to damnation, buoyed up for some brief moments of hope, only to be dragged back to their fate.

It was not a comforting doctrine for those uncertain of their election. Calvin despised those who thought God was making miserable toys of humans, but many must have railed against God's unfairness, as Faustus does when he rejects religion for magic:

If we say that we have no sin
We deceive ourselves, and there is no truth in us.'
Why then, belike, we must sin,
And so consequently die.
Ay, we must die, an everlasting death.
What doctrine call you this? Che sera, sera.
'What will be, shall be.' Divinity, adieu![39]

Hamlet, says Kaufman, expresses the same sensibility in his famous soliloquy, performing the act of self-confession. If the believer was elect, his heart would become "both priest and sacrifice" bringing to him certainty and comfort. If he was not, nothing could disguise the fact. Sinners among the elect could not fool themselves, any more than a Catholic priest could deny in his conscience that he was a priest. Consciences, speaking God's truth, did not lie.[40]

This kind of introspection, with its extreme individuation and meditative stance, can be seen in Grace Mildmay's understanding of her life. When she wrote her huge meditative memoir to instruct her grandchildren, she chose to look at those times when she had been tested, made wretched by events, in order to reach a higher understanding of her relationship with God.

Her understanding of that relationship was channeled through her understanding of scripture. Grace Mildmay represents that first generation of Bible readers freed from the conventions of the text by numbered verses. With the Geneva Bible, first published in 1560, English Christians were introduced to numbered verses, and to the concept that all verses were created equal. For them, taught to rest all judgments on the revealed word of God, a restructuring of their mental universe became possible.

Printed in a handy quarto size in roman type instead of the difficult to read black letter type previously used for sacred printing, the translators, seeking to edify their brethren, had divided it into verses for easy mastery, "Which thing as it is most profitable for memory: so doth it agree with the best translations, and is most easy to find out both by the best concordances."[41] Moreover, the translators provided marginal glosses to explain the meanings of hard passages, so that the Bible became a lesson in theology as well as the word of God. The fact that at least one edition of the Geneva Bible appeared every year between 1575 and 1618 suggests the breadth of its popularity, and the depth of enthusiasm for Bible usage among Elizabethans.

The way of arguing encouraged by this new tool, and by the hundreds of sermons based upon it, tied each person's observations to the word of God directly, verse by verse. In their dedication of the Geneva Bible to Elizabeth, its translators demonstrated the technique. Their prose argument was accompanied with marginal verse citations as thick as cloves in a pomander. With a higher frequency than one citation per sentence of prose, their argument was clearly nothing more than an exposition of divine truth which the Queen could see for herself if she read the verses cited. Thus, in the translators' letter to Elizabeth denouncing idolatry, the argument is a running gloss on: 1 Cor. 3:17; 1 Tim. 3:14; Eph. 1:22; Heb. 3:6; Ezra, 4; 1 Esdras 2:16 (an apocryphal book); Ezra 4:7; Ezra 4:2; Neh. 6:10; Neh. 5:1; John 2:20; Ezra 3:12; 2 Cor. 2:1. They mix and match books of all sorts from all periods, giving all equal weight. Paul's letters combine with the history of the kings of Israel and the prophets to a single end, God's truth.

This way of framing argument crept into the popular conscience in Elizabeth's reign and has never departed. So long as every word of the Bible is considered to be revealed by God, all God's verses can be mixed together to create meaning.

This way of arguing, so natural to Protestants now, was new to Elizabethans, but quickly became common currency, allowing each literate individual to plot his or her own life course using the Bible as a compass. Possessed of a question on any subject, they could find biblical advice. For instance, when puzzled over the role of works in salvation, they could look up works in the table of the Bible and discover that they should read a series of passages demonstrating that by works we are not saved, and that the works of gentiles must be avoided. Converted into daily currency, the works of gentiles might be participation in a prayer book service, or attending a play, but the decision to avoid these could be justified ultimately by a reference to God's command in Ephesians 4:17.

The empowerment of the individual arising from the ready accessibility of the word of God and the emphasis on conscience should not be underestimated. For those who took their religion seriously, priesthood of the believer in combination with access to the Bible created a powerful critical tool, directing their lives and structuring their thoughts. For those who did not take their religion so seriously, it still empowered them, in the sense that their election and their Christian liberty awaited discovery.

It was a new habit of thought, a new way of seeing the world and fashioning the self. It was an important new vision shared by many Elizabethans, but it worried others, such as Archbishop Whitgift and Richard Hooker. How could obedience be maintained in a community which arrogated to the individual conscience the right to make decisions? What about good order? Was that not a Christian value? And if the individual refused to recognize authority beyond the conscience, was not the Queen's authority diminished? If it was, what would happen to the Protestant state she had created? Too much individuality was a recipe for civil disaster and heresy. Therefore, they asserted a different model of Protestant virtue which, while recognizing most of the same theological principles as Perkins, gave the church a central role in determining what proper Christian behavior was. Their individual was bound in conscience to obey the laws of the community, as established by church and crown according to the laws of God.

Hooker knew that Puritanism was popular because it appealed to human pride, stressing Paul's rule in Romans 14:5: "Let every man in his own mind be fully persuaded of that thing which he either alloweth or doth [not]."[42] Glossed by the Geneva Bible as meaning that we must be assured in our conscience by God's word of all that we do, this passage was, to Hooker, a license for the ignorant to criticize their rulers. Is there, he asks, any reason why the average person knows better than the leaders of the church and state what sort of ecclesiastical regiment is the fittest?[43]

This inflated conception of the individual conscience encouraged people to make destructive criticism, without becoming better themselves. Their virtue consists in being critical and mocking everything. Worse, he said, this mocking and destruction were dressed in the garb of charity, attracting ignorant women who, because of their soft natures, were critical of the necessary harshness of magistrates and bishops. Freedom of conscience in the gospel seemed, to Hooker, to create harping, destructive behaviors in men "credulous and over-capable of such pleasing errors," blindly following what they thought was the spirit of God.[44]

For Hooker, many of the things offending the delicate consciences of his coreligionist who wished for further purification of the state church were of no consequence to God. And if a rule was made that did not offend against God's law, it ought to be obeyed in good conscience. As Hooker wrote, "as we live in a civil society, the state of the commonwealth wherein we live both may and doth require certain laws . . ." And since the civil society requires laws, the individual judgment must give way before the judgment of the community embodied in the church.[45]

For Hooker, then, virtue consisted in recognizing one's place in God's plan and living accordingly. Conscience was important to every individual, guiding personal decisions, but it existed within the structure of the state church, which could be trusted to form and guide conscience for the greater good of the whole community. He demonstrates this logically, arguing that all men desire to lead in this world a happy life, and the happiest life is that in which "all virtue is exercised without impediment or let." To this end, civil society was formed in a social contract, minimizing the impediments to virtue by controlling the worst impulses of evil human nature.[46]

For Hooker, all of this rested on a foundation of natural law which was, as it was for Medieval churchmen, divinely ordained. Local customs evolved from natural law, and were binding, even if they differed from place to place, and even if they were not explicitly commanded in the Bible. This was a different spiritual anthropology than that of Perkins, focused on the community rather than the individual. It was an excellent defense of the prayer book liturgy, the use of homilies, and the unreformed structure of the English church.

And so the emerging English Protestant tradition taught two versions of virtue. Resting on many of the same theological principles, they differed over the authority of the individual conscience. They agreed that conscience was the supreme guide to virtue, but they disagreed about when it was to be applied and by whom it was directed. Perkins had the faithful engaged full-time in its application, using it on every issue, while Hooker allowed people to relax about the big issues, such as church government, while still insisting that they be guided in individual choices by godly conscience. They agreed that conscience was guided by the word of God, but they disagreed about the source of understanding. Some held that only the Bible could be used as a guide, while Hooker held that the wisdom of the Bible was encapsulated in the Book of Common Prayer and the ecclesiastical leadership.

There was a political gulf between these two positions. The one empowered conscience and transcended rank, class, and order, permitting individual Christians to ignore social and political structures if their consciences demanded it. They might separate from the Church of England in obedience to God's higher authority. Or they might insist on a Presbyterian church order, as a part of their duty to God. Like William Fuller telling his Queen that she had to stop swearing, people of this conviction were not easily cowed by mere tradition and law.

The other version identified the highest virtue with obedience to God's ordained state and system. These individuals appreciated the power of conscience, but knew it was not to be used too often or applied too strictly, since God had guided the state in developing the law, which set the bounds of proper behavior.[47]

The impossibility of squaring these two conflicting views of the individual's virtue in civil society was to be at the heart of the civil war fought by their grandchildren.

Conscience rightly guided was the purpose of all casuistries. They sought to guide the individual in making decisions in accordance with the word of God, preventing despair and giving assurance of salvation. For most people, their working casuistry was undoubtedly a mix of the principles of conscience, the instincts of custom, legal expectations, and the necessity of obedience. In the pious, it was developed in prayerful contemplations of God's providence in our lives.

Thus Grace Mildmay found joy meditating on her husband's corpse. God had tested her and she had responded. She could prove this to herself by noting the biblical passages which demonstrated how and why she had been tested, noting the marks of her victory.

People like Grace Mildmay were nuisances to those who did not spend their time meditating on God's providence and reading the Bible. As Reverend Greenham, Father Baker and many others commentators noted in the later sixteenth century, some people had become skeptical about religious certainty. The Reformation experience taught them to doubt and dissemble. Greenham expressed his fear of the atheism that was growing up in the post-papist world. Many who had "escaped out of the gulf of superstition are now too far plagued and swallowed up of profaneness, thinking either that there is no God or else that he is not so fearful and merciful as his threatenings and promises commend him to be."[48] Perhaps Greenham was thinking of people like John Minet, the Reader serving the parish of East Drayton, Nottinghamshire, whose parishioners accused him of openly asserting there was no God, no Heaven, and no Hell.[49] It is more likely, however, that he had in mind those who were not so much atheists as Nicodemians and skeptics.

Many of these Nicodemians and skeptics were natural products of the confused times. As the Venetian ambassador remarked in Mary's reign, "in the midst of so much error and confusion" all but a few "make this show of recantation, yet do not effectually resume the Catholic faith." His perception was born out by Ralph Allerton, who told Bishop Bonner that many an English person had become a religious neuter "that is to say, observing all things that are commanded outwardly, as though he were of your part, his heart being yet wholly against the same."[50] William Bullein described four sorts of religion among his early Elizabethan contemporaries: Catholic (Henrician), Papist, Protestant, and *Nulla Fidian*.[51] The translator of Johann Wigand's attack on Nicodemism called them "Jacks of both sides," complaining they try to, "walk as . . . in the middle and most safe way," indifferent to both sides in order "to keep peace, substance, honor and dignity safe, and not altogether nor sluttishly to forsake religion, and yet for all that to seem addict to what religion a man will."[52]

It is not surprising that some Elizabethans were taught by their experiences to find their only sure faith within themselves. By the time the generation of the 1550s and 1560s came of age, many were people who had their opinion, but kept it to themselves. By the 1580s their latent religion enraged Protestant and Catholic clergy alike.

George Gifford, in his lively dialogue between a papist and a Protestant, talks of "church papists," people who conform to the statute law, but who are in conscience papists. On the other side of the doctrinal line, Father Parsons complained about people who, though they claimed to be Catholics, "in going to church show themselves conformable men to the proceedings of them of the contrary religion: and do also think others too scrupulous which do stand in refusal of the same." The Carthusian monk Thomas White complained about these people who outwardly conformed, saying "Some call them Church-papists, other Schismatics, demi-Catholics, or catholic-like Protestants, or external Protestants, and internal Catholics." The Anglican Bishop Cooper of Lincoln called them "cunning papists," and the pursuivant Richard Topcliffe called them "dissembling papists."[53]

Seen through the eyes of the Nicodemites themselves, however, the problem looked rather different. They did not find it worthwhile to suffer for any theology. The Protestants called them "crypto-papists" out of contempt and fear; real Catholics bemoaned their lukewarmness. But they embodied a cool skepticism that may have thought Paris was worth a mass, and wished a plague on all fanatics. They could not be bothered to be more than lukewarm about religion, and they may not have cared if their children were religious, either. Father Garnet, reflecting on the Catholics of his early Elizabethan youth, railed against their neglect of true religion. These so-called Catholics took their families and servants to church, married under heretical rites, had their children baptized by heretics, and took schismatic oaths, because "exterior dissimulation was not even thought to be wrong, provided interiorly a man's faith was sound." Of course, some of their children were lost to Catholicism in the process, as Garnet lamented.[54]

But in the consciences of these conformists, compromise was right, for it was the only response that seemed to have a future. To rebel, or to practice absolute disobedience, would bring death and ruination on their families. To find and maintain a middle position was to survive, and, ironically, their temporizing ensured that English Catholicism survived.[55] By the same token, conscience was recognized as a justification for diverse actions, explaining separatism as well as recusancy. One could, in good conscience, insist on being a Catholic or a separatist and find a sympathetic reception, even in the law courts. In a world of competing systems of virtue, conscience became, in the words of a judge in Richard Lalor's recusancy trial, the "highest tribunal ... wherein the power of the keys is exercised to the highest degree."[56]

As twenty-eight year old Philip Howard, Earl of Arundel, told Queen Elizabeth in 1585, justifying his intention to leave England in order to practice Catholicism, "ask such as ye think hate me most, whether, being of that religion that I profess ... they would not have taken that course for the safety of their souls and the discharge of their conscience, which I did. And either they must tell you directly that they would have done the same, or else plainly acknowledge themselves to be mere Atheists. ..."[57]

In a world in which a young Catholic could imagine the power of a Protestant conscience to prompt independent action, it was increasingly apparent that human laws could not bind God in conscience. Virtue and moral choice were becoming personal. Under these conditions, it is not surprising that academic skepticism was attracting some of the brightest minds.

Like the Stoicism so popular with the middle Tudor generation, philosophical skepticism arrived in England from the classical world via the continent. Once it arrived, it found ready followers, marrying happily with the Tacittean humanism of leading intellectuals like Sir Henry Savile, Warden of Merton and translator of Tacitus' histories. As the disputes over religion raged, some were drawn to a philosophy which denied that the ultimate truth about religion could be empirically known. Their doubt made them politically and religiously moderate, *politiques*, who denied the ability of humanity to puzzle out God's plan.

In 1569 a Latin edition of the works of Sextus Empiricus was published by Gentian Hervet. Hervet, who was anti-Calvinist, saw the Pyrrhonian skepticism of Sextus as the antidote to the Calvinist search for knowledge of election. Simply put, Sextus, the only author of Pyrrho's school whose manuscripts survived, held that nothing can be truly known, so human reason can produce no certainty. This, insisted Hervet, destroyed all claims to know God's will, denied all dogmatism, and forced people to accept Biblical revelation without twisting it into knots.

Hervet's arguments were adopted by Michel de Montaigne and his student, Father Pierre Charron, who developed a fideist skepticism. This inability to know which religion is true, they suggested, permitted people to believe as they felt they must, and denied the need to change religious allegiances. If no church can be known to be true, there is no church better than another. Let your faith be your guide, and whatever seems right is right. Montaigne and Charron remained Catholic, accepting Catholicism on faith alone.

Catholics liked this version of skepticism because it allowed them to attack the very idea that religion could be based entirely on scripture. What, they asked, was scripture? How could one be sure that it was translated and understood properly? Unable to determine the accuracy of one's interpretation, one was left knowing nothing, misled by human frailty.

The people reading Sextus and Montaigne learned that the only certainty they could know came from within them. In the context of ecclesiology, this allowed them to argue that being a member of the state church was as good as being a member of any other church. In a world without certainty, custom and authority provided as much certainty as one could get.[58]

This fideist skepticism was not unchristian, and it aligned with theologians like Augustine and Luther, who knew that knowledge of God came from the operation of grace on the soul. According to them, Christians believed because they wanted to believe, and so the only test of faith was self-administered. It was much more comfortable than Calvinism, and appealed to those who believed, but who did not take battles over ecclesiology seriously. A skeptical fideist really was not concerned whether the Church of England conformed to the organizational model of the primitive church. And a truly skeptical one might agree with Barnabas, the Jew of Malta, when Marlowe made him observe that "religion hides many mischiefs from suspicion."[59] Sir Francis Bacon, citing Montaigne, put it even more bluntly, observing that the greatest liars always enlist religion in their cause.[60]

Bacon, in his little essay "Of Unity in Religion," underscored the way the behaviors of zealots and bigots in the name of religion took people away from it. "Men must beware," he wrote,

that in the procuring . . . of religious unity, they do not dissolve and deface the laws of charity, and of human society. There be two swords amongst Christians, the spiritual and temporal; and both have their due office and place, in the maintenance of religion. But we may not take up the third sword . . . that is, to propagate religion by wars, or by sanguinary persecutions to force consciences. . . . For this is but to dash the first table against the second; and so to consider men as Christians, as we forget that they are men.[61]

Bacon's fear that religious enthusiasm destroyed Christian unity echoed the skeptics' concern that humanity was forgotten in the name of God, the second table of the decalogue assaulted by the first table, making society unworkable. For him, maintaining the laws of human charity and society produced peace, not religion, and peace was the goal.

Bacon's skepticism was clearly influenced by his reading of Roman history. Like Sir Henry Savile, who published his translation of part of Tacitus' *Histories* in 1591, Bacon knew that things were not always what they seemed, and that dissimulation was often a political necessity. This was good "policy," if undertaken for reasons of state. It was necessary, however, for the virtuous man to beware of sycophancy, since all those surrounding a ruler could be expected to lie in their own self-interest. As Savile said in his notes on Tacitus, flatterers can destroy the ruler's ability to use proper reason. Bacon and other members of the Earl of Essex's circle, and the Earl himself, were well-read in Tacitus and consequently skeptical – one might say cynical – about power and religion.[62]

But most in the late sixteenth century could not rest comfortably in Kierkegaardian suspension. By late in Elizabeth's reign the theological and philosophical parties were dividing along the lines of those who accepted absolute predestination and those who believed that election could be influenced by behavior. In short, the question was whether people's wills are free or in bondage. If they were free, they were much more responsible for their own salvation, than if they were not. For those with free will, a guilty conscience had some bearing on salvation.

Large numbers of people aligned themselves with the stance often associated with the theology of Jacob Arminius (1559–1609) because it made easy sense. Arminius, trained by Theodore Beza, was a Calvinist, but he did not believe that election was absolute or that grace was irresistible. God would decree salvation or damnation based on the perseverance of the individual in living a life of faith.

Uncomfortable with double predestination, many people wanted to believe that they were responsible for their own salvation, and that the bad things done by their neighbors would be punished. Some of this attitude may have been retained from the old belief in works, but much of it was rugged common sense. It was reasonable that people who choose to be good should be rewarded. Those who do evil should be punished. To explain their evil in terms of God's eternal decree was not satisfying.

This attitude made them Pelagians in the eyes of the ministers attempting to drum predestination into them, making them suspect as crypto-papists. But it was a ready guide to virtue that linked human action to divine reaction.

Searching for the true order underlying virtue was a pan-European exercise, but in England the most systematic attempt to resolve the problem was made by Sir Francis Bacon. Born in 1561, Bacon met skepticism and anti-Aristotelean arguments early in his youth. Educated at Trinity College, Cambridge when John Whitgift, later Archbishop of Canterbury and foe of Puritans was master, he arrived there in the early 1570s. With people like Gabriel Harvey pushing Ramism into the curriculum and others resisting, the attack on Aristoteleanism was fresh and hot, influencing the young man. His secretary and first biographer tells us that at Cambridge Bacon learned to dislike Aristotle, not because Aristotle was unworthy, but because his method was unfruitful.[63] Apparently this set young Bacon to pondering while he went on to Gray's Inn and took up a legal career.

Born into Elizabeth's political elite, the son of the Lord Keeper and nephew of Lord Burghley, Francis would follow in his father's footsteps, pursuing patronage and a political career. It is certain that his search for a method of achieving knowledge is linked to his practical experiences as a politician. He was equally interested in law, history, political philosophy, and philosophic method. In short, he was the same sort of polymath as Aristotle, and he set out to revise and improve Aristotle's method, replacing Aristotle's *Organon* with his own *Novum Organum*.

Bacon, judging by his confession of faith, written before 1603, was an orthodox Christian who believed in an eternal, almighty, all wise, good God. His treatment of creation, temptation, fall, mediation, election, reprobation and redemption framed his understanding of the world and set the limits within which he believed human reason could work. Not surprisingly for a lawyer, he expressed a belief that God ruled the universe with law. However, as Perez Zagorin remarks, "it is equally evident that his mind was overwhelmingly secular in its interests and that in his reflections as a Christian philosopher he was far more concerned with the advancement of scientific reason and the improvement of mankind's welfare in this world than with religion and the destiny of the immortal soul."[64]

Concerned as a politician with the trouble that religion can make in society, he sought to focus attention on those things which could be beneficial to humanity, rather than worrying about metaphysical problems. His famous method demonstrates this. Critical of Aristotelean induction because it jumps from observations to general axioms, he insisted on a method of testing and observation that led to minor axioms and from them to major axioms. But he never expected his experimentation to lead to knowledge of God. He was content to understand the natural world as it worked under God's natural laws without drawing theological conclusions. Unlike the scholastics, he valued induction for the knowledge it gave of this world, not for its putative ability to reveal knowledge about the Creator.

Bacon represents the late Elizabethan intellectual synthesis well. Absorbing the destructive criticisms of Ramists, skeptics, humanists, and Protestants, he rejected the scholastic methods and interests. But he recognized the vacuum created by that rejection and set out to fill it. As he told Lord Burghley in 1592,

I confess that I have taken all knowledge to be my province; and if I could purge it of two sorts of rovers, whereof the one with frivolous disputations, confutations and verbosities, the other with blind experiments and auricular traditions and impostures, hath committed so many spoils, I hope I should bring in industrious observations, grounded conclusions, and profitable inventions and discoveries; the best state of that province.[65]

Bacon's call for the practical exercise of human reason, undistracted by fruitless arguments over church government and soteriology, was one of the important fruits of the post-Reformation confusion. Convinced that such disputes could never resolve mysteries of faith, he turned his mind elsewhere. And he was not alone.

We can see the arguments of the Ramists, the skeptics, and the humanists, as well as the gusts of theological wind in the curriculum at Merton College. There, two years after Bacon had declared war on the Aristotelean method, one of the disputation propositions set for a candidate for the BA was "Aristotelis obscuritas in philosophia naturalis tradenda reprehendenda est." We do not know if the dons were for or against the assertion that the obscurities of Aristotle retarded natural philosophy, but the proposition joins an increasing number of variation questions challenging the old way of seeing the world. When Edward Lea was examined in 1602, all three of his questions demanded that he argue *contra Aristotelem*. Besides demonstrating a concern about the validity of Aristotle, the examination questions show the increasing unease about humanity's ability to trust its own senses, and about the separation of civic virtue from godly virtue. One scholar had to dispute whether a good citizen was different from a good man, and someone else had to maintain that good lives could be distinguished from bad. In a single examination in 1591 the candidate had to argue whether human nature was inclined to goodness or viciousness, and whether virtuous people feared death less than those without virtue. In a skeptical vein, another had to defend the proposition that humans were less to be believed than other animals. Ironically, perhaps, a student had to prove "Omnis sciencia nobis tantum opinione constat" – that all our knowledge stands only on opinion.[66]

As Marlowe's popular play *The Jew of Malta* opens, Niccolo Machiavelli appears to deliver the prologue. Addressing the audience the notoriously amoral Italian speaks plain truth to the whited sepulchers in the audience:

> Admired am I of those that hate me most,
> Though some speak openly against my books,
> Yet will they read me, and thereby attain
> To Peter's chair; and, when they cast me off,
> Are poisoned by my climbing followers.
> I count religion but a childish toy,
> And hold there is no sin but ignorance.[67]

This bitter, mocking introduction to the tale of Barnabas, the Jew of the title, who enriches himself by amoral pursuit of money, catches another side of the moral reality of Elizabethan England. There were many "Machevills."

Of course there were Machiavellians long before he graced the Florentine chancery, and he himself contended that he only described political behavior as it was, rather than as the moralizers would have it be. But now, in the 1590s, greed and immorality were no longer sins; they were "policy," legitimatized as a philosophical position.

The reality caught by Marlowe's creation appealed to the people born at the beginning of Elizabeth's reign. They looked at the behavior of those around them and found the traditional moral literature naive and useless. If one was to succeed, one had to play the game as it was really played, not demand that the world become what it was not. This was not an opinion officially endorsed in Christian society, but everyone was aware that it was the real philosophy of many aspiring people.

Understanding that the key to success in the world was power, Machiavelli attracted those who sought it. As Anthony Esler remarked about the "generation of 1560," in a world in which many of the traditional moral strictures had been damaged by the Reformation and whose traditional forms of moral reasoning were under assault, Machiavelli's hard edged realism seemed to point the road to success.[68]

Perkins was so aware of this interest in "policy" as a way of getting ahead that he addressed it as an issue of virtue. Can a person, with a good conscience, "use policy in the affairs of this life?" He concluded that one could, as long as it was not against Christian religion, the honor of God, or the laws of men, and that it was appropriate to one's calling.[69] But Perkins' very system admitted moral ambiguity into the equation by putting the emphasis on conscience and calling. Many things could be squared with a conscience which had defined the good as getting ahead in the world, and whose calling was not static. It could change through ambition.

In observers like Christopher Marlowe this bred cynicism. He was as aware as any one of the moral ambiguities of a society that preached one way and lived another. It was ever thus, but in the late Elizabethan period the intense moralizing of some, who seldom lived up to their own expectations, was met with increasing contempt by others. Their cynical ambivalence did not mean that they had ceased to be Christians, but that they, accepting the right of judging in conscience, were very aware that there were few genuine saints in their world.

The moral tension generated by the Reformation was felt in all systems of thought, for people were redefining the signs of a virtuous life. The search for directions for living in the post-Reformation period generated various maps, but they all shared the realization that the individual soul had become the unit of measure. This was a momentous cultural adaptation. Embracing the certainty of faith and election created a culture which tended to reduce religion, not faith, to a matter of organization and political allegiance. The separation of church and state ended by Henry VIII led to the physical union of the two, but one of the unforeseen results was separation of the individual's piety from communal duty. Individuals, following their hearts, made choices about religion in a world that demanded only political conformity. Conscience had become the measure.

When conscience became the measure, it left people confused, willing to grant that individual virtue could only be determined by each individual unless it resulted in actions that damaged secular interests.

A Perkins and a Hooker and a Parsons could agree on the importance of conscience, but they disagreed on what a rightly informed conscience must believe. And there was no way to resolve the disagreement. This left the question of individual virtue in the hands of individuals. The result was ambiguity, a recognition that human behavior and motivation was diverse and complicated. All that could be agreed upon was that there were multiple meanings and interpretations of any act. This had the effect, as Lowell Gallagher has noted, of undermining the communally recognized signs of what belonged inside the structure of cultural norms.[70]

In formal moral discourse this led, across Europe, to the doctrine of Probablism and a search for new descriptive languages like mathematics. In early Stuart England it made moral consensus nearly impossible. For many, this meant license, and for some it meant that they had to become more and more shrill in their attempts to drown out competing consciences. The little God sitting inside us, conscience, that was expected to be an infallible guide to God's will, turned out to be a Trojan horse.

The Post-Reformation World View

If we compare the world of Sir Thomas More with that of Sir Francis Bacon, we catch some glimpse of the Reformation's impact on England. More, a member of Lincoln's Inn and Lord Chancellor of England from 1529 until 1532, died proclaiming the necessity of Christian unity. One of his generation's greatest intellectuals, he spent his energies working for reform of the Church and defending it against heresy. Bacon, a member of Gray's Inn and Lord Chancellor of England from 1618 to 1621, was 83 years More's junior, born 26 years after his death. One of his generation's greatest intellectuals, Bacon spent his energies on a new system of knowledge that would replace the sterile quibbling of theologians, believing that the greatest danger to civil peace was too much religion. Only three generations apart, they belonged to different mental worlds. They had different conceptions of the self, different ideas of a person's place and duties, different perceptions of how salvation worked, different economic values, and different political values. More could never imagine the religious diversity Bacon experienced. The Reformation failed to create a Christian Utopia in England, but it forced English culture to adapt rapidly, changing society in radical ways.

The changes were piecemeal and adaptive, occurring across three or four generations, as English lifestyles and institutions were assaulted and reconstructed. A world view was dismantled in the years between 1532 and 1559, forcing choices on individuals and institutions that were unimaginable shortly before. People met the changes as well as they could, seeking to save what they might, and learning to think about what they valued in new ways.

For individuals, the dissolutions meant the loss of some choices and the opening of others. Monks and nuns expelled from their houses reentered the world; ambitious laymen cynically fattened on church properties; and old people faced eternity without the benefit of the prayers of their families and their priests. Priests lost their cures, or fled, or learned new liturgies and married. Women, emboldened with the freedom of the gospels, learned to approach God directly, without male intervention, charting

FIGURE 7   Sir Francis Bacon, by John Vanderbank, 1731. © National Portrait Gallery, London.

the meaning of their lives in Biblical references. Some women became "Mrs. Priest." Evangelicals, recognizing their election, changed their patterns of socialization. Usurers were transformed into financiers and entrepreneurs.

Each generation's experience of the Reformation produced new uncertainties and challenges that had to be negotiated without maps, for they were traveling where their parents had never been. The confusion over how the virtuous life could be lived sent Elizabethans digging into their consciences, desperately seeking some stable authority that would allow them to differentiate between conflicting religious authorities.

By late in Elizabeth's reign individuals were more alone in their consciences than their grandparents' generation could have imagined. Thomas More knew his opinions were confirmed by Catholic tradition, cemented by the communion of the saints. His grandchildren were taught that he was deluded. They were ordered to check their consciences, individually, against scripture.

For families, the cultural dissolution meant the weakening of hierarchies, reinterpretation of duties, and the invention of new family mythologies. Defensively, all religious ideologies demanded that the true believer put God first, before father or mother, brother or sister. Protestant and papist alike warned people to eschew the evil influence of parental authority over religious choice. Not surprisingly, this meant that families and communities became mixtures of heterodoxy and orthodoxy, often dividing along generational lines. Under such circumstances, traditional pieties were abandoned. Parents could not expect heretical children to pray for their souls, or to execute wills that were theologically repulsive to them. Nor could siblings comfortably agree on the duties owed their parents. Parents, confronted with heretical children, or spouses wedded to heretics, were forced to make compromises that taught them that religion was relative when family solidarity was involved. Many simply gave up, finding it easier to concentrate on the common, secular family good.

For institutions, the dissolutions meant extinction or reconstitution. The seizure of monasteries, chantries, fraternities, and other "superstitious" foundations erased a significant share of the social life of mid-Tudor people. Institutions that were not dissolved changed, too, abandoning many of the forms of their communal lives. Deprived of Purgatory, they could no longer see themselves as communities of the living and the dead. But some kinds of institutions grew stronger and stronger thanks to the dissolutions. Seizing the opportunities they presented, towns and other organizations acquired political independence and new revenues. But however they handled the impacts, they had to reinterpret their reasons for being, inventing new traditions of social solidarity.

As the nation experienced the dissolutions, resistance was low. There were revolts, but Henry VIII's advisers had created a brilliant strategy for success. They replaced heresy with treason and caught those who supported the church but were loyal Englishmen in an impossible position. Conformity and loyalty would become the great tests of Elizabethan orthodoxy.

As the dissolutions forced adaptations, institutions and families narrowed their foci and concentrated on their common business, entering a period of reconstruction that lasted into the 1580s.

Reconstructed individuals learned to redefine sin and self. In keeping with the new theologies, and faced with irreconcilable differences and disillusioning behaviors, individual conscience became the ground on which decisions rested. This put the individual into an uneasy relationship with the community, since self-interest became a legitimate reason for action. Sin, the traditional enemy of humanity, was relegated to the realm of intention, removed from the magistracy's duty roster. This emphasis on intention had major implications for Elizabethan society, since it deregulated some things, and reduced others to mere civil inconveniences. Economic self aggrandizement was licensed in a way never seen before, thanks to the test of intention, creating the opening through which the capitalist mentality emerged.

However, as the seven deadly sins declined in importance, they were replaced with the Ten Commandments, the greatest of which was to honor God. The magistracy, bound in conscience to do its duty, as established by its vocation, was convinced that the nation could only prosper if God's honor was maintained. Consequently, while individual social responsibility declined, offenses like swearing, drinking, and blaspheming were regulated for the good of the community.

The concepts of election taught to young Elizabethans encouraged this reorientation of the self, but, since there was no common template for a "correct" conscience, Elizabethans found certain conflicts insoluble. Surrounded by religious diversity, all of it justified by claims of conscience, they became accustomed to a religiously plural world. Many did not like it, insisting that there was only one true way, and that any conscience that disagreed with their own must be wrong. But they could not get the genie back in the bottle. Toleration, violence, or social separations were possible outcomes in such a circumstance. Luckily, most Elizabethans chose pragmatic tolerance over violence or separation.

From the 1570s the problem of conscience became highly politicized, as recusancy, separatism, and Presbyterianism challenged the authority of the state church. Luckily, the Elizabethan regime refused to test consciences. It demanded only conformity and good order. This, in turn, allowed many people to conform outwardly while dissenting in conscience, preserving the fragile peace.

Reconstructed families invented new folklores to reinforce the values they had evolved. Those that were Protestant told new tales, redefining their sense of themselves. Or they retold old stories, adding Protestant morals. And sometimes, their folklore stressed the suffering of Protestant forebearers and political loyalty.

Catholic families needed stories to reenforce their identities, too. Their folklore portrayed their Catholic forebearers as heroes of the resistance. Those who were not so heroic were forgotten, or their lives were reinvented in order to explain their slackness.

But most families contained both Catholics and Protestants, making religious identity problematic. As a result, families developed treaties of private toleration that permitted the religious mixture to exist by ignoring it as much as possible. Most families quietly accepted their black sheep. Bonds of kinship mitigated demands for conformity, while family members worked to protect property and honor.

Reconstructed institutions redefined good fellowship and the duties of membership, concentrating on common secular concerns. Just as individuals and families were learning how to deal with ideological diversity, so were guilds companies, colleges, towns, and cities. In their records we can see slow cultural adaptations occurring as the first generation raised without clear memories of the old customs displaced the last generation that could remember monks and chantries in England. First, they mimicked the old forms. Later, as the adapted forms became customary, they were further altered, making them less and less religious and more and more about the secular purposes of the organization. By the 1590s the older forms of sociability had been displaced by a secular discourse of membership, commemoration, and occupational identity.

In some institutions, such as colleges in the universities, the Reformation's effects were more sudden, thanks to external interventions. It might take only a decade for a college fellowship to change its religious orientation. But there, too, new forms of membership and commemoration were evolving as governing bodies struggled to fit new expectations into the limitations imposed by ancient statutes.

The younger generation of Elizabethan intellectuals expressed an English Protestant higher culture focused on the individual conscience. Their intellectual interests combined Protestant and humanist traditions in an attempt to discover where virtue and certainty could be found. Their answer was monadic. It was to be found, by testing, in each soul. Every conscience, working out its relationship with God, was charged with following God as best it could. The Elizabethan literature of self-reflection, like Elizabethan casuistry, gave expression to this search within the self for some guiding certainty in a world that was contradictory in its authoritative demands. On the street, this meant self-interest could be read as divinely sanctioned, so long as it was practiced within the general limits of Christian charity.

Luckily, for individuals, families, and institutions, contexts determined the speed and the direction of the adaptations. Local conditions were the key, since Tudor government was essentially local government. In order to make the Reformation work, the Crown depended upon the local magistrates and churchwardens, men who were symbiotic with the monarchy, but who had enormous latitude in enforcement. They knew what they could and could not achieve within local power structures. Ironically, these men were strengthened by the Reformation, and they were its beneficiaries in wealth and power. But they were a difficult group to boss. Members of the leading families, men of influence in their towns, counties, guilds, and companies, they often mitigated the enforcement of laws that did not suit local conditions. This kept the Reformation from being so offensive, or so destructive, or so alien to the magisterial classes that it caused rebellion.

However, they all existed within the structure provided by the Common Law of England. This law, treated by its practitioners as almost another form of divine revelation, stabilized the Reformation by limiting its impacts. What is most important, property law, which recognized even spiritual livings as forms of secular property, guaranteed that the lay elite would benefit from the Reformation. Moreover, it guaranteed that the property they acquired from the church could not be taken away.

The law also prevented mass expulsions of ecclesiastical office holders, stabilizing the church in spite of its ideological joy ride. The Vicar of Bray, and his many, many brothers, cushioned the Reformation in their parishes, and modeled quiet conformity. These conformists made poor ideologues, but they did not stir rebellion. Their conformity allowed their parishes to adjust slowly, keeping some old customs and discarding others until they reached an equilibrium that felt like Protestantism to them.

The example set by the magistracy and the clergy during the Reformation was not edifying to the populace. They were treated to a show of greed and time serving by their leaders, who demonstrated by example how to deal with the frequent religious changes. Keep your opinion to yourself, take care of your property, and seize the day were the watchwords of people as eminent as Elizabeth I and Lord Burghley. Rather than protesting, community leaders maximized their opportunities, both personal and communal, agreeing with the Crown that good order was more valuable than personal risk.

How to maintain that order was always a difficult question. The Crown was its guarantor, but it was threatened by Elizabeth's single state and the possibility of a foreign heiress. By the same token, the new state church had many natural enemies, and it had to be protected from papists and presbyterians alike. To cement English Protestantism and protect the Protestant state, it was easiest to define national identity in relation to the enemy religion. Elizabethans, while practicing pragmatic toleration in their families and communities, were taught to hate the chimerical papist. Of course, after the defeat of the Armada, English people needed no further proof of the Pope's evil intentions or God's love of England.

But hatred is not the same as spiritual conviction. By turning religious identity into political identity the Elizabethans left the spirit free to wander. Elizabeth's church was a house with many rooms, each containing a Book of Common Prayer and a Bible, each open to a different page. Beyond the national church were more and more "communities of conscience" in which politically loyal but religiously diverse people found comfort.

And so by the end of the century a post-Reformation culture was emerging with distinctive characteristics, some of which contradicted others. At its core was the individual conscience, the place where God's plan for the individual could be read. In a separate cell was political loyalty, a thing that could be practiced by people with conflicting consciences. Attached to them both was a new vision of public duty that allowed individuals to be entrepreneurial and progressive in their economic behavior, so long as they did not damage the secular welfare of the community. Enclosing them all was the hazy film of duty and obedience, and it was here the problem lay.

In theory, every English person owed obedience to the monarch and all the rest of God's chosen magistrates, including parents and masters. But the Reformation, though outwardly affirming that obedience, undermined it with its insistence that conscience trumped magistracy. As the Stuart monarchs discovered, for every order issued by a magistrate there was a possible objection in conscience. Magistrates, of course, were bound to do their duty to God, too, which meant that some lesser magistrates felt compelled not only to reform manners, but also to resist ungodly orders from above. Thus, the Elizabethan state was a religious patchwork with varying local standards of conformity. When a more centralizing monarchy tried to impose genuine uniformity on the nation, consciences rose up and smote it.

It was the accidental genius of the Elizabethan Settlement that it was so benign and long lived that this new "Protestant" culture had enfolded the English nation by the early seventeenth century. Elizabeth's refusal to seek definition and the regime's political inability to enforce total conformity had allowed local custom, understood as Protestantism, to emerge. It was the misfortune of the Stuarts that they mistook the diversity of Elizabethan Protestantism for a unified church. There was a reason that Elizabeth I never held a Westminster Conference in her reign. She knew that good order was not about a strict theology.

Elizabeth knew what many, many Tudor people learned across the years of the Reformation. Flexibility was the key to survival in a world that had deposed its certainties. William Paulet, Marquis of Winchester, was born before 1488, living until 1572. Raised to the peerage by Henry VIII, he was Lord Treasurer under Edward VI, Mary, and Elizabeth, conforming to every religious change. Late in his life he revealed his secret for success in the Reformation confusion. "I am sprung from the willow," he said, "not from the oak."[1] The same could have been said for the society in which he lived. Its political culture, sprung from the willow, bent and swayed in the ideological winds, but it was not uprooted and broken. It leaned with the winds until, when they steadied, it developed a permanent, Protestant, bent.

Notes

Chapter 1   Post Reformation Culture

1   Duffy, Eamon, *The Stripping of the Altars. Traditional Religion in England 1400–1580* (New Haven, 1992).
2   BL, Landsdowne 101, fos. 163–4.

Chapter 2   Choosing Reformations

1   Hugh Aveling and W. A. Pantin, eds. *The Letter Book of Robert Joseph Monk-Scholar of Evesham and Gloucester College, Oxford 1530–3*, OHS, MS, 19 (1967), 163; 155.
2   ITL, Petyt Ms 538/10, fo. 25.
3   BL Add. 48064, fo. 25.
4   BL Add. 48064, fo. 9.
5   T. F. T. Plucknett and J. L. Barton, eds. *St. German's Doctor and Student*. Selden Society 91 (1974), xi–xiii.
6   William Roper, *The Life of Sir Thomas More*, E. V. Hitchcock, ed. (Springfield, IL, 1935), 112–14.
7   John Guy, *Thomas More* (London, 2000), 196–202.
8   Nicholas Harpsfield, *The Life and Death of Sir Thomas More*, E. V. Hitchcock, ed. (London, 1932), 84–7. Richard Marius, *Thomas More. A Biography* (Cambridge, MA, 1984), 315.
9   PRO E 314/37/19.
10 HPTD, sub Roper, William.
11 Charles, Nevinson, ed., *Later Writings of Bishop John Hooper* (Cambridge, 1852), 33.
12 Diarmaid MacCulloch, *Thomas Cranmer* (New Haven, 1996), 473–82.
13 CSP Dom. Ed., 196.
14 L&P 12, i, 108 # 212.
15 J. Venn, "Memoir of John Caius," in E. S. Roberts, ed., *The Works of John Caius, M.D. Second Founder of Gonville and Caius College and Master of the College 1559–1573* (Cambridge, 1912), 37–8.

16   PRO, PCC 26 Alen. APC, 1549–50, p. 405.

17   John Caius, *The First Book of the Annals of the Royal College of Physicians, London, 1528–1572,* in Roberts, ed., *Works of John Caius,* 12–71 infra.

18   Norman L. Jones, "William Cecil and the Making of Economic Policy in the 1560s and Early 1570s" in Paul A. Fideler and T. F. Mayer, eds., *Political Thought and the Tudor Commonwealth* (London, 1992), 186. BL Lansdowne 101, nos. 24 and 26, unpaginated.

19   Unless otherwise attributed, this biography is based on HPTD sub Huick, Robert.

20   HPTD sub Markham, Sir John.

21   HMC, Hatfield Mss. IV, 189.

22   HPTD sub Markham, Thomas.

23   HPTD, sub Parker, Thomas I

24   Anthony Esler, *The Aspiring Mind of the Elizabethan Younger Generation* (Durham, NC, 1966), xv.

25   LIBB, 346, 405, 409, 413.

26   HPCD sub Roper, Thomas.

27   Hartley, *Proceedings,* I, 207.

28   Ibid., 351.

29   HPTD sub Snagge, Robert.

30   *Dictionary of National Biography,* entry: Edmund Campion.

31   LGL, 11588/1, fols. 177v; 185

32   Ibid., fo. 186.

33   Ibid., fos. 188; 189.

34   Edmund Campion, "Campion's Brag," in Evelyn Waugh, *Edmund Campion* (London, 1952), Appendix I, 209–13.

35   Puritanism refers to the belief that the English national church has only partially reformed. A generic term, it is used to indicate those who wished to see further "purification" of the Anglican church, but who remained within it. Presbyterians were often Puritans, but they objected to the existence of bishops in the national church, preferring church government by synods of elders or presbyters. Separatists believed that the Anglican church was so far removed from God's plan that they had to separate from it.

36   Esler, *Aspiring Mind,* 244 provides a list of leading courtiers and writers of the "generation of 1560."

37   "Lady Mildmay's Meditations," Northampton, Northamptonshire Libraries, Phillipps Ms. 2569, 9–15.

38   Linda Pollock, *With Faith and Physic The Life of a Tudor Gentlewoman Lady Grace Mildmay 1552–1620* (London, 1993), 42.

39   HPTD sub Mildmay, Anthony. Stanford Lehmberg, *Sir Walter Mildmay and Tudor Government* (Austin, TX, 1964), 304–5.

40   J. H. Baker, ed. *Reports From the Lost Notebooks of Sir James Dyer, Vol. II,* Selden Society 110 (1994), 387–8.

41   HPTD sub Mildmay, Anthony.

42   Pollock, *With Faith and Physic,* 61–2.

43 Ibid., 40–2.
44 Joan Thirsk, *Economic Policy and Projects The Development of a Consumer Society in Early Modern England* (Oxford, 1988), 184.
45 HPTD sub Myddleton, Thomas. Glanmor Williams, *Renewal and Reformation. Wales c. 1415–1642* (Oxford, 1993), 483. Glanmor Williams, *The Welsh and their Religion. Historical Essays* (Cardiff, 1991), 160–1.
46 21 Jac. I, c. 17.
47 Bodl., Rawlinson Ms. D.677, pp. 11–15; 22–3. Norman Jones, *God and the Moneylenders. Usury and Law in Early Modern England* (Oxford, 1989), 145–74.
48 BL, Lansdowne 825, no. 66.
49 HEH HM 8, fo. 200.
50 Don Paterson, ed., *101 Sonnets from Shakespeare to Heaney* (London, 1999), 42.
51 "Divine Poems XIV" in ibid., 299.
52 Elizabeth McClure Thomson, *The Chamberlain Letters. A Selection of the Letters of John Chamberlain Concerning Life in England from 1597 to 1626* (New York, 1965), 165.
53 The details of Donne's life are taken primarily from HPTD sub Donne, John and Oliver, *Donne's Religious Writings*, 20–49.

Chapter 3   Families and Reformations

1 "A Learned Discourse of Justification, Works, and how the Foundation of Faith is Overthrown," Hooker, III, 495–500, 538, 546.
2 Quoted in Joseph Puterbaugh, "'Your selfe be judge and answer your selfe': Formation of Protestant Identity in *A Conference betwixt a Mother a Devout Recusant and Her Sonne a Zealous Protestant*," *Sixteenth Century Journal* 31 (2000), 421.
3 John Whitgift, "Contents of the Archbishop's Sermon Preached at the Cathedral of St. Paul's, London, Nov. the 17, 1583, Being the Anniversary Day of Q. Elizabeth's Coming to the Crown,"*Works*, John Ayre, ed. (Cambridge, 1853), III, 590.
4 Joan Kirby, ed., *Plumpton Correspondence*. Camden Society 5th series, 8 (1996), 205–7. David Danielle, ed., *Tyndale's New Testament* (New Haven, 1989), 207–24.
5 Hastings Robinson, ed., *Original Letters Relative to the English Reformation* (Cambridge, 1856), 86
6 Claire Cross, ed., *The Letters of Sir Francis Hastings 1574–1609*, Somerset Record Society LXIX (1969), 3–5. HEH HA5079.
7 William A. Ringler and Michael Flachmann, eds., *Beware The Cat by William Baldwin. The First English Novel* (San Marino, CA, 1988), 37–9.
8 John Knox, *Selected Writings of John Knox. Public Epistles, Treatises, and Expositions to the Year 1559*. Kevin Reed, ed. (Dallas, 1995), 331.
9 Susan Wabuda, "The Woman with the Rock: The Controversy on Women and Bible Reading," in Susan Wabuda and Caroline Litzenberger, eds., *Belief and Practice in Reformation England* (Aldershot, 1998), 40–59.

10 Thomas Freeman, "The Good Minstrye of Godlye and Vertuouse Women: The Elizabethan Martyrologists and the Female Supporters of the Marian Martyrs," *Journal of British Studies* 39 (2000), 13; 32–3.

11 Charles Nevinson, ed., *Later Writings of Bishop John Hooper* (Cambridge, 1852), 609–11.

12 BL Add. 48064, fo. 20v.

13 Puterbaugh, "Protestant Identity," 425.

14 Susan Brigden, "Youth and the English Reformation," *Past and Present* 95 (1982), 37–67.

15 Ibid., 58.

16 Puterbaugh, "Protestant Identity," 425.

17 Felicity Heal, "Reputation and Honour in Court and Country: Lady Elizabeth Russell, and Sir Thomas Hoby," *Transactions of the Royal Historical Society*, 6th series, 6 (1996), 177.

18 PRO, PROB 11, 57 fo. 25.

19 Foley, I, 183.

20 Richard Gibbings, ed., *An Answer to John Martiall's Treatise of the Cross. By James Calfhill, D.D . . .* (Cambridge, 1856), 65. Bodl. Tanner 50, fos. 44v-45.

21 Andy Wood, "Custom and the Social Organization of Writing in Early Modern England," *Transactions of the Royal Historical Society*, 6th series, 9 (1999), 267.

22 Adam Fox, "Remembering the Past in Early Modern England: Oral and Written Tradition," *Transactions of the Royal Historical Society*, 6th series, 9 (1999), 236. Quoting *The Great Frost* in *Social England Illustrated: A Collection of XVIIth Century Tracts*, Andrew Lang, ed. (1903), 166.

23 Ibid, 234.

24 J. P. Cooper, ed., *The Wentworth Papers 1597–1628*, Camden Society 4th series, 12 (1973), 26–7.

25 M. R. James, *Family, Lineage and Civil Society; a Study of Society, Politics and Mentality in the Durham Region, 1500–1640* (1974), 110.

26 Richard Cust, "Catholicism, Antiquarianism and Gentry Honour: The Writings of Sir Thomas Shirley," *Midland History* 23 (1998), 40–44.

27 John Pits, *Relationum Historicarum de rebus Anglicis* (Paris, 1619) sub "De Antonio Fitzherberto."

28 Gervase Holles, *Memorials of the Holles Family 1493–1656*, Camden Society, 3rd series, 55 (1937), 63.

29 James Whitelocke, *Liber Famelicus of Sir James Whitelocke*, John Bruce, ed. Camden Society OS (1858), 5.

30 John Smith, of Nibley. *The Lives of the Berkeleys Lords of the Honour, Castle and Manor of Berkeley in the County of Gloucester from 1066 to 1618*. John Maclean, ed. (Gloucester, 1883), II, 417.

31 HEH HA 10334.

32 William Camden, *Annales Rerum Anglicarum et Hibernicarum Regnante Elizabetha* (1717), 76. ". . . fraterno intern se amore, at non religione unanimes."

33 BL Add. 48023, fo. 354v. PRO KB 8/40. Nicholas Sander, "Dr Nicholas Sander's

Report to Cardinal Moroni," A. J. Pollen, ed., *Catholic Record Society Miscellanea I* (1905), 45. For the details see Norman Jones, "Defining Superstitions: Treasonous Catholics and the Act against Witchcraft of 1563," in Charles Carlton, Robert L. Woods, Mary L. Robertson, Joseph S. Block, eds., *State, Sovereigns and Society in Early Modern England. Essays in Honour of A. J. Slavin* (Thrupp, Gloucs., 1998), 187–204.

34 Camden, *Annales*, 736.

35 HEH, HA 4714.

36 J. H. Baker, ed., *The Notebook of Sir John Port*, Selden Society 102 (1986), xlvi–l.

37 Ibid., xx.

38 Ibid., lvii. PRO, PCC, 4 Alenger: PROB 11/28, fo. 29v.

39 PRO, PCC 7 Alenger.

40 HEH, HAP Box 9, folder 4. A draft, with editorial comments, perhaps by John Porte himself. Collated with the copy of the probated will at HEH, HA Repton and Etwall, Box 1, folder 1.

41 Repton School: http://www.repton.org.uk/Repton/Repton_History.html. Etwall, Derbyshire: http://www.etwall.demon.co.uk/wells/etwall.html.

42 HEH, HAP Box 14, Folder 15.

43 David Hickman, "From Catholic to Protestant: the Changing Meaning of Testamentary Religious Provisions in Elizabethan London," in Nicholas Tyacke, ed., *England's Long Reformation 1500–1800* (Cambridge, 1998), 117–39.

44 Peter S. Bearman, *Relations into Rhetorics. Local Elite Social Structure in Norfolk, England, 1540–1640* (New Brunswick, NJ, 1993), 71–2.

45 Richard Copley Christie, ed., *Letters of Sir Thomas Copley of Gatton . . . to Queen Elizabeth and Her Ministers* (New York, 1970), 33–34.

46 CSP Ven 1527–33, I, 642, 270. L&P, 20, pt. 2, 231; 21, pt. 2, 96.

47 Ibid, 21, pt. 2, 291.

48 APC, 1549–50, 405.

49 PRO, PCC 24 Loftes.

50 ITL, Petyt Ms. 538/10, fos. 42v-43.

51 Cal. Pat. Rolls, 1565–66, 433, item 2413.

52 ITL, Petyt Ms. 538/10 fo. 78.

53 HPTD sub Alford, Roger.

54 ITL, Petyt Ms. 538/10 fo. 80.

55 Ibid.

56 BL Lansd. 35, fo. 87–87v.

57 HPTD, sub Bacon, Nicholas I; Nicholas II, Edmund, Edward, Nathaniel, Anthony, Francis.

58 Foley, I, 175.

59 Justin McCann and Hugh Connolly, eds., "Memorials of Father Augustine Baker, O.S.B." *Catholic Record Society* 33 (1933), 16–7.

60 Ian Beward, ed., *The Works of William Perkins* (Appleford, 1970), 422.

61 "The Manuscripts of Sir Alexander Acland-Hood, Bart., at St. Audries, co. Somerset," HMC 6th Report, 345–6.

62 BL Add. 48064, fo. 22v.

63 Christopher Marsh, *Popular Religion in Sixteenth-Century England* (New York, 1998), 174.

64 Philip Carman, trans., *William Weston. The Autobiography of an Elizabethan* (London, 1955), 49–51.

65 Cooper, *Wentworth Papers*, 18.

Chapter 4 Dissolutions and Opportunities

1 J. A. Twemlow, ed., *Liverpool Town Books. Proceedings of Assemblies, Common Councils, Portmoot Courts, Etc., 1550–1862. Vol. I, 1550–1571* (London, 1918), 23; 32.

2 Beat A. Kümin, ed., *Reformations Old and New. Essays on the Socio-Economic Impact of Religious Change c. 1470–1630* (Aldershot, 1996), 2.

3 Robert Whiting, *The Blind Devotion of the People. Popular Religion and the English Reformation* (Cambridge, 1989), 265.

4 The best guide to the general law on incorporeal hereditaments is Sir John Doddridge, *A Compleat parson or, A description of advowsons, or church living. Wherein is set forth, the interests of the Parson, Patron, and Ordinarie etc.* (London: 1630).

5 John Strype, *Ecclesiastical Memorials, Relating Chiefly to Religion, and the Reformation of it, and the Emergencies of the Church of England, under King Henry VIII. King Edward VI and Queen Mary I* (Oxford, 1822), II, i, 356–7.

6 PRO E 321/41/284.

7 PRO E 321/41/288.

8 The Dean of St Paul's Case. 3 Dyer, 368b in ER 73, 825.

9 PRO E 321/40/60.

10 J. H. Baker, ed., *Reports From the Lost Notebooks of Sir James Dyer, Vol. I*, Selden Society 109 (1993), 182.

11 R. A. Houlbrooke, ed. *The Letter Book of John Parkhurst Bishop of Norwich compiled during the Years 1571–5* Norfolk Record Society 43 (1974 and 1975), 148.

12 W. H. Frere, ed., *Puritan Manifestoes: A Study of the Origin of the Puritan Revolt* (London, 1907), 10–12, 36. My thanks to Peter Kauffman for reminding me of this.

13 Margaret Spufford, *Contrasting Communities. English Villagers in the Sixteenth and Seventeenth Centuries* (Cambridge, 1979), 251 and 251 n. 49.

14 Rosemary O'Day, *The English Clergy. The Emergence and Consolidation of a Profession 1558–1642* (Leicester, 1979), 45.

15 Christopher Hill, *The Economic Problems of the Church: from Archbishop Whitgift to The Long Parliament* (Oxford, 1956), 144–5.

16 O'Day, *Clergy*, 29–31. Margaret Bowker, "The Henrician Reformation and the Parish Clergy," in Christopher Haigh, ed., *The English Reformation Revised* (Cambridge, 1996), 75–93.

17 Eric J. Carlson, *Marriage and the English Reformation* (Oxford, 1994), 49–66. My understanding of clerical marriage has been enhanced by Nancy Basler Bjorklund, who

allowed me to read her unpublished manuscript, "'A Godly Wife is an Helper': Matthew Parker and the Defense of Clerical Marriage."

18 Nicodemites were named after Nicodemus, the man who only dared visit Jesus at night. Coined by John Calvin, it refers to those Protestants who, for fear of persecution, camouflaged their true convictions and outwardly conformed to Catholic worship.

19 Clair Crosse, "Religion in Doncaster from the Reformation to the Civil War," in Patrick Collinson and John Craig, eds., *The Reformation in English Towns, 1500–1640* (London, 1998), 53–5.

20 Gerald Bray, ed., *The Anglican Canons 1529–1947*. Church of England Record Society 6 (1998), 45–9.

21 21 Henry VIII, c. 13.

22 James C. Spalding, *The Reformation of the Ecclesiastical Laws of England, 1552*. Sixteenth Century Essays and Studies, 19 (1992). See "Concerning those to be admitted to ecclesiastical benefices" 107 ff, and chapters 1, 3, 4, 16 on patrons' and prebendaries' duties.

23 "Legatine Constitutions of Pole, 1556" in Bray, ed., *The Anglican Canons*, 120.

24 13 Eliz. I, c. 12.

25 13 Eliz. I, c. 10.

26 13 Eliz. I, c. 20.

27 Marjorie K. McIntosh, *A Community Transformed: the Manor and Liberty of Havering, 1500–1620* (Cambridge, 1991), 176–87.

28 Patrick Collinson, "The Protestant Cathedral" in Patrick Collinson, Nigel Ramsay and Margaret Sparks, eds., *A History of Canterbury Cathedral* (Oxford, 1995), 159–72.

29 J. E. Cox, ed., *Miscellaneous Writings and Letters of Thomas Cranmer* (Cambridge, 1846), 160, 162, 396–7, 417, 466.

30 Parker Corres., 176, 312, 362.

31 Ibid., 172.

32 W. J. Sheils, "Profit, Patronage, or Pastoral Care: The Rectory Estates of the Archbishopric of York, 1540–1640," in Rosemary O'Day and Felicity Heal, eds., *Princes and Paupers in the English Church 1500–1800* (Leicester, 1981), 91–109.

33 Hill, *Economic Problems*, 50–73.

34 Albert Peel, ed., *The seconde Parte of a Register* (Cambridge, 1915), 100, 104.

35 31 Henry VIII, c. 13 § 14.

36 Ibid., §1.

37 Walter C. Richardson, *History of the Court of Augmentations 1536–1554* (Baton Rouge, 1961), 178.

38 Benjamin Thompson, "Monasteries and Their Patrons at Foundation and Dissolution," *Transactions of the Royal Historical Society* 6th series, 4 (1994), 119–23.

39 Ibid., 118–19.

40 Helen Miller, *Henry VIII and the English Nobility* (Oxford, 1989), 227–9.

41 J. H. Baker, ed., *The Notebook of Sir John Port*. Selden Society 102 (1986), xlviii, xlix.

42 *Lists and Indexes Supplementary Series No. III, vol. 1. List of the Lands of Dissolved Religious Houses. Bedfordshire-Huntingdonshire* (New York, 1964), 82.

43 Ethan Shagan, "Popular Politics and the English Reformation, *c.* 1525–1553" (unpublished Ph.D. dissertation, Princeton University, 2000), 311–58.

44 37 Henry VIII, c. 4 § 1.

45 37 Henry VIII, c. 4 § 3, 4, 5, 10, 12, 13 14.

46 Alan Kreider, *English Chantries. The Road to Dissolution* (Cambridge, MA, 1979), 159–61, 163. J. W. F. Hill, *Tudor and Stuart Lincoln* (Cambridge, 1956), 55.

47 Joyce W. Percy, ed., *York Memorandum Book* Surtees Society 186 (1973), 149–51.

48 Robert Tittler, *The Reformation and the Towns in England. Politics and Political Culture, c. 1540–1640* (Oxford, 1998), 137–8.

49 Robert Whiting, "'For the Health of My Soul': Prayers for the Dead in the Tudor South-West," in Peter Marshall, ed., *The Impact of the English Reformation 1500–1640* (London, 1997), 128.

50 1 Edw. VI, c. 14 § 1.

51 PRO E 315/440, fos. 81v, 87, 89.

52 PRO E 315/441, fos. 120v-121.

53 Parker Corres., 34–6.

54 John Strype, *The Life and Acts of Matthew Parker . . . to which is added, an Appendix Containing Various Transcripts . . .* (Oxford, 1821) I, 41–3.

55 1 Edw. VI, c. 14 § 1, 7.

56 1 Edw. VI, c. 14 § 8–12.

57 Stanford Lehmberg, *Sir Walter Mildmay and Tudor Government* (Austin, 1964), 23–4.

58 PRO SP 46/3/1 fo. 5.

59 Ibid., fo. 16.

60 Ibid., fo. 6.

61 Ibid., fos. 7–8v.

62 Ibid. fos. 9–10.

63 Ibid., fo. 14.

64 PRO E 314/37/33.

65 Kreider, *English Chantries,* 158. J. S. Scarisbrick, *The Reformation and the English People* (Oxford, 1984), 99.

66 PRO STAC 3/5/77. F. E. Warneford, ed., *Star Chamber Suits of John and Thomas Warneford,* Wiltshire Record Society 48 (1993), xvii; 66–7.

67 Lehmberg, *Mildmay,* 24.

68 PRO E 314/63/48. For the dissolution of Fordham see PRO E 322/89.

69 PRO 3114/4/35/piece 15. The date of this must be ca. 1545.

70 Peter Cunich, "The Dissolution of the Chantries," in Patrick Collinson and John Craig, eds. *The Reformation in English Towns, 1500–1640* (London, 1998), 163. Henry Summerson, *Medieval Carlisle: The City and the Borders from the Late Eleventh to the Mid-Sixteenth Century.* The Cumberland and Westmorland Antiquarian and Archaeological Society, Extra Series 25 (1993), II, 611, 632–4.

71 Tittler, *English Towns,* 126.

72 David Harris Sacks, *The Widening Gate. Bristol and the Atlantic Economy 1450–1700* (Berkeley, 1993), 145–6.

73 HPTD sub Pate, Richard. Tittler, *English Towns*, 123–5.

74 Wallace T. MacCaffrey, *Exeter 1540–1640 The Growth of an English County Town*, 2nd edn. (Cambridge, MA, 1975), 184–5.

75 Robert Tittler, "Reformation, Resources and Authority in English Towns: An Overview" in Patrick Collinson and John Craig, eds., *The Reformation in English Towns, 1500–1640* (London, 1998), 192. This argument is worked out in detail in Tittler, *Towns*, summarized on 335–41.

76 BL Add 32091, fo. 147–147v.

77 Jones, *Faith by Statute*, 105–6. HPTD sub Rich, Richard. Michael A. R. Graves, *The House of Lords in the Parliaments of Edward VI and Mary I. An Institutional Study* (Cambridge, 1981), 81–2.

78 CSP Ven., VII, 73.

79 Norman Jones, "Profiting From Religious Reform: The Land Rush of 1559," *Historical Journal*, 22, 1 (1979), 279–94.

80 Jeanette Martin, "Leadership and Priorities in Reading During the Reformation," in Patrick Collinson and John Craig, eds., *The Reformation in English Towns, 1500–1640* (London, 1998), 113–29. HPTD sub Bourne, John II.

81 A. H. Johnson, *The History of the Worshipful Company of the Drapers of London . . . Vol. II 1509–1603* (Oxford, 1915), 82.

82 Joseph P. Ward, *Metropolitan Communities. Trade Guilds, Identity and Change in Early Modern London* (Stanford, 1997), 104.

83 James Christie, ed., *Some Account of Parish Clerks, More Especially of the Ancient Fraternity (Bretherne and Sisterne), of St. Nicholas now known as The Worshipful Company of Parish Clerks* (London, 1893), 100.

84 Cal. Pat. Rolls Ed., III, 386–401.

85 LGL 7086/2 fo. 135v. LGL 7112, fo. 43; 44.

86 LGL 7112, fos. 40–43.

87 LGL, 7086/2 fo. 118v; fo. 165; 176. LGL 7112, fo. 40

88 LGL, 7086/2 fo. 187.

89 Ibid., 232v.

90 Ibid., 247v.

91 Ibid., 278v.

92 Ibid., 332v.

93 Ian Archer reminds me that the cost of the dinner inflated, even though the amount the Company spent remained the same. Those attending were expected to pay the difference.

94 BL Add 32091, fo. 145.

95 J. R. L. Highfield, ed., *The Early Rolls of Merton College Oxford*, OHS n.s. 18 (1964), 446.

96 MCR 169

97 MCR 3348. RACM 1483–1521; 120, 140–1.

98 MCR 804. RACM 1483–1521, 29–30.

99 MCR 133

100   RACM 1483–1521, 499.

101   Ibid., 480. George C. Brodrick, *Memorials of Merton College with Biographical Notices of the Wardens and Fellows*, OHS IV (1885).

102   RACM 1521–1567, 173.

103   The statistics for requiems and obits were compiled from a number of sources. Merton College Records 4022–4048, the Subwardens' Accounts for 1515–1586, and Merton College Records 3839–3960, Bursars' Rolls for 1523–1585, are the backbone of the work, along with John M. Fletcher, and Christopher A. Upton, eds., *The Domestic Accounts of Merton College Oxford 1 August 1482–1 August 1494*, OHS n.s. XXXIV (1996). RACM 1483–1521, RACM 1521–1567; RACM 1567–1603.

104   My thanks to John Cooper for sharing his research on Philipps.

105   L&P 12, i, pg. 108 # 212

106   Brodrick, *Memorials*.

107   S. L. Greenslade, "The Faculty of Theology" in James McConica, ed. *The History of the University of Oxford. Vol. III, The Collegiate University* (Oxford, 1986), 320.

108   L&P, 10, 950. G. H. Martin and J. R. L. Highfield, *A History of Merton College, Oxford* (Oxford, 1997), 151.

109   CSP Dom. Ed., 68 # 164.

110   John M. Fletcher and Christopher A. Upton, "Destruction, Repair and Removal: An Oxford College Chapel during the Reformation," *Oxoniensia* 48 (1983), 123.

111   Ibid., 123.

112   Fletcher and Upton, "Destruction, Repair and Removal," 124.

113   MCR 4043, 1&2 Elizabeth.

114   Ibid., 125–7.

115   MCR 4043. 5 Edward VI; 5&6 Philip and Mary; 1&2 Elizabeth.

116   RACM 15221–1567, 245; 248–9. MCR 4043 7&8 Elizabeth. Each chaplain had a clerk helping him. The numbers later fell to 2 chaplains and 2 clerks.

117   Whiting, " 'Health of my Soul,' " 129–30.

118   Bullein, *Dialogue*, fos. 61–62v, 83v.

Chapter 5   Redefining Communities

1   Kenneth L. Parker and Eric J. Carlson, eds., *'Practical Divinity' The Works and Life of Revd Richard Greenham* (Aldershot, 1998), 134–5.

2   Foley, I, 66–7.

3   L&P, I, # 402.153–4.

4   Gerald Bray, ed., *The Anglican Canons 1529–1947*, Church of England Record Society 6 (1998), 24–39.

5   LGL, 7109. Extracts from Wills, Pewterers' Company. This is a manuscript containing accounts of legacies begun probably in 1563. It is bound in boards with the original leather binding and clasp intact. The front cover is lined with a manuscript account book, in Latin, in a 16th century legal hand. Entered upside down on the left hand side are two entries concerning 1530.

6 Diarmaid MacCulloch, *Thomas Cranmer* (New Haven, 1996), 233–4. Glyn Redworth, *In Defence of the Church Catholic. The Life of Stephen Gardiner* (Oxford, 1990), 87–9.

7 Quoted in Susan Brigden, *London and the Reformation* (Oxford, 1989), 346.

8 Hastings Robinson, ed., *Original Letters Relative to the English Reformation* (Cambridge, 1856), 36.

9 L&P XI (1852), 285. This discussion of the 1540s follows Brigden, *London*, 324–77.

10 Elaine V. Beilin, ed., *The Examinations of Anne Askew* (Oxford, 1996), 127.

11 Ibid., 148.

12 Diarmaid MacCulloch, *Tudor Church Militant. Edward VI and the Protestant Reformation* (London, 1999), 74–5.

13 Philip Caraman, *The Western Rising 1549. The Prayer Book Rebellion* (Tiverton, 1994), 12–16.

14 CSP Dom. Ed. # 302, p. 123.

15 Mark Stoyle, "The Dissendence of Despair: Rebellion and Identity in Early Modern Cornwall," *Journal of British Studies* 38 (1999), 437–8.

16 John Vowell alias Hooker, *The Description of the Citie of Excester*, W. J. Harte, J. W. Schopp, and H. Tapley-Soper, eds. (Exeter, 1919), II, 62–3.

17 Caraman, *The Western Rising*, 47–8; 86–90.

18 CSP Dom. Ed. # 344, p. 131.

19 Ibid., # 333, 334, p. 128–9; # 355, 357, pp. 134–5. LGL, 25630, fos. 270–71.

20 Thomas Norton, ed., *Reformatio legum Ecclesiasticarum* (1571), fos. 9v, 10. [STC 6006], Transubstantiation is referred to as "totum hoc Papistice fecis somnium aufferi volumus." The translation is that of James C. Spalding, *The Reformation of the Ecclesiastical Laws of England, 1552*. Sixteenth Century Essays and Studies 19 (1992), 74, 75.

21 Maitland, *Canon Law in the Church of England*, 178, quoted in Philip Hughes, *The Reformation in England* (New York, 1954), 132. Maitland was following the text as published by Thomas Norton in 1571, fo. 12v. Spalding's translation contains wording added by Peter Martyr Vermigli that suggests exile or imprisonment are acceptable alternatives to burning, since they may encourage repentance. Spalding, *Ecclesiastical Laws*, 79

22 Cal Pat Rolls Ed., III, 347.

23 Jennifer Loach, *Edward VI*, George Bernard and Penry Williams, eds. (New Haven, 1999), 163–4.

24 Robert Parkyn, "Robert Parkyn's Narrative of the Reformation, 1532–54" in David Cressy and Lori Ann Ferrell, eds., *Religion and Society in Early Modern England. A Sourcebook* (London, 1996), 28.

25 H&L, II, 5–7.

26 1&2 Philip and Mary, c. 6. H&L II, 35–8.

27 David Loades, *The Reign of Mary Tudor* (London, 1979), 331–2.

28 Hughes, *The Reformation in England*, II, 274.

29 Christopher Marsh, *Popular Religion in Sixteenth-Century England* (New York, 1998), 184, 186.

30 John Foxe, *Actes and monuments of these latter and perillous dayes* (1563), 1159. [STC 11222]

31 Mark Byford, "The Birth of a Protestant Town: the Process of Reformation in Tudor Colchester, 1530–80," in Patrick Collinson and John Craig, eds., *The Reformation in English Towns, 1500–1640* (Basingstoke, 1998), 34.

32 D. M. Palliser, *Tudor York* (Oxford, 1979), 243. Robert Whiting, *The Blind Devotion of the People. Popular Religion and the English Reformation* (Cambridge, 1989), 163–4. J. W. F. Hill, *Tudor and Stuart Lincoln* (Cambridge, 1956), 59–60.

33 *Certain Sermons or Homilies Appointed to be Read in Churches in the time of Queen Elizabeth of Famous Memory* (London, 1846), 142. John N. Wall, Jr. "Godly and Fruitful Lessons: The English Bible, Erasmus' Paraphrases, and the Book of Homilies," in John E. Booty, David Siegenthaler, John N. Wall, eds., *The Godly Kingdom of Tudor England. Great Books of the English Reformation* (Wilton, Conn., 1981), 95–6.

34 *Certain Sermons*, 154.

35 H&L, II, 102–3.

36 PRO SP 12/1/fos. 147–154.

37 PRO SP 12/1/fos. 156–158.

38 BL Cotton, Julius F. VI, fos. 167v–168v.

39 Peter Ribadeneira, *Patris Petri de Ribadeneira Societatis Jesu Sacerdotis Confessiones, Epistolae aliaque Scripta Inedita*. Monumenta Historica Societatis Jesu 58 (1920), 313–14.

40 Winthrop Hudson, *The Cambridge Connection and the Elizabethan Settlement of 1559* (Durham, 1980), passim. Patrick Collinson, *Archbishop Grindal 1519–1583. The Struggle for a Reformed Church* (Berkeley, 1979), 49–56.

41 Hartley, *Proceedings*, I, 51.

42 HEH, El 2579, fo. 15.

43 Norman Jones, *The Birth of the Elizabethan Age. England in the 1560s* (Oxford, 1993), 4–16.

44 Peter Newman Brooks, *Thomas Cranmer's Doctrine of the Eucharist* 2nd edn. (Basingstoke, 1992), 112–13.

45 Judith Maltby, *Prayer Book and People in Elizabethan and Early Stuart England* (Cambridge, 1998), 15.

46 John Booty, ed., *The Book of Common Prayer 1559 The Elizabethan Prayer Book* (Washington, D. C., 1976), 372–3.

47 Thomas Wilson, *The Arte of Rhetorique Newlie sette forthe again* (1560), prologue. [STC 25800]

48 My analysis of the Grocers' Company follows that in Joseph P. Ward, "Religious Diversity and Guild Unity in Early Modern London," in Eric Josef Carlson, ed., *Religion and the English People 1500–1640. New Voice New Perspectives*, Sixteenth Century Essays and Studies 45 (1998), 77–97. I followed his lead into the records in the Guild Hall.

49 LGL 11588/1, fos. 1, 188, 189.

50 Ibid., fo. 175v.

51 Ibid., fos. 243v, 264, 270.

52 Ibid., fos, 213, 213v.

53 LGL, 11588/2, fo.15.

54   LGL, 11588/1, fo. 179.

55   Ibid., fo. 276.

56   Ibid., fo. 188. LGL, 7086/2, 8v; 126v; fo. 176.

57   LGL, 7086/2, fo. 187.

58   Ibid., 7086/2, fo. 195v.

59   Ibid., fos. 223; 232v. Mervyn Blatch, *A Guide to London Churches* (London, 1978), 9–10.

60   LGL, 7112, fo. 40.

61   Charles Welch, *Additional Appendix to the History of the Pewterers' Company* (London, n.d. [1969]), 9–10. LGL 7086/2, fo. 118v; 126v.

62   LGL, 7086/2, fos. 187; 232v.

63   Ibid., 7086/2, fo. 247v.

64   Ibid., 7086/2, fo. 271.

65   LGL, 7086/3, fo. 328v.

66   *ER*, 41, 276–7. S. C. 5 Mylne & Craig 11. The Companies, having bought back the properties given to them to support obits, got an act of Parliament, 4 Jac. I, private act 10, to protect them from charges of concealed lands. However, the Act did not stop the criticism. The issue was settled in Victoria's reign by Attorney General V. Fishmongers Company (Kneseworth's Charity) 2 Beav. 151 in ER 48, 1137.

67   Bower Marsh, ed., *Records of the Worshipful Company of Carpenters. Vol. IV. Wardens' Account Book 1546–1571* (Oxford, 1916), 5, 6, 16, 56, 69, 77, 78, 82, 83, 87, 90, 91, 95, 98, 99, 102, 106, 110, 114, 120, 125, 126, 130, 131, 177, 182, 183, 199, 201, 207, 213, 214, 221, 227, 236, 238, 243.

68   Bower Marsh and John Ainsworth, eds., *Records of the Worshipful Company of Carpenters. Vol. V., Wardens' Account Books 1571–1591* (London, 1937), 29. The index lists no payments for preachers.

69   Guy Parsloe, ed., *Wardens' Accounts of the Worshipful Company of Founders of the City of London 1487–1681* (London, 1964), 150, 164, 326, n. 1.

70   Tittler, *Reformation and the Towns*, 272. Ian Archer, "The Art and Acts of Memorialisation in Early Modern London." Forthcoming in Julia Meritt, ed., *Imagining the City. Portraits of London*. My thanks to Dr. Archer for allowing me to see this before publication.

71   Joe Ward, "London's Livery Companies and Metropolitan Government, c. 1500–1725," (Unpublished dissertation, Stanford University, 1992), 240.

72   G. H. Martin, and J. R. L. Highfield, *A History of Merton College* (Oxford: Oxford University Press, 1997), 15–8. Millar MacLure, *Register of Sermons Preached at Paul's Cross 1534–1642*, revised and augmented by Peter Pauls and Jackson Campbell Boswell (Ottawa, 1989), 28.

73   Martin and Highfield, *Merton*, 155. RACM 1521–1567, 189.

74   Ibid., 191, 169. 181.

75   Ibid., 192. W. H. Frere, ed., *Registrum Matthei Parker Diocesis Cantuarensis A.D. 1559–1575*. Canterbury and York Society 36 (1916–28), 707–8.

76   Ibid., 709.

77   Ibid., 713–4.

78   Ibid. 707, 711.
79   Ibid., 711–12.
80   Ibid., 199; 207.
81   PRO SP 12/15/fo. 38. Martin and Highfield, *Merton*, 209.
82   RACM 1521–1567, 202.
83   PRO SP 12/15/ fo. 38.
84   PRO SP 12/21/ fo. 109. RACM 1521–67, 210.
85   RACM 1521–67, 211.
86   Ibid., 701, 705, 716
87   Ibid., 216.
88   Ibid., 219.
89   Ibid., 227–8.
90   Ibid., 256.
91   Ibid., 246, 249.
92   Ibid., 280.
93   John M. Fletcher and Christopher A. Upton, "Destruction, Repair and Removal: An Oxford College Chapel during the Reformation," *Oxoniensia* 48 (1983), 127–8.
94   Ibid., 128.
95   MCR 4043, 1568–9.
96   RACM 1567–1603, 101.
97   MCR 4043, 1570/71.
98   MCR 4048, 1586.
99   W. G. Searle, *The History of the Queens' College of St. Margaret and St. Bernard in the University of Cambridge, 1446–1662.* Cambridge Antiquarian Society 9 (1867), 266–7.
100 Ibid., 283. BL Add 5808, fos. 134–8.
101 John Buxton and Penry Williams, eds., *New College Oxford 1379–1979* (Oxford, 1979), 46–52.
102 RACM 15221–1567, 143.
103 *Statuta antiqua universitatis oxoniensis* ed. Strickland Gibson (Oxford, 1931), 297.
104 RACM 1521–67, 229.
105 Nicholas Sander, *The Rise and Growth of the Anglican Schism*, David Lewis, trans. and ed. (London, 1877), 264.
106 Geoffrey de C. Parmiter, *Elizabethan Popish Recusancy in the Inns of Court* Bulletin of the Institute of Historical Research, Special Supplement No. 11 (1976), 54.
107 Ibid., 32.
108 LIBB, 273, 274–5.
109 Rodney Munro Fisher, "The Inns of Court and the Reformation 1530–1580" (Unpublished Ph.D. Dissertation, Cambridge University, Ph.D. # 8757, 1974), Appendix 1, 334.
110 LIBB, 313–14.
111 Ibid., 308–9
112 Fisher, "Inns and Reformation," Appendix 5, II, 348.
113 LIBB, 323, 408. HPTD sub Cordell, William; Dalton, James.

114   ITL, Petyt Ms. 47, fo. 47.
115   PRO SP 12/60/fo. 202–202v.
116   ITR, 265.
117   PRO SP 12/60/fos. 130–130v; 135.
118   ITR, 472. Parmiter, *Recusancy in the Inns*, 46–7. HPTD sub Plowden, Edmund.
119   LIBB, 346, 361, 365, 366. HPTD sub Roper, William and Roper, Thomas.
120   Ibid., 365, 398, 405, 408.
121   Ibid., 398.
122   Fisher, "Inns and Reformation," Appendix 5, 348.
123   LIBB, 408.
124   Ibid., 308. "Hic ordo propter stolidam abhominacionem [et] superstitionem aboletur ad Consilium tentum 16 die Novembris, anno regni Domine Regine Elizabeth', 23."
125   Charles Trice Martin, ed., *Minutes of the Parliament of the Middle Temple. Vol. I. 1501–1603* (London, 1904), I, 224.
126   Fisher, "Inns and Reformation," Appendix 2, 336. LIBB, 458, 459.
127   ITR, 333.
128   Izaak Walton, *Lives*, A. H. Bullen, ed. (London, 1884), 208.
129   "A Learned Discourse of Justification, Works, and how the Foundation of Faith is Overthrown," in *Hooker*, III, 495–500, 538, 546. BL, Harley Ms. 291, fo. 184v.
130   BL, Harley Ms. 291, fo. 183–4. Albert Peel, ed., *The seconde Parte of a Register* (Cambridge, 1915), II, 48. Jennifer Loach, "Reformation Controversies" in James McConica, ed., *The History of the University of Oxford. Vol. III, The Collegiate University* (Oxford, 1986), 391. Benjamin Hanbury, ed., *The Ecclesiastical Polity and other Works of Richard Hooker with his Life by Izaak Walton and Strype's Interpolations: To which are now first added: The "Christian Letter" to Mr. Hooker; and Dr Covel's "Just & Temperate Defence" in Reply to it . . .* (London, 1830), III, 344–51.
131   Parmiter, *Recusancy in the Inns of Court*, 54.
132   Norman Jones, "The Adaptation of Tradition: The Image of the Turk in Protestant England," *East European Quarterly*, XII, 2 (1978), 161–75.
133   Muriel McClendon, "A Moveable Feast: St. George's Day Celebrations and Religious Change in Early Modern England," *Journal of British Studies* 38 (1999), 12–27.

Chapter 6   Reinventing Public Virtue

1   Bodl. Tanner 50, fos. 21v-22.
2   Steve Hindle, *The State and Social Change in Early Modern England, c. 1550–1640* (New York, 2000), 237. Hindle's entire book is dedicated to demonstrating this.
3   Bob Scribner, "Preconditions of Tolerance and Intolerance in Sixteenth-Century Germany," in Ole Peter Grell and Bob Scribner, eds., *Tolerance and Intolerance in the European Reformation* (Cambridge, 1996), 38.
4   Edmond Bicknoll, *A Sword Agaynst Swearyng* (London, 1579) fo. 2v. [STC 3048]
5   David Cressy, *Bonfires and Bells. National Memory and the Protestant Calendar in Elizabethan and Stuart England* (Berkeley, 1989), 50–4.

6   Eric Kerridge, *Trade and Banking in Early Modern England* (Manchester, 1988), 84.

7   Richard Tuck, *Philosophy and Government 1572–1651* (Cambridge, 1993), 104–19.

8   Thomas Morton, *A Full Satisfaction Concerning a Double Romish Iniquitie; Hainous Rebellion, and more then Heathenish Aequivocation, Containing the Reply upon the Moderate Answerer* (1606), part 3, 49–52.

9   Dana F. Sutton, ed., *Unpublished Works by William Alabaster (1568–1640)*. University of Salzburg Studies in English Literature Elizabethan and Renaissance Studies, 126 (1997), 105–6.

10 John Bossy, "Moral Arithmetic: Seven Sins into Ten Commandments," in Edmund Leites, ed., *Conscience and Casuistry in Early Modern Europe* (Cambridge, 1988), 214–34.

11 Janet E. Halley, "Equivocation and the Legal Conflict Over Religious Identity in Early Modern England," *Yale Journal of Law and the Humanities* 3 (1991), 46.

12 Hindle, *State and Social Change*, 139.

13 Quoted in Patrick Collinson, "The Cohabitation of the Faithful with the Unfaithful," in Ole Peter Grell, J. I. Israel and N. Tyacke, eds., *From Persecution to Toleration: The Glorious Revolution and Religion in England* (Oxford, 1991), 58.

14 Diarmaid MacCulloch, "Archbishop Cranmer: Concord and Tolerance in a Changing Church," in Ole Peter Grell and Bob Scribner, eds., *Tolerance and Intolerance in the European Reformation* (Cambridge, 1996), 199–215.

15 William Bullein, *A Dialogue . . . Against the Fever Pestilence* (1573), fos. 85–86v. [STC 4037]

16 Foley, I, 183.

17 HPTD sub Stonor, Francis.

18 Anthony Milton, "A Qualified Intolerance: The Limits and Ambiguities of Early Stuart Anti-Catholicism," in Arthur F. Marotti, ed., *Catholicism and Anti-Catholicism in Early Modern English Texts* (Basingstoke, 1999), 99–102.

19 Hugh Bowler, ed., *Recusant Rolls No. 3 (1594–1595) and Recusant Roll No. 4 (1595–1596) An Abstract*, in English Catholic Record Society 61 (1970), 72; 201.

20 HPTD, sub Stonor, Francis.

21 PRO, PCC 26 Alen. A. H. Johnson, *The History of the Worshipful Company of the Drapers of London: Preceded by an Introduction on London and Her Gilds up to the close of the XVth Century. Vol. II From the Accession of King Henry VIII to the Death of Queen Elizabeth 1509–1603* (Oxford, 1915), 101, n. 2. Robert Alford did not win the good will of his Company, since he failed to provide money for a funeral potation: "Obit of Robert Alford kept at St. Swithun London Stone. In the forenoon he had his service done and a sermon for him and after was buried. To whose burial came Mr. Wardens, and of the whole Livery as most in number, and iiij of the Ancients went on every side of the corpse, the whole Company offered (their pence) and so departed without potation or anything given towards this house or them."

22 HPTD sub Alford, Roger.

23 William Fleetwood to Lord Burghley, 14 April, 1582. BL Lansd. 35, fo. 87–87v. J. H. Pollen, ed., *Unpublished Documents Relating to the English Martyrs, I, 1584–1603*, Catholic Record Society 4 (1908), 26.

24　Hartley, *Proceedings*, I, 326.

25　Ibid., I, 361. G. R. Elton, *The Parliament of England 1559–1581* (Cambridge, 1986), 345.

26　Ibid., I, 315. J. E. Neale, *Elizabeth I and her Parliaments 1559–1581* (London, 1966), 253–4.

27　Ibid., I, 334.

28　Ibid., I, 334–5; 315.

29　Ibid., I, 335.

30　IT, Petyt Ms. 538/10 fo. 11.

31　Hartley, *Proceedings*, I, 222

32　Hartley, *Proceedings*, II, 105–6

33　David Dean, *Law-Making and Society in Late Elizabethan England. The Parliament of England 1584–1601* (Cambridge, 1996), 111. Hartley, *Proceedings*, II, 391.

34　IT, Petyt ms 538/10 fo. 73v.

35　Ibid., fo. 54.

36　Ibid., fo. 36v.

37　HPTD, sub Brokesby, Robert.

38　John Gwynfor Jones, *Law, Order and Government in Caernarfonshire, 1558–1640. Justices of the Peace and the Gentry* (Cardiff, 1996), 158–9.

39　PRO, STAC 5 O9/18 Thomas Owen against Richard Vaughan. APC 11, 67.

40　STAC 5 O8/17, STAC 5 O8/17, PRO STAC 5 O7/22. E. G. Jones, "The Lleyn Recusancy Case, 1578–81" *Transactions of the Honorable Society of Cymmrodorion* (1936), 97–123.

41　Milton, "Qaulified Intolerance," 105.

42　Marjorie K. McIntosh, *A Community Transformed: the Manor and Liberty of Havering, 1500–1620* (Cambridge, 1991), 196.

43　Christopher Marsh, "Piety and Persuasion in Elizabethan England: The Church of England Meets the Family of Love," in Nicholas Tyacke, ed., *England's Long Reformation 1500–1800. The Neale Colloquium in British History* (Cambridge, 1998), 141–66.

44　HPTD, sub Topcliffe, Richard.

45　RACM 1567–1603, 339.

46　Sir S. D'Ewes, *Journals of all the Parliaments of Queen Elizabeth* (London, 1682), 661.

47　Justin McCann and Hugh Connolly, eds., "Memorials of Father Augustine Baker, O.S.B." *Catholic Record Society* 33 (1933), 16–7.

48　CSP Span. 1558–67, pp. 636–7.

49　Hastings Robinson, ed., *Original Letters Relative to the English Reformation* (Cambridge, 1856), 34.

50　CUL, Mm.1.29, fos. 1,

51　J. J. Muskett, ed., "The Diary of Adam Winthrop" in *Winthrop Papers Vol. I 1498–1628* (Boston, 1929), 71.

52　Foley, I, 66–7. Sutton, ed., *Unpublished Works by William Alabaster*, 118.

53　Quoted in John Racster, *A Booke of the seven planets, or, seven wandring motives, of W. Alablasters [sic] wit, retrograded or removed* (1598), Sig. F3. [STC 20601]

54 Foley, I, 620–1.
55 Muskett, ed., "The Diary of Adam Winthrop," 110.
56 Racster, *A Booke of the seven planets*, Sig M3v.
57 "Satyre III," 93–9 in Herbert Grierson, ed., *Donne Poetical Works* (London, 1973), 139–40.
58 LIBB, 371.
59 Ibid., 372, 381.
60 HPTD, sub Egerton, Thomas I.
61 HEH, HAP Box 15, Folder 4, 3–6.
62 4 Co. Rep. 36b-40a in ER 76, 982.
63 5&6 Edward VI, c. 20.
64 Keith Wrightson, *Earthly Necessities. Economic Lives in Early Modern Britain* (New Haven, 2000), 202.
65 John Ayre, ed., *The Works of John Jewel* (Cambridge, 1847), II, 851.
66 Martin Bucer, *Praelectiones Doctiss. In epistolam D.P. ad Ephesios, eximii doctoris D. Martini Buceri, habitae Cantabrigiae in Anglia, anno MDL & LI* (Basel, 1562), 168–9. Martin Bucer, "Tractatus de usuris," in *Martini Buceri Scripta Anglicana* (Basel, 1577), 792–6.
67 B. M. C. Kervyn de Lettenhove, ed., *Relations Politiques des Pays-Bas et de L'Angleterre, sous le règne de Philippe II* (Brussels, 1882–1900), IV, 367.
68 Norman Jones, *God and the Moneylenders. Usury and the Law in Early Modern England* (Oxford, 1989), 47–66.
69 BL, Lansdowne 101, 24 and 26. Norman Jones, "William Cecil and the Making of Economic Policy in the 1560s," in *The Commonwealth of Tudor England*, P. Fideler and T. Mayer, eds. (London, 1992), 169–93.
70 Bodl. Rawlinson Ms. D.677, 22–3, 36, 59.
71 David H. Wilson, ed., *The Parliamentary Diary of Robert Bowyer 1606–1607* (New York, 1971), 151.
72 DeLloyd J. Guth, "The Age of Debt, the Reformation and English Law," in D. J. Guth and J. W. McKenna, eds., *Tudor Rule and Revolution. Essays for G. R. Elton from his American Friends* (Cambridge, 1982), 69–86.
73 Northampton Record Office, Finch-Hatton Ms. 50, fo. 35. LJ, III, 322, 323. Jones, *God and the Moneylenders*, 175–98.
74 Wrightson, *Earthly Necessities*, 209–13.
75 James C. Spalding, *The Reformation of the Ecclesiastical Laws of England, 1552. Sixteenth Century Essays and Studies* 19 (1992), 82–3.
76 Norman Jones, "Elizabethan Parliaments and the Reform of the Ecclesiastical Law: New Evidence," *Parliamentary History* 4 (1985), 171–188. Thomas S. Freeman, "'The Reformation of the Church in this Parliament': Thomas Norton, John Foxe and the Parliament of 1571," *Parliamentary History* 16 (1997), 131–47.
77 *Certain Sermons or Homilies appointed to be read in Churches in the Time of Queen Elizabeth of Famous Memory* (London, 1846), 71–80.
78 David Harris Sacks, *The Widening Gate. Bristol and the Atlantic Economcy 1450–1700* (Berkeley, 1993), 161–2.

79   Ibid., 184–5.

80   Bicknoll, *A Sword Agaynst Swearyng*, fos. 2v, 4–4v.

81   Quoted in Hindle, *State and Social Change*, 180.

82   Ibid.

83   R. H. Helmholz, *Roman Canon Law in Reformation England* (Cambridge, 1990), 110, 178.

84   F. G. Emmison, *Elizabethan Life: Morals and the Church Courts* (Chelmsford,1973), 290.

85   Richard Rawlidge, *A Monster late Found Out* (Amsterdam, 1628), Sig. F. [STC 20766]

86   William Fuller, "A copie of Mr Fullers booke to the Queene," in Albert Peel, ed., *The Seconde Parte of a Register* (Cambridge, 1915), II, 54.

87   John Downame, *Foure Treatises Tending to Diswade all Christians from foure no less hainous then common sinnes; namely, the abuses of swearing, drunkennesse, whoredoem, and bribery* (1613). [STC 7142]

88   Ibid., 33–4.

89   PRO SP 12/282/56. There is also a breviate, PRO SP 12/282/57.

90   PRO SP 12/283/24.

91   Sir S. D'Ewes, *Journals of all the Parliaments of Queen Elizabeth* (London, 1682), 660–1.

92   Claire Cross, ed., *The Letters of Sir Francis Hastings 1574–1609* Somerset Record Society LXIX (1969), 117–18.

93   Hindle, *State and Social Change*, 187.

94   Richard Dean Smith, "Social Reform in an Urban Context: Colchester, Essex, 1570–1640" (Unpublished dissertation, University of Colorado, 1996), 128–61, 193.

Chapter 7   Learning Private Virtue

1   George Downame, *A Treatise upon John 8.36. Concerning Christian Libertie. The Chiefe Points whereof were delivered in a sermon at Pauls Crosse, Novemb. 6, 1608* (1609), 67. [STC 28513]

2   David Siegenthaler, "Religious Education For Citizenship: Primer and Catechism," in John E. Booty, ed., *The Godly Kingdom of Tudor England: Great Books of the English Reformation* (Wilton, Conn., 1981), 240.

3   Strype, *Annals*, I, ii, 567–8. William Haugaard, *Elizabeth I and the English Reformation* (Cambridge, 1968), 170–1.

4   Haugaard, *English Reformation*, 277–8.

5   G. E. Corrie, ed., *A Catechism written in Latin by Alexander Nowell . . . together with the same Catechism translated into English by Thomas Norton* (Cambridge: 1853), 130–1.

6   Sir Thomas Wilson, *The Rule of Reason, Conteinyng the Arte of Logike* (London, 1563), fos. 28v; 29. [STC 25812]

7   John Bossy, *Peace in the Post-Reformation* (Cambridge, 1998), 73–100.

8 Debora Kuller Shuger, *Habits of Thought in the English Renaissance. Religion, Politics, and the Dominant Culture* (Berkeley, 1990), 12, 67–8.

9 Kenneth L. Parker and Eric J. Carlson, eds., *'Practical Divinity' the Works and Life of Revd Richard Greenham* (Aldershot, 1998), 138.

10 Ibid., 137–8.

11 Ibid., 141.

12 Ibid., 146–7.

13 Ibid., 145–6.

14 David Cressy, *Birth, Marriage, and Death. Ritual, Religion, and the Life-Cycle in Tudor and Stuart England* (Oxford, 1997), 398–9.

15 Parker and Carlson, *Greenham*, 249.

16 Ibid., 248.

17 Eric Carlson, "'Practical Divinity' Richard Greenham's Ministry in Elizabethan England," in Eric Carlson, ed., *Religion and the English People 1500–1640. New Voices New Perspectives*. Sixteenth Century Essay and Studies 45 (1998), 180–1.

18 L&P IX,350.

19 J. M. Fletcher, "The Faculty of Arts" in James McConica, ed., *The History of the University of Oxford. Vol. III, The Collegiate University* (Oxford, 1986), 301, 305.

20 Sir Philip Sidney, *The Defence of Poesie* (1595). Ian Lancashire, ed., http://www.library.utoronto.ca/utel/rp/criticism/defen_il.html. Ll. 463–78. Katherine Duncan-Jones, *Sir Philip Sidney Courtier Poet* (New Haven, 1991), 232–8.

21 Peter Ivor Kaufman, *Prayer, Despair and Drama. Elizabethan Introspection* (Urbana, 1996), 8–11.

22 Quoted in Parker and Carlson, *Greenham*, 46.

23 Edward John Lang Scott, ed., *The Letter Book of Gabriel Harvey*, Camden Society n.s. 33 (1884), 78–82.

24 Erika. Rummel, *The Humanist-Scholastic Debate in the Renaissance and Reformation* (Cambridge, MA, 1995), 150.

25 Margo Todd, *Christian Humanism and the Puritan Social Order* (Cambridge, 1987), 68–9.

26 Walter J. Ong, *Ramus, Method and the Decay of Dialogue, from the Art of Discourse to the Art of Reason* (Cambridge, MA, 1983), 23.

27 Patrick Collinson, *The Birth Pangs of Protestant England. Religious and Cultural Change in the Sixteenth and Seventeenth Centuries* (New York, 1988), 95.

28 Petrus Ramus, *The logike of the moste excellent philosopher P. Ramus martyr, newly translated, and in divers places corrected, after the mynde of the author. Per M. Roll. Makylmenaeum Scotorum* (1574), 8–10. [STC 15246]

29 Dudley Fenner, *The artes of logike and rethorike, plainelie set foorth in the English tounge, easie to be learned and practised togeather with examples for the practise of the same, for methode in the government of the familie, prescribed in the word of God: and for the whole in the resolution or opening of certaine partes of Scripture, according to the same* (Middleburgh, 1584). [STC 10766]

30 "A Discourse of Conscience" in Perkins, I, 548.

31 Ibid., 510.

32 "Three Books of Cases of Conscience," Perkins, II, 134–5.
33 "A Treatise of Christian Equity and Moderation," Perkins, II, 506.
34 Geoffrey Fenton, *A Forme of Christian Pollicie* (1574), 1–5. [STC 10793a]
35 M. M. Knappen, ed., *Two Elizabethan Puritan Diaries* (Chicago, 1933), 105, 108.
36 Kaufman, *Prayer and Despair*, 22–3.
37 Christopher Marlowe, "The Tragical History of Doctor Faustus," in *The Complete Plays*. J. B. Steane, ed. (Harmondsworth, 1969), 5, 2, 155–9.
38 Kaufman, *Prayer and Despair*, 79–92.
39 Marlowe, "Faustus," I, i, 42–8.
40 Kaufman, *Prayer and Despair*, 139, 63. Paul R. Sellin, "The Hidden God: Reformation Awe in Renaissance Literature," in Robert S. Kinsman, ed., *The Darker Vision of the Renaissance. Beyond the Fields of Reason* (Berkeley, 1974), 179–87.
41 "To the Reader," *The Geneva Bible. A Facsimile of the 1560 Edition* (Madison, 1969), v.
42 Hooker, II, 143.
43 Ibid., II, 145.
44 Ibid., II, 150–3.
45 Ibid., I, 284–5, 295.
46 Ibid., II, 239–40.
47 David Little, *Religion, Order and Law. A Study in Pre-Revolutionary England* (Chicago, 1984), 163–6.
48 Parker and Carlson, *Greenham*, 150.
49 York, Borthwick Institute, HC.CP 1590/5.
50 Quoted in Robert Whiting, *Local Responses to the English Reformation* (London, 1998), 103.
51 Bullein, *Dialogue*, fos. 8–8v.
52 Johann Wigand, *De Neutralibus et Mediis. Grossly Englished, Jacke of both Sides.* Anon. trans. (London, 1562), Sig. B.i. [STC 25612]
53 Alexandra Walsham, *Church Papists. Catholicism, Conformity and Confessional Polemic in Early Modern England* (London, 1993), 1–2, 9.
54 Philip Caraman, *Henry Garnet 1555–1606 and the Gunpowder Plot* (New York, 1964), 110.
55 Elliot Rose, *Cases of Conscience. Alternatives Open to Recusants and Puritans Under Elizabeth I and James I* (Cambridge, 1975), 240–1.
56 Lowell Gallagher, *Medusa's Gaze. Casuistry and Conscience in the Renaissance* (Stanford, 1991), 9.
57 IT Petyt 538/10, f. 25.
58 Richard H. Popkin, *The History of Skepticism from Erasmus to Spinoza* (Berkeley, 1979), 1–86.
59 Christopher Marlowe, "The Jew of Malta," in *The Complete Plays*. J. B. Steane, ed. (Harmondsworth, 1969), 363, l. 290.
60 "Of Truth," at gopher://gopher.vt.edu:10010/02/43/1.
61 "Of Unity in Religion," at ibid.
62 Richard Tuck, *Philosophy and Government 1572–1651* (Cambridge, 1993), 105–18.

Paul Hammer, *The Polarisation of Elizabethan Politics. The Political Career of Robert Devereux, 2nd Earl of Essex, 1585–1597* (Cambridge, 1999), 335–6 and n. 86.

63 Markku Peltonen, *The Cambridge Companion to Bacon* (Cambridge, 1996), 3.
64 Perez Zagorin, *Francis Bacon* (Princeton, 1998), 50–1.
65 Peltonen, *Companion to Bacon*, 5.
66 RACM 1567–1603, 276, 284, 295, 296, 304, 334, 339, 340, 346, 347.
67 Marlowe, "The Jew of Malta," in *Complete Plays*, 347, ll. 9–15.
68 Anthony Esler, *The Aspiring Mind of the Elizabethan Younger Generation* (Durham, 1966), 156–7.
69 Perkins, "Three Books of Cases of Conscience," *Works*, II, 134–5.
70 Gallagher, *Casuistry and Conscience*, 2.

Chapter 8   The Post-Reformation World View

1 HPTD sub Paulet, William.

Select Bibliography

Primary

Aveling, Hugh and W. A. Pantin, ed. *The Letter Book of Robert Joseph Monk-Scholar of Evesham and Gloucester College, Oxford 1530–3*, Oxford Historical Society, n.s., 19 (1967).

Ayre, John, ed. *The Works of John Jewel*, 4 volumes. Cambridge: Parker Society, 1847.

Baker, J. H., ed. *Reports From the Lost Notebooks of Sir James Dyer*, 2 vols. Selden Society 109 and 110 (1993, 1994).

Baker, J. H., ed. *The Notebook of Sir John Port*. Selden Society 102 (1986).

Baker, J. H., ed. *The Reports of Sir John Spelman*. Selden Society XCIII, XCIV (1976, 1977).

Basing, Patricia, ed. *Parish Fraternity Register. Fraternity of the Holy Trinity and SS. Fabian and Sebastian in the Parish of St. Botolph without Aldersgate*. London Record Society 18 (1982).

Becon, Thomas. *The Governance of Virtue* in John Ayre, ed., *The Early Works of Thomas Becon, S.T.P., Chaplain to Archbishop Cranmer. . . .* Cambridge, 1843, 395–485.

Beilin, Elaine V., ed. *The Examinations of Anne Askew*. Oxford: Oxford University Press, 1996.

Bettey, J. H., ed. *Calendar of the Correspondence of the Smyth Family of Ashton Court 1548–1642*. Bristol Record Society 35 (1982).

Bicknoll, Edmond. *A Sword Agaynst Swearyng*. 1579. [STC 3048]

Booty, John, ed. *The Book of Common Prayer 1559. The Elizabethan Prayer Book*. Washington, D.C., 1976.

Bowler, Hugh, ed. *Recusant Roll No. 3 (1594–1595) and Recusant Roll No. 4 (1595–1596) An Abstract*, in English Catholic Record Society 61 (1970).

Bradford, John. *The Writings of John Bradford*. 2 vols. Aubrey Townsend, ed. Cambridge, 1848.

Bray, Gerald, ed. *The Anglican Canons 1529–1947*. Church of England Record Society 6 (1998).

Brigden, Susan. "The Letters of Richard Scudamore to Sir Philip Hoby, Sept. 1549–March 1555," *Camden Miscellany* XXX 4th ser. (1990), 67–148.

Brodrick, George C., ed. *Memorials of Merton College with Biographical Notices of the Wardens and Fellows* Oxford Historical Society IV (1885).

Bucer, Martin. *Praelectiones Doctiss. In epistolam D.P. ad Ephesios, eximii doctoris D. Martini Buceri, habitae Cantabrigiae in Anglia, anno MDL & LI*. Basel, 1562.

Bucer, Martin. "Tractatus de usuris," in *Martini Buceri Scripta Anglicana*. Basel, 1577.

Bullein, William. *A Dialogue . . . Against the Fever Pestilence*. 1573. [STC 4037]

Caius, John. *The First Book of the Annals of the Royal College of Physicians, London, 1528–1572*, E. S. Roberts, ed. *The Works of John Caius, M.D. Second Founder of Gonville and Caius College and Master of the College 1559–1573*. Cambridge, 1912. 1–71.

Camden, William. *Annales Rerum Anglicarum et Hibernicarum Regnante Elizabetha*. 1717.

Carman, Philip, trans. *William Weston. The Autobiography of an Elizabethan*. London, 1955.

Cardwell, Edward, ed. *Documentary Annals of the Reformed Church of England*. 2 vols. Oxford, 1854.

Certain Sermons or Homilies Appointed to be Read in Churches in the time of Queen Elizabeth of Famous Memory. London, 1846.

Chambers, D. S., ed. *Faculty Office Registers 1534–1549. A Calendar of the First Two Registers of the Archbishop of Canterbury's Faculty Office*. Oxford, 1966.

Christie, James, ed. *Some Account of Parish Clerks, More Especially of the Ancient Fraternity (Bretherne and Sisterne), of St. Nicholas now known as The Worshipful Company of Parish Clerks*. London, 1893.

Coke, Edward. *The First Part of the Institutes of the Laws of England; or, a Commentary Upon Littleton*. 2 vols. Philadelphia, 1853.

Collinson, Patrick, ed. *Letters of Thomas Wood, Puritan, 1566–1577*. Bulletin of the Institute of Hisorical Research Spec. Supp. 5 (1960).

Cooper, J. P. ed. *The Wentworth Papers 1597–1628*. Camden Society 4th series, 12 (1973).

Corrie, George F. ed. *Sermons and Remains of Hugh Latimer*. Cambridge, 1845.

Cox, J. E. ed., *Miscellaneous Writings and Letters of Thomas Cranmer*. Cambridge, 1846.

Dasent, John Roche, ed. *The Acts of the Privy Council of England*, n.s., 37 vols. London, 1890–1904.

Dickens, A. G., ed. *Tudor Treatises*. Yorkshire Archaeological Society Record Series 125 (1959).

Doddridge, John, Sir. *A Compleat Parson or, A description of advowsons, or church living. Wherein is set forth, the interests of the Parson, Patron, and Ordinarie etc. . . . delivered . . . Anno 1602, 1603*. London: 1630. [STC 6980]

Dowling, Maria, ed. "William Latymer's Chronickille of Anne Boeleyne," *Camden Miscellany XXX* 4th Ser. 39 (1990), 23–66.

Downame, George. *A Treatise upon John 8.36. Concerning Christian Libertie. The Chiefe Points whereof were delivered in a sermon at Pauls Crosse, Novemb. 6, 1608*. London: 1609. [STC 28513]

Downame, John. *Foure Treatises Tending to Diswade all Christians from foure no less hainous then common sinnes; namely, the abuses of swearing, drunkennesse, whoredome, and bribery . . . 1613*. [STC 7142]

Fenton, Geoffrey. *A Forme of Christian Pollicie* (1574). [STC 10793a]

Fenton, Roger. *An answere to William Alablaster [sic] his motive.* 1599. [STC 10799]

Foley, B. C. "The Breaking of the Storm," *Essex Recusant* III (1961), 1–21.

Foley, Henry, ed. *Records of the English Province of the Society of Jesus, Vol. I–IV.* London, 1875–8.

Foxe, John. *Actes and monuments of these latter and perillous dayes.* London:1563. [STC 11222].

Frere, W. H., ed. *Puritan Manifestoes: A Study of the Origin of the Puritan Revolt.* London, 1907.

Frere, W. H., ed. *Registrum Matthei Parker Diocesis Cantuarensis A.D. 1559–1575.* Canterbury and York Society 35 (1907–14); 36 (1916–28); 39 (1932–3).

Fuller, William. "A copie of Mr Fullers booke to the Queene," in Albert Peel, ed. *The Seconde Parte of a Register.* Cambridge, 1915.

Gibbings, Richard, ed. *An Answer to John Martiall's Treatise of the Cross. By James Calfhill, D.D* . . . Cambridge, 1856.

Gibbons, A., ed. *Ely Episcopal Records. A Calendar.* n.p., 1890.

Granville, Henry, ed. *The Life of St. Philip Howard.* Chichester, 1971.

Grierson, Herbert, ed. *Donne Poetical Works.* Oxford, 1973.

Harrison, William. *The Description of England. The Classic Contemporary Account of Tudor Social Life,* Georges Edelen, ed. 2nd edn. Washington, 1994.

Haddon, Walter. D. *Gualteri Haddoni, Legum Doctoris, serenissimae reginae Elizabethae, a supplicum libellis, Poemata, studio et labore Thomae Hatcheri Cantabrigiensis sparsim collecta, et edita.* 1567. [STC 12596]

Halliwell, James Orchard, ed. *The Autobiography and Personal Diary of Dr.Simon Forman, the Celebrated Astrolger, from A.D. 1552 to A.D. 1602.* London, 1849.

Harpsfield, Nicholas. *The Life and Death of Sir Thomas More,* E. V. Hitchcock, ed. London, 1932.

Highfield, J. R. L., ed. *The Early Rolls of Merton College Oxford.* Oxford Historical Society n.s. 18 (1964).

Hitchcock, Elsie Vaughan and P. E. Hallett, eds. *The Life of Syr Thomas More sometymes Lord Chancellour of England by Ro:Ba:.* Oxford, 1950.

Holles, Gervase. *Memorials of the Holles Family 1493–1656.* Camden Society, 3rd series, 55 (1937).

James, Montague Rhodes. *A Descriptive Catalogue of the Manuscripts in the Library of Corpus Christi College Cambridge.* Cambridge, 1912.

Jordan, W. K. ed. *The Chronicle and Political Papers of King Edward VI.* Ithaca, 1966.

Kervyn de Lettenhove, B. M. C., ed. *Relations Politiques des Pays-Bas et de L'Angleterre, sous le règne de Philippe II.* 11 volumes. Brussels: 1882–1900.

Kitching, C. J. ed. *The Royal Visitation of 1559. Act Book of the Northern Province.* Surtees Society 187 (1975).

Kirby, Joan, ed. *Plumpton Correspondence.* Camden Society 5th series, 8 (1996).

Knappen, M. M., ed. *Two Elizabethan Puritan Diaries.* Chicago, 1933.

Knox, John. *Selected Writings of John Knox. Public Epistles, Treatises, and Expositions to the Year 1559.* Kevin Reed, ed. Dallas, 1995.

Lamb, John, ed. *Collection of Original Documents from the Manuscript Library of Corpus Christi College, Illustrative of the History of the University of Cambridge, 1500–1572.* London, 1838.

McCann, Justin and Hugh Connolly, eds. *The Memorials of Father Augustine Baker.* Catholic Record Society 33 (1933).

Marlowe, Christopher. *The Complete Plays.* J. B. Steane, ed. Harmondsworth, 1969.

Marsh, Bower, ed. *Records of the Worshipful Company of Carpenters. Vol. III Court Book 1533–1573.* Oxford, 1915.

Marsh, Bower, ed. *Records of the Worshipful Company of Carpenters. Vol. IV Wardens' Account Book 1546–1571.* Oxford, 1916.

Marsh, Bower, and John Ainsworth, eds. *Records of the Worshipful Company of Carpenters. Vol. V. Wardens' Account Book 1571–1591.* London, 1937.

Mellows, W. T. and Daphne H. Gifford, eds. *Peterborough Local Administration. Elizabethan Peterborough. The Dean and Chapter as Lords of the City (Part III of Tudor Documents).* Northamptonshire Record Society 18 (1956).

Moody, Joanna, ed. *The Private Life of an Elizabethan Lady. The Diary of Lady Margaret Hoby 1599–1605.* Stroud, 1998.

Mullen, James A., ed. *The Letters of Stephen Gardiner.* Cambridge, 1933.

Muskett, J. J., ed. "The Diary of Adam Winthrop" in *Winthrop Papers Vol. I, 1498–1628.* Boston, 1929, pp. 39–145.

Nevinson, Charles, ed. *Later Writings of Bishop John Hooper together with his Letters and Other Pieces.* Cambridge, 1852.

Nichols, John Gough, ed. *Chronicle of the Grey Friars of London.* Camden Society o.s. 53 (1857).

Nichols, John Gough ed. *The Diary of Henry Machyn.* Camden Society o.s. 42 (1846).

Nichols, John Gough ed. *Narratives of the Reformation.* Camden Society o.s. 77 (1859).

Norfolk, Duke of, ed. *The Lives of Philip Howard, Earl of Arundel, and of Anne Dacres, His Wife.* London, 1857.

Norton, Thomas, ed. *Reformatio Legum Ecclesiasticarum, Ex Authoritate Primum Regis Henrici.8. inchoata: Deinde per Regem Edouardem .6. provecta, adauctaque in hunc modum, atque nunc ad pleniorem ipsarum reformationem in ludem aedita.* 1571. [STC 6006]

O'Day, Rosemary, ed. "The Letter-Book of Thomas Bentham, Bishop of Coventry and Lichfield, 1560–1561," *Camden Miscellany* 4th series 22 (1979), 113–238.

Palmer, Anthony, ed. *Tudor Churchwardens' Accounts.* Hertfordshire Record Society 1 (1985).

Parker, Kenneth L. and Eric J. Carlson, eds. *'Practical Divinity' The Works and Life of Revd Richard Greenham.* Aldershot, 1998.

Parkyn, Robert. "Robert Parkyn's Narrative of the Reformation, 1532–54" in David Cressy and Lori Ann Ferrell, eds. *Religion and Society in Early Modern England. A Sourcebook.* London, 1996. 24–9.

Parsloe, Guy, ed. *Wardens' Accounts of the Worshipful Company of Founders of the City of London 1497–1681.* London, 1964.

Percy, Joyce W., ed. *York Memorandum Book* Surtees Society 186 (1973).

[Persons, Robert]. *An Answere to the fifth part of Reportes lately set forth by Syr Edward*

Cooke Knight, the Kinges Attorney generall. Concerning the ancient and moderne Municipall lawes of England which do apperteyne to Sprituall Power and Iurisdiction (1606), English Recusant Literature, 1558–1640. (1975) 245.

Pits, John. *Relationum historicarum de rebus Anglicis.* Paris, 1619.

Plucknett, T. F. T. and J. L. Barton, eds. *St. German's Doctor and Student* Selden Society 91 (1974).

Pollen, John Hungerford, ed. *Unpublished Documents Relating to the English Martyrs, I, 1584–1603.* Catholic Record Society 4 (1908).

Prideaux, Walter Sherburne, ed. *Memorials of the Goldsmiths' Company being Gleanings from their Records between the Years 1335 and 1815,* vol. I. London, 1896.

Racster, John. *A Booke of the seven planets, or, seven wandring motives, of W. Alablasters [sic] wit, retrograded or removed.* 1598. [STC 20601, 20601.5]

Ramus, Petrus *The logike of the moste excellent philosopher P. Ramus martyr, newly translated, and in divers places corrected, after the mynde of the author. Per M. Roll. Makylmenaeum Scotorum.*1574. [STC 15246]

Rawlidge, Richard. *A Monster Late Found Out and Discovered or The Scourging of Tiplers, the ruine of Bacchus, and the bane of the Tapsters. Wherein is plainly set forth all the lawes of the kingdome, that be now in force against Ale-house keepers, Drunkards, and Haunters of ale-houses, with all the paines and penalties in the same lawes . . .* Amsterdam: 1628. [STC 20766]

Ribandeneira, Peter. *Patris Petri de Ribadeneira Societatis Jesu Sacerdotis Confessiones, Epistolae aliaque Scripta Inedita.* Monumenta Historica Societatis Jesu 58 (1920), 313–14.

Ringler, William A. and Michael Flachmann, eds. *Beware The Cat by William Baldwin. The First English Novel.* San Marino, CA, 1988.

Robinson, Hastings, ed. *Original Letters Relative to the English Reformation.* Cambridge, 1856.

Robinson, Hastings, ed. *The Zurich Letters, Comprising the Correspondence of Several English Bishops and others with some of the Helvetian Reformers, During the Early Part of the Reign of Queen Elizabeth.* Cambridge, 1842.

Roper, William. *The Life of Sir Thomas More.* E. V. Hitchcock, ed. Springfield, IL, 1935.

Sander, Nicholas. "Dr Nicholas Sander's Report to Cardinal Moroni," A. J. Pollen, ed. *Catholic Record Society Miscellanea I* (1905).

Sander, Nicholas. *The Rise and Growth of the Anglican Schism,* David Lewis, trans. and ed. London, 1877.

Scott, Edward John Lang, ed. *The Letter Book of Gabriel Harvey.* Camden Society NS 33 (1884).

Shakespeare, Joy and Maria Dowling, eds. "Religion and Politics in Mid Tudor England Through the Eyes of an English Protestant Woman: the Recollections of Rose Hickman," *Bulletin of the Institute of Historical Research* 55 (1982), 94–102.

Sidney, Sir Philip. *The Defence of Poesie* (1595). Ian Lancashire, ed. http://www.library.utoronto.ca/utel/rp/criticism/defen_il.html.

Smith, A. Hassell, Gillian M. Baker and R. W. Kenny, eds. *The Papers of Nathaniel Bacon of Stiffkey volume I, 1556–1577.* Norfolk Record Society 46 (1978, 1979).

Smith, John, of Nibley. *The Lives of the Berkeleys Lords of the Honour, Castle and Manor of*

Berkeley in the County of Gloucester from 1066 to 1618. 2 vols. John Maclean, ed. Gloucester, 1883.

Spalding, James C. *The Reformation of the Ecclesiastical Laws of England, 1552.* Sixteenth Century Essays and Studies, 19 (1992).

Spelman, Henry. *De non temerandis ecclesiis, Churches not to be Violated.* J. Spelman, ed. Oxford, 1646.

Strype, John. *Ecclesiastical Memorials, Relating Chiefly to Religion, and the Reformation of it, and the Emergencies of the Church of England, under King Henry VIII, King Edward VI and Queen Mary I.* 3 vols. in 6 parts. Oxford, 1822.

Strype, John. *The History of the Life and Acts of the Most Reverend Father in God, Edmund Grindal.* Oxford, 1821.

Strype, John. *The Life and Acts of Matthew Parker.* 3 vols. Oxford, 1821.

Strype, John. *The Life of the Learned Sir John Cheke.* London, 1705.

Strype, John. *Memorials of the Most Reverend Father in God Thomas Cranmer.* Philip E. Barnes, ed. London, 1853.

Sutton, Dana F. ed. *Unpublished Works by William Alabaster (1568–1640).* University of Salzburg Studies in English Literature Elizabethan and Renaissance Studies, 126 (1997).

Thomson, Elizabeth McClure. *The Chamberlain Letters. A Selection of the Letters of John Chamberlain Concerning Life in England from 1597 to 1626.* New York, 1965.

Trice, Charles Martin, ed. *Catalogue of the Archives in the Muniment Rooms of All Souls' College.* London, 1877.

Tymms, Samuel, ed. *Wills and Inventories from the Registers of the Commissary of Bury St. Edmund's and the Archdeacon of Sudbury.* Camden Society OS 49 (1850).

Vowell, John, (alias Hooker). *The Description of the Citie of Excester.* W. J. Harte, J. W. Schopp, and H. Tapley-Soper, eds. Exeter: 1919.

Welch, Charles. *Additional Appendix to the History of the Pewterers Company.* London 1969.

Welch, Charles. *History of the Worshipful Company of Pewterers of the City of London Based upon their Records.* 2 vols. London, 1902.

Wigand, John. *De Neutralibus et Mediis. Grossly Englished, Jacke of Both Sides. A Godly and necessary Catholike Admonition, Touching those that be neuters, . . .* 1562. [STC 25612]

Willson, David H., ed. *The Parliamentary Diary of Robert Bowyer 1606–1607.* New York: 1971.

Wilson, Janet, ed. *Sermons very fruitfull, godly and learned by Roger Edgeworth. Preaching in the Reformation c. 1535–1553.* Cambridge, 1993.

Wilson, Sir Thomas. *The Arte of Rhetorique Newlie sette forthe again.* 1560. [STC 25800]

Wilson, Sir Thomas. *The Rule of Reason, Conteinyng the Arte of Logike.* 1563. [STC 25812]

Whitelocke, James. *Liber Famelicus of Sir James Whitelocke, A Judge of the Court of King's Bench in the Reigns of James I and Charles I.* John Bruce, ed. Camden Society OS (1858).

Whitgift, John. *The Works of John Whitgift.* 3 vols. John Ayre, ed. Cambridge, 1853.

Winthrop Papers Vol. I, 1498–1628. Boston, 1929.

Wright, Thomas, ed. *Three Chapters of Letters Relating to the Suppression of the Monasteries* Camden Society, OS 26 (1843).

Secondary Sources

Bearman, Peter S. *Relations into Rhetorics, Local Elite Social Structure in Norfolk, England, 1540–1640.* New Brunswick, NJ, 1993.

Bossy, John. "Moral Arithmetic: Seven Sins into Ten Commandments," in Edmund Leites (ed.), *Conscience and Casuistry in Early Modern Europe.* Cambridge, 1988, 214–34.

Bossy, John. *Peace in the Post-Reformation.* Cambridge, 1998.

Bowker, Margaret. "The Henrician Reformation and the Parish Clergy," in Christopher Haigh, ed. *The English Reformation Revised.* Cambridge, 1996. 75–93.

Bowler, Gerald. " 'An Axe or an Act': The Parliament of 1572 and Resistance Theory in Early Elizabethan England," *Canadian Journal of History* 19 (1984), 349–59.

Brigden, Susan. *London and the Reformation.* Oxford, 1989.

Brigden, Susan and Nigel Wilson, "New Learning and Broken Friendship," *English Historical Review* 112 (1997), 396–411.

Brigden, Susan. "Religion and Social Obligation in Early Sixteenth-century London," *Past and Present* 103 (1984), 67–112.

Brigden, Susan. "Youth and the English Reformation," *Past and Present* 95 (1982), 37–67.

Brooks, Peter Newman. *Thomas Cranmer's Doctrine of the Eucharist,* 2nd edn. Basingstoke, 1992.

Byford, Mark. "The Birth of a Protestant Town: the Process of Reformation in Tudor Colchester, 1530–80," in Patrick Collinson and John Craig, eds. *The Reformation in English Towns, 1500–1640.* Basingstoke, 1998. 23–47.

Caraman, Philip. *The Western Rising 1549 The Prayer Book Rebellion.* Tiverton, 1994.

Carlson, Eric J. *Marriage and the English Reformation.* Oxford, 1994.

Carlson, Eric J. " 'Practical Divinity' Richard Greenham's Ministry in Elizabethan England," in Eric Carlson, ed. *Religion and the English People 1500–1640. New Voices New Perspectives.* Sixteenth Century Essay and Studies 45 (1998), 147–93.

Collinson, Patrick. *Archbishop Grindal 1519–1583. The Struggle for a Reformed Church.* Berkeley, 1979.

Collinson, Patrick. *The Birth Pangs of Protestant England. Religious and Cultural Change in the Sixteenth and Seventeenth Centuries.* New York, 1988.

Collinson, Patrick. "The Cohabitation of the Faithful with the Unfaithful," in Ole Peter Grell, J. I. Israel and N. Tyacke, eds. *From Persecution to Toleration: The Glorious Revolution and Religion in England.* Oxford, 1991. 51–76.

Collinson, Patrick "Comment on Eamon Duffy's Neale Lecture and the Colloquium," in Nicholas Tyacke, ed. *England's Long Reformation 1500–1800. The Neale Colloquium in British History.* Cambridge, 1998. 71–86.

Collinson, Patrick "John Knox, the Church of England and the Women of England," in Roger Mason, ed. *John Knox and the British Reformations.* Aldershot, 1998, 74–96.

Collinson, Partick. "Magistracy and Ministry: A Suffolk Miniature" in *Reformation Conformity and Dissent,* R. Buick Knox, ed. London, 1977, 70–91.

Comartie, Alan. 'The Constitutionalist Revolution: The Transformation of Political Culture in Early Stuart England," *Past and Present* 163 (1999), 76–120.

Crawford, Patricia *Women and Religion in England 1500–1700*. London, 1996.

Cressy, David. *Birth, Marriage, and Death. Ritual, Religion, and the Life-Cycle in Tudor and Stuart England*. Oxford, 1997.

Cressy, David. *Bonfires and Bells. National Memory and the Protestant Calendar in Elizabethan and Stuart England*. Berkeley, 1989.

Crosse, Clair. "Religion in Doncaster from the Reformation to the Civil War," in Patrick Collinson and John Craig, eds. *The Reformation in English Towns, 1500–1640*. London, 1998. 48–62.

Cunich, Peter. "The Dissolution of the Chantries," in Patrick Collinson and John Craig, eds. *The Reformation in English Towns, 1500–1640*. London, 1998. 159–74.

Cust, Richard. "Catholicism, Antiquarianism and Gentry Honour: The Writings of Sir Thomas Shirley," *Midland History* 23 (1998), 40–70.

Davies, Horton. *Worship and Theology in England. Vol. I, From Cranmer to Hooker, 1534–1603*. Grand Rapids, MI, 1996.

Dean, David. *Law-Making and Society in Late Elizabethan England. The Parliament of England 1584–1601*. Cambridge, 1996.

Dent, C. M. *Protestant Reformers in Elizabethan Oxford*. Oxford, 1983.

Dooley, Brendan. "*Veritas Filia Temporis*: Experience and Belief in Early Modern Culture," *Journal of the History of Ideas* 60 (1999), 487–504.

Dooley, Brendan. *The Social History of Skepticism: Information and Belief in Early Modern Europe* Baltimore, 1990.

Drees, Clayton J. *The Prosecution of Heresy and Religious Non-Conformity in the Diocese of Winchester, 1380–1547*. Lewiston, NY, 1997.

Duffy, Eamon. *The Stripping of the Altars. Traditional Religion in England 1400–1580*. New Haven, 1992.

Duncan-Jones, Katherine. *Sir Philip Sidney Courtier Poet*. New Haven, 1991.

Edwards, A. C. *John Petre. Essays on the Life and Background of John, 1st Lord Petre, 1549–1613*. London, 1975.

Emmison, F. G. *Elizabethan Life: Morals and the Church Courts*. Chelmsford, 1973.

Emmison, F. G. *Tudor Secretary. Sir William Petre at Court and Home*. Cambridge, MA, 1961.

Esler, Anthony. *The Aspiring Mind of the Elizabethan Younger Generation*. Durham, 1966.

Ferrell, Lori Anne. *Government by Polemic. James I, the King's Preachers, and the Rhetorics of Conformity, 1603–1625*. Stanford, 1998.

Fletcher, John M. and Christopher Upton "Destruction, Repair and Removal: An Oxford College Chapel during the Reformation," *Oxoniensia* 48 (1983), 119–130.

Fox, Adam. "Remembering the Past in Early Modern England: Oral and Written Tradition," *Transactions of the Royal Historical Society*, 6th series, 9 (1999), 233–56.

Frankforter, A. Daniel. "Elizabeth Bowes and John Knox: A Woman and Reformation Theology," *Church History* 56 (1987), 333–47.

Freeman, Thomas. "The Good Minstrye of Godlye and Vertuouse Women": The Elizabethan Martyrologists and the Female Supporters of the Marian Martyrs," *Journal of British Studies* 39 (2000), 8–33.

Freeman, Thomas S. " 'The Reformation of the Church in this Parliament': Thomas Norton, John Foxe and the Parliament of 1571," *Parliamentary History* 16 (1997), 131–47.

Gallagher, Lowell. *Medusa's Gaze. Casuistry and Conscience in the Renaissance.* Stanford, 1991.

Gammon, Samuel Rhea. *Statesman and Schemer. William, First Lord Paget Tudor Minister.* Hamden, Conn.: 1973.

Garrod, H. W. "Sir Henry Savile: 1549–1949," *The Study of Good Letters.* J. Jones, ed. Oxford, 1963, 101–119.

Graham, Timothy and A. G. Watson, *The Recovery of the Past in Early Elizabethan England: Documents by John Bale and John Joscelyn from the Circle of Matthew Parker.* Cambridge Bibliographic Society Monograph 13 (1998).

Grassby, Richard. *The Business Community of Seventeenth-Century England.* Cambridge, 1995.

Green, Ian. " 'Puritan Prayer Books' and 'Geneva Bibles': an Episode in Elizabethan Publishing," *Transactions of the Cambridge Bibliographical Society* 11, 3 (1998), 313–49.

Guth, DeLloyd J. "The Age of Debt, the Reformation and English Law," in D. J. Guth and J. W. McKenna, eds. *Tudor Rule and Revolution. Essays for G. R. Elton from his American Friends.* Cambridge, 1982, 69–86.

Guy, John. *Thomas More.* London, 2000.

Haigh, Christopher. "1546 Before and After. The Making of Christ Church. A Commemorative Lecture . . . given on 2 November 1996 to celebrate the 450th anniversary of the foundation." Oxford, 1996.

Haigh, Christopher, ed. *The English Reformation Revised.* Cambridge, 1996.

Halley, Janet E. "Equivocation and the Legal Conflict Over Religious Identity in Early Modern England," *Yale Journal of Law and the Humanities* 3 (1991), 33–52.

Hammer, Carl. I. "The Oxford Martyrs in Oxford: The Local History of their Confinements and their Keepers," *Journal of Ecclesiastical History* 50, 2 (1999), 235–50.

Heal, Felicity, and Clive Holmes. *The Gentry in England and Wales, 1500–1700.* Basingstoke, 1994.

Heal, Felicity. *Hospitality in Early Modern England.* Oxford, 1990.

Heal, Felicity. "Reputation and Honour in Court and Country: Lady Elizabeth Russell, and Sir Thomas Hoby," *Transactions of the Royal Historical Society* 6th series, 6 (1996), 161–78.

Helmholz, R. H. *Roman Canon Law in Reformation England.* Cambridge, 1990.

Hickman, David "From Catholic to Protestant: the Changing Meaning of Testamentary Religious Provisions in Elizabethan London," in Nicholas Tyacke, ed. *England's Long Reformation 1500–1800.* Cambridge, 1998. 117–39.

Hickman, David. "Religious Belief and Pious Practices Among London's Elizabethan Elite," *Historical Journal* 42 (1999), 941–60.

Hill, Christopher. *The Economic Problems of the Church: from Archbishop Whitgift to The Long Parliament.* Oxford, 1956.

Hill, J. W. F. *Tudor and Stuart Lincoln.* Cambridge, 1956.

Hindle, Steve. *The State and Social Change in Early Modern England, c. 1550–1640.* New York, 2000.

Holmes, Peter. *Resistance and Compromise. The Political Thought of Elizabethan Catholics.* Cambridge, 1982.

Hudson, Winthrop. *The Cambridge Connection and the Elizabethan Settlement of 1559.* Durham, 1980.

Hughes, Philip. *The Reformation in England.* 3 vols. New York, 1954.

Jones, John Gwynfor. *Law, Order and Government in Caernarfonshire, 1558–1640. Justices of the Peace and the Gentry.* Cardiff, 1996.

Jones, Norman. "Defining Superstitions: Treasonous Catholics and the Act against Witchcraft of 1563," in Charles Carlton, Robert L. Woods, Mary L. Robertson, Joseph S. Block, eds. *State, Sovereigns and Society in Early Modern England. Essays in Honour of A. J. Slavin.* Thrupp, Gloucs., 1998, 187–204.

Jones, Norman. "Elizabethan Parliaments and the Reform of the Ecclesiastical Law: New Evidence," *Parliamentary History* 4 (1985), 171–88.

Jones, Norman L. *Faith by Statute. Parliament and the Settlement of Religion, 1559.* London, 1982.

Jones, Norman. *God and the Moneylenders. Usury and Law in Early Modern England.* Oxford, 1989.

Jones, Norman. "Profiting From Religious Reform: The Land Rush of 1559," *Historical Journal,* 22, 1 (1979), 279–94.

Jones, Norman L. "Living the Reformation: Generational Experience and Political Perception in Early Modern England," *The Huntington Library Quarterly* 60, 3 (1999), 273–88.

Jones, Norman L. "Matthew Parker, John Bale and the Madgeburg Centuriators," *Sixteenth Century Journal* 12 (1981), 35–49.

Jones, Norman L. "William Cecil and the Making of Economic Policy in the 1560s and early 1570s" in Paul A. Fideler and T. F. Mayer, eds. *Political Thought and the Tudor Commonwealth* London, 1992. 169–93.

Jordan, W. K. *The Development of Religious Toleration in England from the beginning of the English Reformation to the Death of Queen Elizabeth.* London, 1932.

Kaufman, Peter Ivor. *The "Polytyque Churche" Religion and Early Tudor Political Culture, 1485–1516.* Macon, GA, 1986.

Kaufman, Peter Ivor. *Prayer, Despair and Drama. Elizabethan Introspection.* Urbana, 1996.

Kaushik, Sandeep. "Resistance, Loyalty and Recusant Politics: Sir Thomas Tresham and the Elizabethan State," *Midland History* 21 (1996), 37–72.

Kerridge, Eric. *Trade and Banking in Early Modern England.* Manchester, 1988.

Kreider, Alan. *English Chantries. The Road to Dissolution.* Cambridge, MA, 1999.

Loades, D. M. *The Reign of Mary Tudor. Politics, Government and Religion in England, 1553–1558.* London, 1979.

Low, Anthony. *Augustine Baker.* New York: 1970.

MacCaffrey, Wallace T. *Exeter 1540–1640 The Growth of an English County Town.* 2nd edn. Cambridge, MA, 1975.

McClaren, Anne. "Reading Sir Thoms Smith's *De Republica Anglorum* as a Protestant Apologetic," *Historical Journal* 42 (1999), 911–40.

McClendon, Muriel. "A Moveable Feast: St. George's Day Celebrations and Religious Change in Early Modern England," *Journal of British Studies* 38 (1999), 1–27.

McClendon, Muriel C. *The Quiet Reformation. Magistrates and the Emergence of Protestantism in Tudor Norwich.* Stanford, 1999.

MacCulloch, Diarmaid. "Archbishop Cranmer: Concord and Tolerance in a Changing Church," in Ole Peter Grell, and Bob Scribner, eds. *Tolerance and Intolerance in the European Reformation.* Cambridge, 1996. 199–215.

MacCulloch, Diarmaid. *Thomas Cranmer.* New Haven, 1996.

MacCulloch, Diarmaid. *Tudor Church Militant. Edward VI and the Protestant Reformation.* London, 1999.

McCullough, Peter E. *Sermons at Court. Politics and Religion in Elizabethan and Jacobean Preaching.* Cambridge, 1998.

McIntosh, Marjorie K. *A Community Transformed: the Manor and Liberty of Havering, 1500–1620.* Cambridge, 1991.

McIntosh, Marjorie K. *Controlling Misbehavior in England, 1370–1600.* Cambridge, 1998.

McKim, Donald K. *Ramism in William Perkins' Theology.* New York, 1987.

MacLure, Millar. *Register of Sermons Preached at Paul's Cross 1534–1642,* revised and augmented by Peter Pauls and Jackson Campbell Boswell. Ottawa, 1989.

Maltby, Judith. *Prayer Book and People in Elizabethan and Early Stuart England.* Cambridge, 1998.

Manning, Roger. *Religion and Society in Elizabethan Sussex.* Leicester, 1969.

Marius, Richard. *Thomas More. A Biography.* Cambridge, MA, 1984.

Marotti, Arthur F. "Alienating Catholics in Early Modern England: Recusant Women, Jesuits and Ideological Fantasies," in Arthur F. Marotti, ed. *Catholicism and Anti-Catholicism in Early Modern English Texts.* Basingstoke, 1999. 1–34.

Marsh, Christopher. "Piety and Persuasion in Elizabethan England: The Church of England Meets the Family of Love," in Nicholas Tyacke, ed. *England's Long Reformation 1500–1800.* Cambridge, 1998, 141–66.

Marsh, Christopher. *Popular Religion in Sixteenth-Century England.* New York, 1998.

Marshall, Peter. *The Catholic Priesthood and the English Reformation.* Oxford, 1994.

Marcombe, David. *English Small Town Life. Retford 1520–1642.* Oxford, 1993.

Martin, G. H. and J. R. L. Highfield. *A History of Merton College.* Oxford, 1997.

Martin, Jeanette. "Leadership and Priorities in Reading During the Reformation," in Patrick Collinson and John Craig, eds. *The Reformation in English Towns, 1500–1640.* London, 1998. 113–29.

Mason, Roger, ed. *John Knox and the British Reformations.* Aldershot, 1998.

Meigs, Samantha A. *The Reformations in Ireland. Tradition and Confessionalism, 1400–1690.* Basingstoke, 1997.

Miller, Helen. *Henry VIII and the English Nobility.* Oxford, 1989.

Milton, Anthony. "A Qualified Intolerance: The Limits and Ambiguities of Early Stuart Anti-Catholicism," in Arthur F. Marotti, ed. *Catholicism and Anti-Catholicism in Early Modern English Texts.* Basingstoke, 1999. 85–115.

Moreton, C. E. *The Townshends and their World: Genty, Law, and Land in Norfolk, c. 1450–1551.* Oxford, 1992.

Newman, Christine M. "The Reformation and Elizabeth Bowes: A Study of a Sixteenth-Century Northern Gentlewoman," in W. J. Sheils and Diana Wood, eds. *Women in the Church*, Studies in Church History 27 (1990), 325–33.

Oberman, Heiko A. "The Travail of Tolerance: Containing Chaos in Early Modern Europe," in Ole Peter Grell and Bob Scribner, eds. *Tolerance and Intolerance in the European Reformation*. Cambridge, 1996. 13–31.

O'Day, Rosemary. *The English Clergy. The Emergence and Consolidation of a Profession 1558–1642*. Leicester, 1979.

Oliver, P. M. *Donne's Religious Writing. A Discourse of Feigned Devotion*. London, 1997.

Ong, Walter J. *Ramus, Method and the Decay of Dialogue, from the Art of Discourse to the Art of Reason*. Cambridge, 1983.

Palliser, D. M. *Tudor York*. Oxford, 1979.

Parmiter, Geoffrey de C. *Elizabethan Popish Recusancy in the Inns of Court*. Bulletin of the Institute of Historical Research, Special Supplement No. 11 (1976).

Patterson, Catherine F. *Urban Patronage in Early Modern England. Corporate Boroughs, the Landed Elite, and the Crown, 1580–1640*. Stanford, 1999.

Peltonen, Markku. *The Cambridge Companion to Bacon*. Cambridge, 1996.

Pettegree, Andrew. "The Clergy and the Reformation: From 'Devilish priesthood' to New Professional Elite," in Andrew Pettegree, ed. *The Reformation of the Parishes. The Ministry and the Reformation in Town and Country*. Manchester, 1993. 1–21.

Pettegree, Andrew. "Nicodemism and the English Reformation," in Andrew Pettegree, *Marian Protestantism. Six Studies*. Aldershot, 1996. 86–117.

Pettegree, Andrew. "The Politics of Toleration in the Free Netherlands, 1572–1620," Ole Peter Grell and Bob Scribner, eds. *Tolerance and Intolerance in the European Reformation*. Cambridge, 1996. 182–98.

Pollock, Linda. *With Faith and Physic. The Life of a Tudor Gentlewoman Lady Grace Mildmay 1552–1620*. London, 1993.

Popkin, Richard H. *The History of Skepticism from Erasmus to Spinoza*. Berkeley, 1979.

Pritchard, Arnold. *Catholic Loyalism in Elizabethan England*. Chapel Hill, 1979.

Puterbaugh, Joseph. "'Your selfe be judge and answer your selfe': Formation of Protestant Identity in *A Conference betwixt a Mother a Devout Recusant and Her Sonne a Zealous Protestant*," *Sixteenth Century Journal* 31 (2000), 419–431.

Redworth, Glyn. *In Defence of the Church Catholic. The Life of Stephen Gardiner*. Oxford, 1990.

Richardson, Walter C. *History of the Court of Augmentations 1536–1554*. Baton Rouge, 1961.

Rowe, Joy. "'The Lopped Tree': the Re-formation of the Suffolk Catholic Community," in Nicholas Tyacke, ed. *England's Long Reformation 1500–1800*. Cambridge, 1998. 167–94.

Rose, Elliot. *Cases of Conscience. Alternatives Open to Recusants and Puritans Under Elizabeth I and James I*. Cambridge, 1975.

Rummel, Erika. *The Humanist-Scholastic Debate in the Renaissance and Reformation*. Cambridge, MA, 1995.

Ryan, Lawrence V. *Roger Ascham*. Stanford, 1963.

Sacks, David Harris. *The Widening Gate. Bristol and the Atlantic Economy 1450–1700*. Berkeley, 1993.

Sands, Kathleen R. "Word and Sign in Elizabethan Conflicts with the Devil," *Albion* 31, 2 (1999), 238–56.

Scarisbrick, J. S. *The Reformation and the English People*. Oxford, 1984.

Scribner, Bob. "Preconditions of Tolerance and Intolerance in Sixteenth-Century Germany," in Ole Peter Grell and Bob Scribner, eds. *Tolerance and Intolerance in the European Reformation*. Cambridge, 1996. 32–47.

Searle, W. G. *The History of the Queens' College of St. Margaret and St. Bernard in the University of Cambridge, 1446–1662*. Cambridge Antiquarian Society 9 (1867).

Sellin, Paul R. "The Hidden God: Reformation Awe in Renaissance Literature," in Robert S. Kinsman, ed. *The Darker Vision of the Renaissance. Beyond the Fields of Reason*. Berkeley, 1974. 147–96.

Sheils, W. J. "Profit, Patronage, or Pastoral Care: The Rectory Estates of the Archbishopric of York, 1540–1640," in Rosemary O'Day and Felicity Heal, eds. *Princes and Paupers in the English Church 1500–1800*. Leicester, 1981. 91–109.

Shuger, Debora Kuller. *Habits of Thought in the English Renaissance. Religion, Politics, and the Dominant Culture*. Berkeley, 1990.

Simpson, A. W. B. *A History of the Common Law of Contract. The Rise of the Action of Assumpsit*. Oxford, 1975.

Smith, Alan G. R., ed. *The "Anonymous Life" of William Cecil, Lord Burghley*. Studies in British History 20. Lampeter, 1990.

Smith, David L. "Catholic, Anglican or Puritan? Edward Sackville, Fourth Earl of Dorset and the Ambiguities of Religion in Early Stuart England," *Transactions of the Royal Historical Society* 6th series, 2 (1992), 105–24.

Spufford, Margaret. *Contrasting Communities. English Villagers in the Sixteenth and Seventeenth Centuries*. Cambridge, 1979.

Stoyle, Mark. "The Dissidence of Despair: Rebellion and Identity in Early Modern Cornwall," *Journal of British Studies* 38 (1999), 423–44.

Stretton, Tim. *Women Waging Law in Elizabethan England*. Cambridge, 1998.

Summerson, Henry. *Medieval Carlisle: The City and the Borders from the Late Eleventh to the Mid-Sixteenth Century*. 2 vols. The Cumberland and Westmorland Antiquarian and Archaeological Society, Extra Series 25 (1993).

Terry, Reta A. "'Vows to the Blackest Devil'": Hamlet and the Evolving Code of Honor in Early Modern England." *Renaissance Quarterly* 51 (1999), 1070–86.

Thirsk, Joan. *Economic Policy and Projects The Development of a Consumer Society in Early Modern England*. Oxford, 1988.

Thompson, Benjamin. "Monasteries and Their Patrons at Foundation and Dissolution," *Transactions of the Royal Historical Society* 6th series, 4 (1994), 103–26.

Tittler, Robert. *The Reformation and the Towns in England. Politics and Political Culture, c. 1540–1640* Oxford, 1998.

Tittler, Robert. "Reformation, Resources and Authority in English Towns: An Overview," in Patrick Collinson and John Craig, eds. *The Reformation in English Towns, 1500–1640*. London, 1998. 190–201.

Tittler, Robert. *Townspeople and Nation. English Urban Experiences 1540–1640*. Stanford, 2001.

Todd, Margo. *Christian Humanism and the Puritan Social Order*. Cambridge, 1987.

Tuck, Richard. *Philosophy and Government 1572–1651*. Cambridge, 1993.

Twigg, John. *A History of Queens' College, Cambridge, 1448–1986*. Woodbridge, Suff., 1987.

Wall, John N. Jr. "Godly and Fruitful Lessons: The English Bible, Erasmus' Paraphrases, and the Book of Homilies," in John E. Booty, David Siegenthaler, and John N. Wall, eds. *The Godly Kingdom of Tudor England. Great Books of the English Reformation*. Wilton, Conn., 1981. 47–138.

Ward, Joseph P., *Metropolitan Communities. Trade Guilds, Identity and Change in Early Modern London*. Stanford, 1997.

Ward, Joseph P. "Religious Diversity and Guild Unity in Early Modern London," in Eric Josef Carlson, ed. *Religion and the English People 1500–1640. New Voice New Perspectives*, Sixteenth Century Essays and Studies 45 (1998), 77–97.

Williams, Glanmor. *Renewal and Reformation. Wales c. 1415–1642*. Oxford, 1993.

Williams, Glanmor. *The Welsh and their Religion. Historical Essays*. Cardiff, 1991.

Wilson, Alison. "An Elizabethan Miniature in the Parker Library, Corpus Christi College, Cambridge," *Transactions of the Cambridge Bibliographical Society* 10 (1994), 461–88.

Venn, J. "Memoir of John Caius," in E. S. Roberts, ed. *The Works of John Caius, M.D. Second Founder of Gonville and Caius College and Master of the College 1559–1573*. Cambridge, 1912, 1–78.

Wabuda, Susan. "The Woman with the Rock: The Controversy on Women and Bible Reading," in Susan Wabuda and Caroline Litzenberger, eds. *Belief and Practice in Reformation England*. Aldershot, 1998, 40–59.

Walsham, Alexandra. *Church Papists. Catholicism, Conformity and Confessional Polemic in Early Modern England*. London, 1993.

Waugh, Evelyn. *Edmund Campion*. London, 1952.

White, Micheline. "A Biographical Sketch of Dorcas Martin: Elizabethan Translator, Stationer, and Godly Matron," *Sixteenth Century Journal* 30 (1999), 775–92.

Whiting, Robert *The Blind Devotion of the People. Popular Religion and the English Reformation*. Cambridge, 1989.

Whiting, Robert. "'For the Health of My Soul': Prayers for the Dead in the Tudor South-West," in Peter Marshall, ed. *The Impact of the English Reformation 1500–1640*. London, 1997. 121–41.

Whiting, Robert. *Local Responses to the English Reformation*. London, 1998.

Wood, Andy. "Custom and the Social Organization of Writing in Early Modern England," *Transactions of the Royal Historical Society*, 6th series, 9 (1999), 257–69.

Wright, Jonathan. "Surviving the English Reformation: Commonsense, Conscience, and Circumstance," *Journal of Medieval and Early Modern Studies* 29 (1999), 381–402.

Wrightson, Keith. *Earthly Necessities. Economic Lives in Early Modern Britain*. New Haven, 2000.

Zagorin, Perez. *Francis Bacon*. Princeton, 1998.

Theses and Dissertations

Fisher, Rodney Munro. "The Inns of Court and the Reformation 1530–1580." Unpublished Ph.D. Dissertation, Cambridge University, Ph.D. #8757, 1974.

Shagan, Ethan Howard. "Popular Politics and the English Reformation, c. 1525–1553." Unpublished Ph.D. dissertation, Princeton University, 2000.

Smith, Richard Dean. "Social Reform in an Urban Context: Colchester, Essex, 1570–1640." Unpublished Ph.D. dissertation, University of Colorado, 1996.

Ward, Joseph P. "London's Livery Companies and Metropolitan Government, c. 1500–1725." Unpublished Ph.D. dissertation, Stanford University, 1992.

Wenig, Scott A. "The Ecclesiastical Vision and Pastoral Achievements of the Progressive Bishops under Elizabeth I, 1559–1579." Unpublished Ph.D. dissertation, University of Colorado, 1994.

Index